Teaching Art and Design

Addressing Issues and Identifying Directions

Edited by

Roy Prentice

CONTINUUM
London and New York

For Jeni

Continuum
Wellington House,
125 Strand
London WC2R 0BB

370 Lexington Avenue
New York
NY 10017 – 6503

© Roy Prentice 1995

Reprinted 1998, 2000

British Library Cataloguing-in-Publication Data
A catalogue record for this book is available from the British Library.

ISBN 0–304–33074– 4 (hardback)
0–8264–5264–7 (paperback)

Phototypeset by Intype, London
Printed and bound in Great Britain by
Redwood Books, Trowbridge, Wilts

Contents

Notes on Contributors

Roy Prentice is a senior lecturer and chair of the Department of Art and Design at the Institute of Education, University of London. His experience in the field of art and design education is wide-ranging and includes curriculum development, teaching and examining at PGCE course and MA degree levels. Formerly he was head of an art and design department in a comprehensive school in London and county art adviser for East Sussex Education Authority. In 1994 he was invited by the School Curriculum and Assessment Authority to serve as a member of the Art Advisory Group to review the National Curriculum for Art. His main research interest is the education and training of teachers of art and design. He is a practising painter.

Michael Buchanan has taught art and design in both primary and secondary schools. He is currently senior adviser in Redbridge Local Education Authority and an OFSTED Registered Inspector. Experience of university teaching has been gained through his contributions to PGCE and MA art and design in education courses at the Institute of Education, University of London. He is a member of the editorial board of the *Journal of Art and Design Education* and secretary of the Association of Advisers and Inspectors for Art and Design. He was a member of the Art Advisory Group which reviewed the National Curriculum Order for Art for the School Curriculum and Assessment Authority.

Lesley Burgess is a lecturer in the Art and Design Department at the Institute of Education, University of London, and course tutor for the PGCE course in art and design. She has taught in London schools and most recently held the post of head of art and design at Parliament Hill School in Camden. Her main research interests are curriculum development and resource-based learning, particularly residencies.

Robert Ferguson trained as a painter and graphic designer and became a teacher of art. Later, he taught in the Film Department of Hornsey College of Art. After a period as a film editor and sound recordist, he worked in the Teacher Training

Department at Hornsey. He is at present head of media studies at the Institute of Education, University of London, and has written, lectured and broadcast internationally on a range of media issues. His main research interest is in the ideological dimension of media messages, with particular reference to representations of history on television.

James Hall taught art and design in secondary schools in Durham, Cleveland and Cambridgeshire before taking up a joint appointment in 1985 as a teacher tutor with the University of Reading School of Education and Berkshire Education Department. Since 1988 he has taught full-time on the PGCE secondary course at Reading, and he is now co-director and course leader for art and design. He completed his MA in Art and Design in Education at the Institute of Education, University of London in 1989 and is currently researching into the initial training and professional development of teachers of art and design, in the context of partnerships between schools and universities. He is a printmaker with a particular interest in limited edition artists' books.

Arthur Hughes is professor and head of the Department of Art at the University of Central England. Previously held posts include head of the School of Art Education and director of the PGCE art and design course at Birmingham Polytechnic, and head of an art department in a secondary school. Additional experience has been gained as an external examiner and in his role as co-editor of the *Journal of Art and Design Education.* He is a past president of the National Society for Education in Art and Design and a visiting professor at Simon Fraser University, Vancouver. He continues to work as a practising artist.

Martin Kennedy is head of the Faculty of Expressive Arts at Crofton School in Lewisham, London. He is a senior assessor for the General Certificate of Secondary Education in London. He is also the elected chair of the London Association for Art and Design Education (LAADE). As a visiting lecturer he contributes to courses of initial teacher education and has worked closely with groups of student teachers during the school-based components of their PGCE course.

Lucy Dawe Lane is community education organizer at the Whitechapel Art Gallery, where she has been leading the community education team since 1990. Educated at Cambridge University, and subsequently at Oxford, she read philosophy and history of art and then moved directly into gallery education, working at Kettle's Yard in Cambridge, before joining the Whitechapel. Over the last four years the schools' programme has continued to flourish, expanding its programme for the secondary sector through the introduction of Saturday GCSE classes. These attract a wide following from schools across East London and involve participants in working directly with contemporary exhibitions and young artists, with activities taking place first in the galleries and then in schools.

John Reeve is Head of Education at the British Museum. After teaching history in comprehensive schools and with adults in Avon, he established a museum education service for North Yorkshire based at the Castle Museum in York. His publications include *Living Arts of Japan* (British Museum Press, 1990), aimed primarily at helping art and design teachers work with a rapid turnover of exhibitions; and the chapter on the British Museum in *Culture, Education and the State* (ed. Stephens, Routledge, 1988). He is a Visiting Fellow in the Art and Design Department at the Institute of Education and was a member of the History Advisory Group reviewing the National Curriculum for the School Curriculum and Assessment Authority in 1994.

Colin Robinson started his career as an art teacher in Yorkshire before becoming a lecturer in the Art Education Department of Cardiff College of Art. He then moved back into the secondary sector as head of the first open-plan art and design department in Leicestershire. From there he moved to Brighton Polytechnic, working mainly with intending secondary art and design teachers. In 1987 he was appointed as one of Her Majesty's Inspectors of Schools, with responsibilities for art and design in schools and for teacher education. In 1992 he took early retirement, and he is currently engaged in printmaking, inspecting art and design departments in schools, and evaluating the PGCE Course Partnership Scheme at Nottingham University.

Phillida Salmon has worked as a psychologist first in clinical contexts, and then in a variety of educational ones. She is currently Visiting Fellow at London University Institute of Education. Throughout her work she has tried to make links between educational and personal concerns, and between the ways in which we understand crises on the one hand, and development on the other. Her most recent books are *Psychology for Teachers* (Hutchinson Education, 1988) and *Achieving a PhD* (Trentham Books, 1992).

Kate Schofield is a lecturer in the Department of Art and Design at the Institute of Education, University of London. She is course tutor for the MA degree Museums and Galleries in Education, and teaches on the PGCE course. After training as a textile designer, she gained extensive teaching experience in further education in Nottinghamshire before studying for an MA degree at London University. In her capacity as chief examiner, senior examiner and reviser for each of three examination groups, she has gained additional experience of the examination system in art and design. The focus for her current research is designer objects, their meanings and their relationship with museums and galleries.

Foreword

When a motionless Rodin figure places elbow on knee and chin on hand, we all know what is happening: someone is thinking. Everyone also understands what is happening when someone lays one brick on top of another: action is occurring. Someone is doing something.

It is the very clarity of these two perceptions that leads to the damaging dichotomy of theory versus practice: either one is thinking or one is doing. Yet thinking and doing are not distinct activities. We simply lack confidence in our ways of describing what all of us can recognize, thoughtful action.

The function of this book is to show that, as in other areas of teaching and learning, the theory versus practice, form versus content, dichotomies cannot be allowed to apply. As Yeats once put it in *Among School Children*: 'How can we know the dancer from the dance?'

Art and design educators, at the Institute of Education and elsewhere, have a long tradition of thinking hard and causing students to think hard about what they see and do, and encouraging those they teach to do likewise.

It is important that this tradition be maintained within art and design departments. Some of the externally imposed pressures on schools inhibit rather than enhance the sensitive and intelligent work of well-run art and design departments. Hence this book. It raises the issues, encourages thought and invites action. That it does so without stridency adds, I believe, to the force of what it has to say.

Sir Peter Newsam
Director,
Institute of Education, University of London

Preface

Many people, directly and indirectly, have influenced the preparation of this book. I am indebted to the eleven contributors from whom chapters were commissioned for the creative thought and energy they invested in this venture; along with their strong commitment to it. For their sustained support I am also indebted to my colleagues in the Department of Art and Design at the Institute of Education, University of London. A book published nearly a quarter of a century ago – *Change in Art Education* by Dick Field – is an enduring reference point, and the first sentence in the present introduction reflects the spirit of this source. My ideas about the role of practical workshops in courses of art and design teacher education have been shaped over many years. In particular I have learned much from the student teachers with whom I have worked at the Institute and from my collaborations with Alfred Harris and Peter Burton. To Tony Dyson and Keith Gentle for their editorial advice and constructive criticism of my original proposal respectively I offer my sincere thanks. I am also grateful to Sir Peter Newsam for his belief in the value of art and design in education and for supporting the development of the Department of Art and Design at the Institute during his period as Director. My thanks are also due to Magdalen Meade for her meticulous typing and to Naomi Roth for her sensitive understanding of the issues involved in the hazardous journey from idea to published book. Above all, I am indebted to Jeni, my wife, for her enthusiastic encouragement at all stages of this project.

Roy Prentice
Institute of Education, University of London

Introduction

Roy Prentice

This book addresses contemporary issues in art and design education. It also identifies directions for future curriculum development in art and design, with particular
reference to the secondary phase of schooling. It came into being as a response to
the debates about two far-reaching government initiatives: the introduction of the
National Curriculum and the reform of teacher education and training. In rapid
succession, art and design teachers have had to implement the National Curriculum
for Art (DES, 1992) and prepare themselves for a new role within school-based
courses of initial teacher education (DFE, 1992).

It is the purpose of this book to support the professional development of specialist
teachers of art and design: those who are preparing to teach as well as newly
qualified and experienced teachers. In particular, it should be seen as a rich resource
to be used by all participants in the teacher education enterprise: student teachers,
teacher tutors and tutors in higher education institutions. Each chapter has a different focus and aims to stimulate debate and inform practice through creative thought
and action in relation to a range of key and often controversial issues.

This being the case, the content of this book is also relevant to a wider audience
than art and design teachers in secondary schools and those directly involved in the
preparation of specialist teachers of art and design. Ideas are located in theoretical
frameworks, but their bearing on classroom practice is made explicit throughout;
thus the interdependence of theory and practice is reaffirmed. Above all, it is
important that this book avoids being regarded as a manual or handbook; indeed,
to do so would run counter to the concept of reflective practice on which it is
founded, and to the model of professionalism which it seeks to strengthen.

THE WIDER CONTEXT OF PROFESSIONAL DEBATES

It is essential that art and design educators are fully aware of the wider and rapidly
changing context in which subject-specific and subject-related issues are addressed.
Only then is it possible for them to grasp a proper understanding of the ways in

which change in art and design education continues to be influenced by initiatives generated within the subject community and by external developments, directives and pressures. Since the Education Reform Act (DES, 1988) central government has gained an increasing amount of control over the content, organization and assessment of the National Curriculum and over the arrangements for funding and inspecting schools. The reform of initial teacher education and training (DFE, 1992) requires institutions of higher education in partnership with local schools to establish school-based Postgraduate Certificate in Education (PGCE) courses which meet the government's newly imposed competence-based criteria. Alternative routes into the teaching profession are also being promoted and directly funded by central government. In addition – as this book is being prepared – there is before Parliament a proposal to create a Teaching Agency through which central government would acquire control over the allocation of funds for courses of initial teacher education and related areas of research.

At the same time, major changes are taking place within the worlds of arts education and the professional arts, with far-reaching implications for the future of art and design education in schools. Many well-established structures that traditionally have supported the professional development of teachers, along with agencies through which curriculum development has been initiated and disseminated, are at risk. Already the effectiveness of some is severely diminished, while others have been dismantled.

An Arts Council survey undertaken by Rogers (1993) 'to map what is happening to the main source of current provision of advice, support and funding to schools on the arts' reveals the extent to which many Local Education Authorities (LEAs) have reduced their specialist advisory services and in-service provision for teachers. A similar situation is to be found at a national level following the drastic contraction of Her Majesty's Inspectorate for Schools (HMI) together with a redefinition of role. In the higher education sector, evolving schemes for school-based courses of initial teacher education point towards a slimmed-down network of specialist centres for art and design education at PGCE, in-service, higher degree and research levels.

Specialist centres for the initial education of teachers of art and design have enjoyed a long and distinguished history with roots that can be traced back to Marion Richardson's course at the London Day Training College (later the Institute of Education, University of London). Writing in 1970, Dick Field (then head of the art department at the Institute) considers such centres to be 'among the more progressive institutions in art education'. He goes on to say:

> But probably their most persistent problem has been that of bringing together practical and theoretical studies.
> One cannot conceive of a course concerned with the education of art teachers which does not include some practical art: for technical reasons, as preparation for practical teaching, as a workshop for the study of creative activity, and so on. Centres have devised a whole range of ways of integrating their courses; but this area of study seems to be the crucial point at which changing attitudes, changing methods and changing needs meet; there may always be flux here.
>
> (Field, 1970, p. 100)

During the twenty-four years since the publication of Field's influential book *Change in Art Education* – from which the above extract is taken – these centres have strengthened their pivotal role in the development of art and design education in secondary schools through their involvement in curriculum development, teaching and research activities. They function as sources of creative energy through which innovative ideas are generated and as a national network through which ideas about contemporary issues and models of good practice are disseminated.

In principle, the intention to strengthen the relationship between theory and practice in initial teacher education should be welcomed. So, too, should the move to regulate the often long-standing, fruitful but informal arrangements between higher education institutions and schools. It is vital that those engaged in the design, management, teaching and assessment of school-based courses of initial teacher education over the next few years approach the task creatively and with a sense of vision. The subject-specific strengths of existing courses must be acknowledged, and conditions conducive to their future development must be accommodated within new course structures.

THE SCOPE OF THE BOOK

The focus for each chapter is a contemporary issue in art and design education viewed from a particular perspective. As the discussion progresses, key concepts and concerns emerge which can be identified as recurring themes through which creative connections can be made between chapters. In this way they serve to illuminate and reinforce, extend or challenge ideas rather than merely to repeat them. Enduring concerns include the relationship between theory and practice, between art and design and art and design education, and between practical, studio-based work and critical, historical and contextual studies. In addition, the fundamental basis for learning in and through art and design activities – experience of quality – is considered along with the notion of reflective practice and ways of approaching curriculum planning and assessment.

The aim of this book is to capture the spirit of a rigorous debate in which individual voices contribute towards the advancement of a single conversation. Each chapter was commissioned and retains the distinctive voice of an educator who is well qualified to explore an issue with which teachers of art and design have to grapple. Collectively, the contributions represent a wealth of experience of curriculum development, course design, teaching and examining at school, college and university levels. A wider perspective is provided by a Local Education Authority Inspector, a former member of Her Majesty's Inspectorate, and museum and gallery educators.

The first chapter raises issues about the education and training of specialist teachers of art and design at a time when all courses of initial teacher education are in a state of flux. Drawing upon practical experience and relevant theoretical material, a case is made to support the retention of a strong subject presence in the new school-based PGCE courses. Learning to teach and the reciprocal relationship which evolves between an artist and work-in-progress is likened to a conversational exchange. This provides the basis for an exploration of the concept of reflective practice in relation to art and design activity and to pedagogy. It is argued that engagement in studio-based workshops in art and design education provides student teachers with unique opportunities to make creative connections between their professional practice as artist or designer and their deepening understanding of their role as teacher. The rationale for workshop studies within the PGCE art and design course at the Institute of Education, University of London, is discussed in some detail in order to demonstrate the nature of the relationship between theory and practice and between teaching and learning. The discussion about reflective practice and experiential learning continues beyond this chapter, thus reaffirming their importance in the on-going debate about the nature of teaching and learning in art and design.

In Chapter 2, Phillida Salmon examines the nature and value of experiential learning in a psychological context. She argues for a wider acknowledgement of the profoundly personal nature of the learning process in which 'knowledge is not divorced from knowers'. This provides the key to the relationship between Salmon's ideas and art and design education. The position she adopts within the field of psychology is influenced by construct theory – in particular, the work of George Kelly. It is to such ideas and their implications for classroom practice that this chapter provides access. As a psychologist, Salmon is equally critical of traditional approaches to psychology in education and mechanistic approaches to teaching. She firmly believes in the capacity of each individual to construct and reconstruct personal meanings, but it is made clear that to do so involves more than merely 'doing things'. Like most artists, designers and teachers of art and design, Salmon is familiar with the widely held but inadequate conception of what is entailed when people learn from experience. It is made clear that, in order to make meanings, learners must reflect on practical experience and articulate their growing understanding. It is here that Salmon reinforces the importance the previous chapter attaches to the development of reflective teachers of art and design. For Salmon 'the curriculum can only come mediated through the person of the teacher ... the tasks, materials, goals of the lesson come infused with the teacher's personal identity'. Of particular significance for teachers of art and design – given the diverse specialisms included in the subject-field along with the problematic nature of art – is the claim that teachers represent more than their subject: they represent their personal stance towards it. In conclusion, discussion focuses on each of four components of experiential learning: integration, personal learning, evaluative stance and reflection.

In Chapter 3, Michael Buchanan examines further the nature of art and design in the curriculum and the opportunities it offers pupils to construct, reconstruct and communicate meanings that have personal significance. He is critical of organizational structures which seem to separate practical work from critical, historical and contextual studies. Central to his argument is the need for the National Curriculum for Art to develop an interactive and mutually dependent relationship between Attainment Target 1 (Investigating and Making) and Attainment Target 2 (Knowledge and Understanding). A reciprocal relationship between the making of art and critical literacy is proposed in order to maximize the conceptual integrity of the art and design experiences in which pupils engage. It is useful to consider Buchanan's concern for the preservation of the holistic nature of art activity in the light of Colin Robinson's criticism of the two-Attainment Target structure of the present National Curriculum, which, he claims, lacks conceptual integrity. Issues relating to the place and content of art history, ways in which it might be introduced and the context in which it might be located are discussed. The skills associated with critical appraisal are examined in relation to other subjects in the school curriculum – English, religious education and history – and in so doing the basis on which cross-curricular collaboration is discussed by Arthur Hughes in Chapter 11 is underpinned. Through his use of the term 'critical literacy', Buchanan enriches and extends the familiar debate about the inseparability of practical, studio-based activity and critical, historical and contextual studies in art and design. Creative connections can also be invited between his concept of critical literacy and what Robert Ferguson, in Chapter 4, refers to as the 'politics of vision' in his critical analysis of the treatment of race, gender and class by the mass media.

Ferguson – a former art and design teacher and a practising painter – is well placed to investigate the possibilities for teaching about representation. His aim is to equip all pupils with a range of skills through which they can gain access to and make informed judgements about a world in which diverse modes of representation coexist and compete for attention. The ideas advanced address 'the ways in which meanings are constructed in media texts, and the ways in which those meanings are negotiated by different audiences in different contexts'. It is argued that the critical analysis of media representation should be an essential element of art and design education rather than an optional extra. Through a detailed analysis of case studies which focus on issues of race, gender and class, Ferguson demonstrates how the critical dimension of art and design education can be strengthened. It is claimed that the social and political aspects of the teaching of art and design have been denied or evaded for too long, and a strong case is made for pupils to develop an understanding of art and design in a social context. It is suggested that in many schools the art and design curriculum is deficient because it fails to subject to rigorous intellectual interrogation the different ways in which the media signify meaning.

Like Ferguson – but from a designer's stance – Kate Schofield in the chapter which follows advocates a broader base for art and design in the curriculum. Attention is drawn to the limitations of design projects that leave unchallenged the relationship between form and function and the concept of truth to materials. Teachers are encouraged to *use* designer objects in ways that maximize their potential for generating meanings. In particular, the ways in which commercial, domestic and museum settings, in their different ways, determine how a given object is perceived are discussed in detail. Overall, Chapter 5 reveals how working with objects can extend the contribution made by design to the art and design curriculum. Five domains are identified within which material culture can be interrogated.

Chapters 6 and 7 focus on the ways in which museums and galleries can be *used* to support resource-based learning across a continuum of art, craft and design. From their respective vantage points – the British Museum and the Whitechapel Art Gallery – John Reeve and Lucy Dawe Lane critically consider issues of policy and pedagogy with reference to particular exhibitions and projects.

John Reeve provides a brief review of museum education in order to locate current policy, provision and practice in an historical framework. He declares that the role of a museum educator is to 'problematise an exhibition ... make its basic methodology apparent' and 'suggest alternative structures for interpretation'. From this position he examines the impact of the development of critical and historical studies in art and design on museum and gallery education services. In particular, he identifies ways in which gender issues and multiculturalism can be approached by teachers of art and design supported by museum and gallery resource material. Selected teaching projects are discussed in detail to make explicit their contributions to the National Curriculum for Art and to reveal further potential for cross-curricular collaborations. Reeve subscribes to the view that 'school practice could profitably become more like that of a museum educator: starting from the specific object'. (He is critical of teaching projects that reduce the role of museum and gallery resources solely to an illustrative function.) Certainly the substantial evidence he offers to support this view highlights the potential contribution to be made by museums and galleries as an integral part of the evolving National Curriculum and newly established school-based PGCE courses.

Like Reeve, Lucy Dawe Lane recognizes that contemporary art can provide a 'route into art history'. However, her main thrust in Chapter 7 is to demonstrate how a wide range of contemporary art practice can be made accessible to both pupils and teachers and to acknowledge the role it has to play in shaping the future. Teachers of art and design are encouraged to 'plunder' contemporary art 'for all its worth'. Its potential as a unique resource to support practical work and critical, historical and contextual studies is explored. Key issues with which contemporary artists are preoccupied are examined, and their relevance to the requirements of the National Curriculum for Art is made explicit. Practical ways in which teachers can keep abreast of developments in contemporary art and gain access to resource material to support its use in teaching projects are suggested. Central to this chapter is a desire to broaden pupils' ideas about art through their growing awareness of the range of possibilities available to living artists. Concepts considered in some detail include originality and art as commodity, whilst the relationship between the environment, technology and art raises important questions that should be addressed in art and design lessons.

Many of the issues raised by Dawe Lane inform the discussion about the role of artists in education presented in Chapter 8. Lesley Burgess examines the 'elaborate network of support structures' developed by arts organizations over the last two decades 'to bring the worlds of practising visual artists into a closer working partnership with educational institutions'. The origins of artists in schools programmes in both the United Kingdom and America are traced, their influences charted and emergent problems identified. Burgess recognizes the need to overcome organizational and financial problems in order to secure a sound basis on which practising artists can make substantial contributions within the framework of the National Curriculum for Art. She also draws attention to potential conflicts between the orthodoxy of much 'school art' and the innovative work of living artists. It is proposed that artists working in schools should contribute to the professional development of teachers and fulfil a curriculum development function. For this shift of emphasis to be achieved, it is advocated that artists should be trained to work in education, and artists' responses to training programmes – particularly to schemes offering accreditation – provide support for this proposal. Burgess makes a strong case for practising artists, craftspersons and designers to play a more prominent role in art and design education in schools. It is claimed that where 'teachers continue to rely exclusively on monographs of well-documented painters, they will be discounting not only many black and female artists, but equally important histories of craft, design and popular culture'. Thus the case for residencies is extended beyond the realm of fine art to embrace the concerns expressed by Schofield and Ferguson about design and the mass media respectively, and their place in an art and design curriculum.

Throughout this book reference is made to the National Curriculum for Art. It should be noted that each country in the United Kingdom has a different curriculum structure. The original proposal of the Art Working Group in England was for three Attainment Targets: 'Understanding', 'Making' and 'Investigating'. While the resulting Order for National Curriculum Art in England contains two Attainment Targets – 'Investigating and Making' and 'Knowledge and Understanding' – that for Wales, developed separately, maintains the three-Attainment Target model. In Scotland and Northern Ireland separate guidelines apply. At the time of writing the National Curriculum is under review.

In Chapter 9 Colin Robinson draws attention to issues central to the translation of the National Curriculum for Art into practice. In so doing he stresses the need to take into account the distinctive features of both art and design activity and the rich contributions that practising artists and designers can make to art and design education. The conceptual integrity of the present Order for Art is examined, and the educational validity of a structure consisting of two Attainment Targets is challenged. Nevertheless further critical analysis of the requirements of the National Curriculum for Art reveals ways in which teachers can design and teach courses that build upon existing strengths. Throughout this chapter Robinson demonstrates that the National Curriculum offers scope for creative teachers of art and design to meet the required criteria while retaining their professional integrity. Above all, he highlights the conditions under which externally imposed curricular requirements and the personal commitment of teachers can be integrated to improve the quality of pupils' learning in art and design.

James Hall also is mindful of the seemingly irreconcilable demands of externally imposed directives and pressures on the one hand, and personal beliefs and values on the other. In Chapter 10 he identifies a range of factors to be addressed by teachers when planning an art and design curriculum. The notion of curriculum planning as 'a creative and imaginative process' is proposed, along with the need to differentiate between the curriculum as it is planned and taught and the curriculum as it is experienced by pupils. The need to achieve a balance between freedom and constraint within frameworks that are neither too flexible nor too rigid is also emphasized. It is recognized that the ways in which teachers approach curriculum planning is 'guided by their personal orientations as artists or designers' together with their capacity to reflect upon, evaluate and develop their teaching. Here Hall echoes the support advanced in Chapter 1 for courses of initial teacher education rooted in models of reflective practice. With reference to the approaches adopted in two schools, a structure is introduced consisting of seven tiers within which ways of thinking about and ways of planning an art and design curriculum can be articulated.

Chapter 11 brings a refreshing perspective to the long-running debate about the problematic nature of cross-curricular connections. It moves beyond the manipulation of slogans and stereotyped examples of projects and themes to which this debate is too often reduced. Arthur Hughes argues for a curriculum to be conceptualized and implemented in such a way that opportunities are maximized for pupils to make *personal* linkages between disciplines and between different areas within a subject-field. Reference is made to the work of Bruner, Gardner, Postman and Weingartner, and Warnock to support the view of learning on which his ideas about the curriculum are founded.

Not surprisingly, Hughes expresses his dissatisfaction with the traditional structure of the present subject-oriented National Curriculum. He regards it as a missed opportunity and favours a more radical approach to facilitate creative connections between different areas of knowledge and experience. He is also concerned about the separation of art from design and craft – a situation for which he partly blames the National Curriculum. The introduction of Technology into the school curriculum is heralded as a development in which art and design teachers could and should have played a major role; but they were prevented from doing so. Hughes, with regret, points out how 'the original intentions for Technology were thwarted as this new cross-subject area of knowledge and experience became entrusted to the stewardship of one of the more educationally conservative subjects, CDT'. This example fuels a deeper disquiet about the shift towards vocational plans for education, in which instrumental functions rather than intrinsic values dominate the curriculum and in which the transmission of knowledge occurs at the expense of personal understanding. It is to assist the making of personal meaning that Hughes counters such a position and encourages pupils and teachers to explore uncharted and potentially rich, exciting and rewarding cross-curricular 'liaisons'.

In the final chapter, Martin Kennedy deals in a down-to-earth manner with what is widely regarded as the most controversial issue that teachers of art and design have to confront: assessment. He draws attention to two major influences on current approaches to assessment in art and design in secondary schools. Firstly, the impact of teacher involvement in GCSE assessment criteria is considered at Key Stage 4. Secondly, the more rigorous approach to record-keeping, instigated by the National Curriculum, is considered in relation to work at Key Stage 3. It is Kennedy's purpose to help teachers of art and design 'formulate assessment systems for their own schemes of work' rather than to perpetuate the myth of a definitive format for assessment that can be applied in all situations. To emphasize this point, reference is made to several 'customized' assessment schemes to indicate how the particular requirements of pupils and teachers can be accommodated. A number of important dimensions of assessment are addressed; they include differentiation, formative and summative assessment, and moderated and self-assessment. Throughout the discussion the difficulties associated with the mechanics of and attitudes towards assessment are squarely faced and examined. In conclusion, the chapter stresses the need for assessment to be established as an integral part of each course, 'conceived as an organic whole'.

REFERENCES

Department for Education (DFE) (1992) *Initial Teacher Training (Secondary Phase)*. Circular 9/92. London: HMSO.
Department of Education and Science (DES) (1988) *Education Reform Act*. London: HMSO.
Department of Education and Science (DES) (1992) *Art in the National Curriculum (England)*. London: HMSO.
Field, R. (1970) *Change in Art Education*. London: Routledge & Kegan Paul.
Rogers, R. (1993) *Looking Over the Edge: The Survey*. London: Arts Council of Great Britain.

Chapter 1

Learning to Teach: A Conversational Exchange

Roy Prentice

This chapter sets out to explore the relationship between teaching and learning. The concept of reflective practice in art and design is considered as a basis for the professional development of specialist teachers of art and design. In this way, the centrality of art and design and experiential learning in initial courses of art and design teacher education is reaffirmed. As Field and Newick (1973) point out:

> In claiming that the experience of art is at the heart of the study of art education we are thinking of a quality of experience which is fundamentally aesthetic ... This experience shades into other kinds of human experience but in the process of merging its experiential nature is inviolable. It is a 'natural' experience yet it is sometimes undervalued; it is available to everyone although it is not necessarily availed *of*; it is always potent yet its potential can remain unexplored. (p.4)

The term 'reflective practice' is used in a variety of professional settings supported by an extensive literature. While alternative conceptual models have been adopted to develop reflective practice in different professional contexts, they share a fundamental concern for active learning, through which investigative, practical and attitudinal skills and capacities are combined. Reflective practice is rooted in the ideas on which 'learning through doing' (Dewey, 1933), personal construct theory (Kelly, 1955) and person-centred learning (Rogers, 1983) are founded. Further influences that are particularly relevant to the present discussion include the work of Schon (1983, 1987) on the nature and development of the reflective practitioner, and alternative models of professionalism such as those proposed by Elliott (1991) and Day (1993). An amalgam of such ideas, enriched by artists' and designers' insights into their own creative processes, underpins the rationale for the art and design Postgraduate Certificate in Education (PGCE) course at the Institute of Education, University of London. Within this course a series of workshops make a distinctive contribution to the development of reflective teachers. Later in the chapter, the nature of this contribution and its wider implications are discussed in greater detail.

It is useful to pause for a moment to reflect upon the educational route which the majority of art and design teachers have followed. The pattern of national provision for undergraduate courses in art and design is broad and complex. Highly specialized degree courses differ enormously in their declared aims, ethos, content and structure. Overall, they represent a continuum of professional practice in art, craft and design which constitutes the subject-field. Such degree courses are predominantly practical, their nature being studio-workshop rather than book-based. Their main focus is on making and their main aims are to develop students' creative capacities and technical skills within a context of professional practice as artists, craftspersons or designers.

For an artist or designer, the decision to train as a teacher raises fundamental and complex questions about professional integrity, creative energy, belief system and self-image. Attitudes that influence responses to such questions include those which support a strong commitment to personal creative work. This is even more apparent when an increasing number of entrants to courses of initial teacher education in art and design have gained invaluable, and often substantial, experience of employment in an area of art, craft or design practice. It is significant that the vast majority of intending teachers of art and design are motivated by a very strong subject allegiance and by an equally strong sense of personal identity. First and foremost they see themselves as beginning teachers of art and design, with roots firmly embedded in their identity as person-as-artist, -craftsperson or -designer. Their interest in, and understanding of, a teacher's wider professional role evolves gradually during the period of initial education and training and the induction year. This growth process, through which a wider perspective on teaching is cultivated, cannot be enforced. It is important that this development pattern is acknowledged by those involved in teacher education from both school and higher education sectors. It is vital that they display an empathetic understanding of creative artists, craftspersons and designers in order to help student teachers make personal connections between art and design and pedagogy.

It is desirable that the content and form of any course of professional education and training is experienced by all participants as having coherence. Traditionally, attempts to achieve coherence within PGCE courses have too often been limited to structures and strategies to facilitate connections between subject-specific content and professional concerns and competences of a general nature that are common to teachers of all subjects. The government's introduction of new criteria for secondary PGCE courses from 1994 offers an opportunity for schools and institutions of higher education, working in partnership, to provide school-based courses that promote a wider interpretation of coherence. By subscribing to a model of professionalism in which reflective practice is central, such courses would be shaped by evolving interrelationships between:

- previous and present experience;
- theory and practice;
- teaching and learning;
- school-based and higher education-based activities; and
- teacher tutor and higher education tutor roles.

REFLECTIVE PRACTICE IN ART AND DESIGN

A brief consideration of reflective practice in art and design highlights the inherent duality of creative activity: at one moment the artist or designer functions as maker, engaged in the manipulation of visual images, tools and expressive media, while at the next the role of critic is adopted. The painter Ben Shahn (1967, p. 49) draws attention to the fact that 'painting is both creative and responsive', requiring an artist to function as 'two people not one', being both 'the imaginer and the producer' as well as 'the critic'. Central to such creative behaviour is a capacity to evaluate from within the activity that which evolves through the activity: the realization of intention in concrete form. When describing their working methodologies, it is common for artists and designers to stress the importance of the periods of time they spend looking at and thinking about work in progress: making far exceeds the skills of mere production.

Growth points exist within the processes and procedures of art and design, and they are located at the interface between intention and expressive media. Plastic unity comes about through a dynamic interaction between an artist's projections and the intrinsic qualities of the medium through which intention is embodied. This is achieved through the construction of a life-line between ideas and feelings that inhabit a personal, private world and a chosen medium that exists as part of a shared, public world.

To embark on a piece of creative work is likely to be an experience that is simultaneously exhilarating and terrifying. Feelings are prone to oscillate between confidence and timidity. The first marks to be made, as an artist reaches out to establish a presence in the public world of things, activate a surface or three-dimensional space, and confirm a personal commitment to particular images and forms. In particular, the early phases of creative activity consume a lot of energy. As the energy generated from within the making process gains momentum, the maker is compelled to absorb it and make decisions about future transactions in relation to an image of increasing complexity and intensity. More importantly, the development of a reciprocal relationship between an artist and a work-in-progress enables ideas and feelings to be presented and articulated in ways which were unknown at the outset. Thus there emerges through the interdependence of content and form what Reid (1969, p. 279) calls 'a discovery in union'. Expressing this in terms of painting, Ben Shahn (1967), a painter who has experienced this condition from the inside, says:

> From the moment at which a painter begins to strike figures of colour upon a surface he must become acutely sensitive to the feel, the texture, the light, the relationships which arise before him. At one point he will mold the material according to an intention. At another he may yield intention – perhaps his whole concept – to emerging forms, to new implications within the painted surface. Idea itself, ideas, many ideas move back and forth across his mind as a constant traffic ... Thus idea rises to the surface, grows, changes as a painting grows and develops. (p. 49)

In the above account, the creative process in art is analogous to conversational exchange. A fruitful conversation is defined by Britton (1972, p. 239) as one in which 'the participants profit from their own talking ... from what others contribute, and above all from the interaction'. The duration of a conversation cannot be predetermined: every conversation evolves at its own irregular pace with periods of animated exchange interspersed with periods of silence. For a conversation to be deemed successful, it must have been allowed to develop from the inside.

It is important to differentiate between exchanges that are mechanistic and productive, and those that are organic and generative. In order to be truly generative a conversation demands more than regular alternation between talking and listening. Timing is crucial for an uninterrupted flow of ideas. The moment at which a particular interjection is made, the speed with which it is made, phrasing and accentuation, both influence the meaning of that specific contribution and alter the balance of the conversation up to that point. Subsequent contributions may accept or reject, build upon or demolish previous statements, but nothing should be ignored if dislocations are to be avoided; every utterance extends the debate.

A visual image retains embedded in its material substance the character of the encounter through which it was made. Skid marks on tarmac, peeling posters on a wall, a scratch on a cheek – all survive as legacies of actions. In a painting each additional mark introduced into pictorial space 'gives a resonance to the other marks; and this leads on to a further development of the image' (Francis Bacon, quoted in Sylvester, 1975, p. 121). A mark on a surface is simultaneously a particular colour, shape, texture, in an active relationship with all the other elements in pictorial space. The way in which an artist responds to cues embedded in this continually changing whole provides the key to future action. Uncertainties must be lived with, courted rather than merely tolerated, if situations are to remain open for sufficiently long periods of time to encourage explorations of alternatives. Risks must be taken. Having struggled to realize an intention in concrete form, an artist has to be prepared to let go, to exchange that which exists for something which might exist. The destruction of an image, together with the relinquishment of the stability that present reality promotes, in favour of the pursuit of the potential it offers, is a painful but inevitable condition of creative behaviour. Similarly, the visual consequences of actions judged to be unsuccessful can also be used to advantage, to provide a means through which the work may be renegotiated. Matisse states, 'At the next sitting, if I discover some weakness in the whole canvas, I use this flaw as a point of re-entry' (quoted in Guichard-Meili, 1967, p. 31).

There is no ultimate fact to which a painting is an equivalent. A painting exists as one way of dealing with a problem within a specific context. There are endless alternatives which would require other paintings to give them a concrete existence.

REFLECTIVE PRACTICE IN TEACHING

> Learning to be a reflective practitioner is learning to reflect about one's experience of complex human situations holistically. It is always a form of experiential learning. The outcome of such learning is not knowledge stored in memory in propositional form, but 'holistic understandings' of particular situations which are stored in memory as case repertoires.
>
> (Elliott, 1991, p. 313)

The act of teaching is a complex and subtle performance that is determined by knowledge and understanding, skills and attitudes. Reflective teachers acknowledge the problematic nature of teaching and systematically reflect upon their practice in order to improve it. In so doing they simultaneously engage in teaching and learning: a relationship that echoes the quality of creative activity in art and design. Such a view of teaching exploits the range of personal experience that teachers as well as pupils bring to each educational enterprise in which they participate. Personal growth and the professional development of teachers are seen as being inextricably entwined. A reflective teacher is valued as a resourceful individual rather than as someone who functions routinely in a predetermined role.

A creative model of professionalism which acknowledges the need for 'qualitative indicators' rather than 'performance indicators', and central to which is the development of the reflective practitioner, is advocated by Elliott (1991). His concept of professional practice runs counter to the traditional image of teacher as 'infallible expert': a role which government policy seems intent on perpetuating. While the 'infallible expert' matches 'a stable and unchanging' society, the reflective practitioner is better equipped to respond to change which is 'continuous and unpredictable' in a social setting which lacks 'stable definitions and explanations'. Elliott (1991) goes on to point out that:

> The quality of open-mindedness manifests a capacity for understanding situations holistically, for looking at them from a variety of perspectives. Tactfulness in communicating with others manifests a capacity for empathy. Reflective and non-defensive responses to criticism manifest a capacity for self-monitoring. Exercising initiative in proposing, implementing and evaluating problem solutions manifests a capacity to take risks in the face of uncertainty, to believe in and trust oneself as an agent of change. (p. 313)

Other writers on reflective practice reinforce Elliott's view and draw attention to the relationship between essential skills and attitudes on which effective teaching is founded. Pollard and Tann (1987) identify six key skills. *Empirical skills* are those through which teachers gain access to that which is actually going on in their lessons. *Analytical skills* are the tools of interpretation and a means of making connections, while *evaluative skills* are necessary in order to make judgements based on evidence and with its implications for the future in mind. Effective planning requires *strategic skills, practical skills* provide the means through which ideas are translated into action, and well-developed *communication skills* enable teachers to share their ideas about aims and methodologies.

Attitudinal dimensions can be traced back to the three conditions which Dewey (1933) refers to as 'open-mindedness', 'responsibility' and 'wholeheartedness'. Open-mindedness makes possible the coexistence of alternatives as a result of which reflective processes and procedures gain in rigour. The means through which teachers can influence ends as well as means relies upon 'intellectual responsibility', through which integrity is secured. Wholeheartedness – an apt, if quaintly unfashionable term – encapsulates the level of energy and enthusiasm generated by those teachers who are immersed in subject content and committed to its propagation and dissemination.

In drawing attention to the importance of reflection within the professional development of teachers, it is necessary to focus more sharply on the facets of reflective practice that need to be addressed. As Day (1993, p. 83) points out, 'much "lip service" is paid to the need for teachers to reflect upon their work, but ... not enough is understood about the benefits of opportunities and challenges for reflection of different kinds at different levels'. Some critics have discredited the notion of reflective practice in education by claiming that it is limited to highly subjective judgements made in a vacuum, and that it is preoccupied with means and process at the expense of outcomes and curriculum content. Effective reflective behaviour requires teachers to subject their own practice to scrutiny within a conceptual framework: a framework which does not limit itself to one particular theoretical interpretation or one practical approach to school-based work. It is the richness of reciprocal relationships between theory and practice that provides the basis for reflective teaching: the means through which experience is contextualized, understandings are extended and insights are deepened.

The concept of the reflective practitioner promoted by Schon (1983) relies on a dynamic interrelationship between three phases of reflection: reflection-in-action, reflection-on-action and reflection on reflection-on-action. In his consideration of research relating to different levels of reflective behaviour, Day (1993) reveals a need for the articulation of reasons and justifications for practice as well as for the more familiar ground of planning and immediate action. Traditionally, the main focus for reflection has been on process rather than on curriculum content. However, when reflective dimensions of teaching fail to take into account issues relating to content, the potency of reflection is reduced. It is essential that teachers who do not aspire to the role of infallible expert consider critically the nature of lesson content in order to challenge assumptions about subject knowledge. In so doing, they should be encouraged to take the evidence of their sense impressions seriously. Feelings and intuitive responses should be allowed to influence situations in which historically an overdependence on cognitive aspects of reflection has prevailed. Above all, it is necessary to recognize and accept the value of insights into experience that can be gained through modes of human functioning other than linear, logical, rational patterns of behaviour.

Central to successful reflective practice is the ability to make explicit those aspects of professional practice that too often remain implicit. Well-developed verbal communication skills enable ideas about teaching and learning across a wide spectrum, from immediate action to long-term aims, to be articulated and shared in a public arena. First and foremost, the activity of talking benefits the speaker. The process of organizing and communicating ideas through language leads to their further clarification and a deepening of understanding. Placing thoughts and feelings 'out there' in the public domain means that they are subjected to external influences, require an increasingly confident defence and become modified in the light of alternative positions. Alternative views are accommodated and legitimized. (For a classic account of the ways in which exposure to alternatives influences judgements, see Abercrombie, 1960.) Unavoidably, reflective teachers need time to grow and develop; to become confident in their belief in self and in their capacity to make informed professional judgements about teaching and learning; and to generate their own ideas and identify creative directions within a shifting educational, social, political and economic landscape.

While discussing an approach to reflection in courses of teacher education based on life-history accounts, Knowles (1993) makes the following significant observation:

The process of cultivating reflexive practices is, in the end, both a vehicle and catalyst for professional development. It is an avenue to induce, in prospective and beginning teachers, alternative approaches to thinking about practice, about the relationships between cause and effect of those practices within the communities of classroom, school and society. The construction and use of life-history accounts in preservice teacher education provide opportunities for preservice teachers to learn from both the process and substance of their engagement in reflexive practical inquiry. (p. 88)

The section which follows goes on to discuss the nature of 'engagement in reflexive inquiry' within the context of a course of art and design teacher education.

WORKSHOP STUDIES IN ART AND DESIGN EDUCATION

Artists simultaneously experience the evidence of their sense impressions and examine it to find ways in which it can be used. Teachers simultaneously reflect upon their practice in order to learn more about teaching by doing it. Workshops in art and design education provide an organic framework within which student teachers following the PGCE art and design course at the Institute of Education can simultaneously address subject knowledge and subject application.

Workshops are defined as environments for enquiry into the making of, and response to, art and design, and ways of teaching and learning. Each workshop focuses on one of the following: ways of recording, ways of investigating, ways of developing, and ways of presenting ideas. Activities are supported by a range of two- and three-dimensional materials and resources, including information technology. Through a series of visual displays with accompanying written rationales, supported by discussion and guided reading, students deepen their understandings of the intricate relationship between concepts and skills, and visual and verbal modes of communication and expression, and thus between Attainment Targets 1 and 2 in the National Curriculum for Art (see Figure 1.1).

Every member of a workshop is a rich resource for learning. Each workshop group consists of students from a wide range of fine art, craft and design backgrounds. A climate is created in which alternative philosophical positions and working methodologies can coexist, and in which theoretical understandings grow out of engagement in practical activity that is school-focused. Conceptual clarity emerges through experiential learning and an increasing ability to reflect upon it: it can hardly precede it. In her advocacy of small-group discussion to develop in students the processes of perception and reasoning, Abercrombie (1960) states:

> The main difference between this and traditional methods of teaching is in the amount of attention that is paid to the *processes* of observing or thinking, as distinct from the results. In traditional teaching the student makes an observation, and finds it to be correct or incorrect by comparison with the teacher's (or the currently accepted) version . . .
>
> In the discussion technique of teaching, the student learns by comparing his observations with those of ten or so of his peers. He compares not only the results, but how the results were arrived at, and in doing this the range of factors taken into consideration is much wider than is usual in didactic teaching. (p. 18)

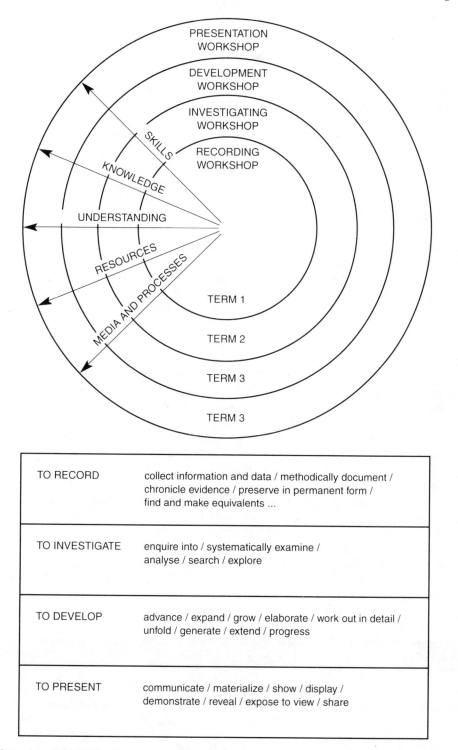

Figure 1.1 *Workshop studies in art and design education: PGCE Art and Design Course, Institute of Education, University of London*

As the PGCE course progresses, workshops provide opportunities for the acquisition – and in increasingly challenging ways, the application – of a range of reflective skills. While engagement in practical work in art and design – making – relies on reflection-in-action that occurs through a kind of *thinking in qualities*, students are expected to keep on-going records of workshop activities and their implications for structuring an art and design curriculum. Records – in the form of personal logs or diaries – contain both written and visual material and retain the substance of reflection-on-action, through which the implicit is made explicit. Students develop strategies to reflect on these reflections-on-action, both individually and in small groups. As a result there evolves an awareness of potential connections between: past experience as artist, craftsperson or designer; the present activity; and future possibilities as a teacher of art and design.

At the commencement of the PGCE course, it cannot be assumed that art and design graduates possess the breadth of knowledge and range of practical skills required to implement the National Curriculum for Art. Neither can it be assumed that all degree courses help students to acquire highly developed skills of critical analysis and verbal communication. In order to avoid students' feeling deskilled in the first term of the PGCE course, it is important to capitalize upon their individual strengths. The recording workshop offers a structure within which students engage in practical activities that draw upon and extend the experience and expertise they bring to this new situation. The brief – to find and invent different ways of recording experience using the processes and procedures of art and design – encourages individuals to respond by moving from familiar towards unfamiliar ways of working. Materials and processes are explored and exploited in new combinations as traditional approaches to craft skills are questioned. Making is informed and enriched by being located in a wider historical, social and cultural context. Everything is subjected to scrutiny.

By reflecting on their own creative behaviour and identifying the factors which determine their own preferred patterns of working, students gain insight into the nature of the creative process in art and design and the conditions required to support and develop creative responses in others. The ways in which ideas are generated, shaped, developed and refined are explored, along with strategies through which connections can be made between ideas and skills, form and content, process and product. The influence on the creative process of such constraints as time, scale and materials is addressed, as are ways of dealing with variables of this kind when planning projects for teaching practice. Throughout the workshop, the various means through which ideas are transformed into action are brought sharply into focus.

Workshop studies gather momentum in the second term. The work that students undertake is informed by the experience gained during their first period of teaching practice, and this in turn helps them to plan and resource projects to be implemented during their second teaching practice. With growing confidence and competence, students address an extended agenda. They assume greater responsibility for the form and content of their work, the context in which it is located, the issues it addresses or reveals, and the criteria by which it should be evaluated. Each student is required to construct a conceptual and organizational framework within which a key concept – arising out of the recording workshop – is investigated in depth.

Central to this activity is an increasing awareness of the role and power of visual metaphor and analogy: the found and invented equivalents through which art communicates personal response to experience.

Engagement in workshops enables students to acquire, develop and apply a range of reflective skills. Written and visual records and displays provide the basis for individual tutorials and structured group discussions. Intentions and working methodologies are clarified, and made explicit by being shared. Assumptions about the functions, nature and content of art and design and art and design education are challenged. Justifications for adopted positions are articulated, and in the process of being communicated, ideas are open to modification.

In the final term of the course, projects undertaken with pupils are further reflected upon, informed by wider reading and used as a basis for curriculum development. A key issue is identified for study in depth. This becomes the focus for a major assignment in the field of art and design education, for which conceptual and organizational frameworks have to be designed.

The presentation workshop culminates in a series of visual displays supported by written rationales which make explicit connections between subject knowledge and subject application by drawing upon both workshop and teaching practice experiences. Above all, it is the function of workshops to help students gain insight into the factors which determine their own creative behaviour – while exposing them to alternative ways of working – in order to understand the range of possibilities available to teachers and pupils.

SHAPING THE FUTURE OF ART AND DESIGN TEACHER EDUCATION

The underlying strength of the workshop component of the PGCE course, described above, is its potential for the development of the kinds of human capacity which lie at the heart of Elliott's model of professionalism. It is argued that such workshops provide a powerful means through which student teachers progressively gain insights into the nature of, and implications for, reflective practice, both as professional artists or designers and as professional teachers of art and design. A detailed analysis of the process and procedures through which students gain such insights provides a fruitful starting point for teachers and higher education tutors engaged in planning school-based, competence-led PGCE courses to meet the government's criteria as outlined in Circular 9/92 (DFE, 1992) and the additional notes of guidance (CATE, 1992).

If such courses are to be founded upon a genuine partnership between schools and institutions of higher education, the roles of serving teachers and higher education tutors must be differentiated and made explicit to all participants in the enterprise. Too often, the differences between these roles remain blurred, or it is assumed that they are interchangeable. Indeed, for some years, tutors teaching on PGCE courses were required by the government to return periodically to teach in schools, to gain 'recent and relevant' experience: a pressure, according to Rudduck (1991, p. 324), to make 'higher education tutors ... more like teachers'. This simplistic notion, if allowed to dictate the nature of future support for PGCE students, 'will foster more rapid socialisation into a redundant occupational culture and the practice it sustains' (Elliott, 1991, p. 315). As Edwards (1992) makes clear:

> Higher Education Institutions' distinctive contribution comes from making reference to and drawing on evidence from a wider range of contexts, curriculum developments and teaching strategies than any one school can provide. It also comes from making the theories and assumptions about children's learning embedded in classroom practice more explicit than they are for many teachers, and so more open to reflection and investigation. (p. 4)

It is vital that teachers of art and design and PGCE art and design tutors are proactive in order to secure within evolving structures for courses of initial teacher education a firmly established place for art and design education. There needs to be a clear definition of roles and clearly articulated rationales for course content and the modes and locations in which it is most appropriately experienced. Above all, there is a need for subject specialist provision to remain central in the emerging pattern of PGCE partnership schemes. Only in this way can art and design be fully exploited as the richest resource for the study of art and design education. When organizational structures are in place, it will be too late for art and design educators to have a significant influence on the way in which distinctive elements of art and design courses are accommodated within the new arrangements for initial teacher education.

REFERENCES

Abercrombie, J. (1960) *The Anatomy of Judgement*. London: Penguin.

Britton, J. (1972) *Language and Learning*. London: Penguin.

Council for the Accreditation of Teacher Education (CATE) (1992) *A Note of Guidance*. London: HMSO.

Day, C. (1993) Reflection: a necessary but not sufficient condition for professional development. *British Educational Research Journal* **19**(1), 83–93.

Department for Education (DFE) (1992) *Initial Teacher Training (Secondary Phase)*. Circular 9/92. London: HMSO.

Dewey, J. (1933) *How We Think: A Restatement of the Relation of Reflective Thinking to the Educative Process*. Chicago: Henry Regnery.

Edwards, T. (1992) *Change and Reform in Initial Teacher Education*. National Commission on Education, Briefing Paper No. 9.

Elliott, J. (1991) A model of professionalism and its implications for teacher education. *British Educational Research Journal* **17**(4), 309–18.

Field, D., and Newick, J. (1973) *The Study of Education and Art*. London: Routledge and Kegan Paul.

Guichard-Meili, J. (1967) *Matisse*. London: Thames and Hudson.

Kelly, G. (1955) *The Psychology of Personal Constructs*. New York: Norton.

Knowles, J. (1993) Life-History Accounts as Mirrors: A Practical Avenue for the Conceptualization of Reflection in Teacher Education. In Calderhead, J. and Gates, P. (eds), *Conceptualising Reflection in Teacher Development*. London: Falmer Press.

Pollard, A., and Tann, S. (1987) *Reflective Teaching in the Primary School*. London: Cassell.

Reid, L.A. (1969) *Meaning in the Arts*. London: Allen and Unwin.

Rogers, C. (1983) *Freedom to Learn for the Eighties*. London: Charles E. Merrill.

Rudduck, J. (1991) The language of consciousness and the landscape of action: tensions in teacher education. *British Educational Research Journal* **17**(4), 319–331.

Schon, D. (1983) *The Reflective Practitioner*. New York: Basic Books.

Schon, D. (1987) *Educating the Reflective Practitioner*. San Francisco: Jossey-Bass.
Shahn, B. (1967) *The Shape of Content*. Cambridge, Mass.: Harvard University Press.
Sylvester, D. (1975) *Interviews with Francis Bacon*. London: Thames and Hudson.

Chapter 2

Experiential Learning

Phillida Salmon

Art and design has always been a prime candidate for experiential learning. And while the imposition of the National Curriculum may have curtailed and constrained some of its possibilities in schools, nevertheless the subject remains defined in ways which presuppose the salience of first-hand experience. Of the two broad Attainment Targets, one concerns investigating and making: learning through doing. Gaining knowledge and understanding, the other target, is seen as integral with the first; pupils work towards a grasp of artistic traditions through making connections with their own artistic endeavours. This is a view of learning which sees theory and practice as essentially linked. Visual literacy and critical appreciation develop not as independent, abstract capacities, but out of direct experience of actual doing.

Learning from experience calls for educational modes that are as far removed as they could be from traditional classroom teaching. Instead of didactic transmission of information, such modes need to engage learners actively and purposefully in their own learning. In place of top-down knowledge, pupils must construct things for themselves. And what is learned must go beyond merely doing things; the learner must come to reflect on that practical experience, to articulate something of what it means.

Though learning modes such as these seem suited *par excellence* to art and design, there are also many teachers outside this curriculum area who would equally subscribe to them: for if school learning is not experiential, how can young people acquire an understanding which is real to them, and personally meaningful? Learning modes which genuinely, actively engage the learner are perhaps ultimately the only way of learning. Yet actually to adopt such modes – to set up classroom conditions which will allow pupils to learn from experience – is far from easy. As teachers all too often find, pupils themselves may resist this kind of learning; they fail to engage with the material, they do not identify themselves with the activity. The opportunity seems to be there, and yet the learning does not take.

For all the richness of their promise, experiential modes of learning are far more difficult to set up than are traditional forms of classroom learning. There are clearly many reasons for this. One fundamental difficulty arises out of an educational tradition in which experiential kinds of learning are entirely alien. But a further and related problem is the inadequacy of our conception. Too little thought has been given to the question of what is entailed when people learn from their own experience. Glib references to experiential learning may go no further than the phrase itself. What this kind of learning really means, how it happens, how it may be brought about: on these fundamental questions we have mostly only the vaguest, the sketchiest of ideas.

Experiential learning is sometimes used synonymously with life learning. People who emphasize the parallel generally see no need for further explanation. Nothing very complicated is involved, they might say, if pressed; we all learn all the time in our everyday lives, just by picking up the events around us. It is merely a matter of opportunity. In this perspective, school learners need only be exposed to situations that are of interest to them, and learning will just happen. Yet real-life learning is surely far from being as simple and as easy as this optimistic picture would portray it. Certainly we all learn from life. But what is just as striking is how much we do not learn. A man boasts of having twenty years' experience; yet, as George Kelly (1955) acidly remarked, he may have only one year's experience repeated twenty times.

When experiential learning is theorized, it is characteristically within the model of education of Carl Rogers (1983). Rogers believed that learning flourishes in the same conditions as those from which psychotherapy clients also benefit. Learning, in this view, is a basic, natural human urge, only thwarted by the emotionally damaging effects of disabling relationships. A good teacher, like a good therapist, may gradually rebuild inner confidence by providing the learner with genuine warmth and empathy. In this interpersonal atmosphere, people will naturally learn.

In countering the mechanistic and depersonalizing views which have so often dominated education at secondary level, the Rogerian model of learning is welcome. But for teachers trying to enable young people to learn through their own experience, it proves in the end an inadequate guide. It fails to flesh out the process of learning: to say what actually happens, what needs to happen, for real learning to occur. And though Rogers writes eloquently of the personal encouragement which teachers ought to offer, he is strangely silent as to teaching itself – as to what to do after the necessary establishment of mutual trust. Again this is because learning is seen as essentially unproblematic: something that can be safely left to look after itself.

In the Rogerian view, teaching is defined as facilitating, and teachers as facilitators. Facilitator: it is a term entirely devoid of social particularity. Like 'teacher', the word makes no reference to race or gender. But unlike 'teacher', it carries no allusion to collective professional identity, with all its social, economic and political connotations. Bland and neutral, it conjures up a somewhat blurred and two-dimensional silhouette: of a vaguely defined individual, standing apart, characterized only by the possession of a generalized skill.

This picture seems a world away from how young people actually experience their classroom teachers. For pupils, each teacher encountered is a highly distinctive physical presence: someone with a very definite social and cultural identity, invested with positive or with negative feeling and value. And this presence is not incidental in classroom learning, for the curriculum can only come mediated through the person of the teacher. And this is all the more clearly the case when learning modes are experiential. Where knowledge is not divorced from knowers, where personal feeling, spontaneity and intuitive responses are encouraged, pupils and teacher necessarily meet as persons – not hidden behind the masks of their institutionalized roles. And the ground on which they meet is not the curriculum in abstract, but what this curriculum means personally to each of them. For young people in school, art and design is inseparable from the art and design teacher: the tasks, materials, goals of the lesson come infused with the teacher's personal identity.

The profoundly personal nature of the learning process has generally gone unrecognized in traditional educational accounts. Concomitantly, traditional teaching methods tend to ride rough-shod over the delicate, vulnerable human responses involved in truly personal learning. A practitioner of experiential methods cannot, of course, disregard these features, since the whole basis of such methods is an assumption that meaningful learning is integral with the personal identity of the learner. This philosophy is thoroughly learner-centred. Yet what is characteristically left out of account by the advocates of experiential methods is that the logic which integrates learning with learners applies equally to the position of the teacher.

Meaningful learning entails taking an altered orientation towards things, an orientation which, though new and different, can yet be felt to be one's own, an orientation in which one can still recognize oneself. And the teaching through which such learning comes about is itself essentially the exemplification of what that orientation means. In teaching we do not merely pass on a free-standing package of knowledge – of the different periods, cultures and traditions in art, say, or the skills involved in working with different materials. What we do is rather to offer, however indirectly, a sense of the personal meaning which our curriculum has for us: its value, its relevance, its implications for us as particular human beings. In teaching we are, in some sense, our own curriculum, because we represent not only our subject, but, more importantly, the stance we take towards it.

Advocates of experiential learning rightly emphasize the uniqueness of the learner. But their simple portrayal of teachers as mere facilitators obscures both the significance and the complexity of the teacher's role. Defining teaching as facilitating renders it impersonal and essentially unproblematic. Yet teaching is a highly personal activity, and one which is far from simple. To teach is to reveal, both intentionally and unwittingly, what the curriculum really means to the teacher. Integrity and enthusiasm: those are qualities often cited in defining good teachers. And what they indicate is a real consonance of values; for such teachers, there is a wealth, a personal richness of meaning within the curriculum, which touches the deepest reaches of feeling and response.

Yet for many teachers this sense of wholeness, of perfect consonance between their inmost values and their classroom work, seems unachievable. This is no less true of art and design specialists than of their colleagues in other departments. The teaching situation is an increasingly beleaguered and complicated one. The constant barrage of new, often conflicting educational directives disallows a sense of purpose and consolidation; teachers must keep running in order to stay still. In art and design, the curriculum remains under permanent threat and must be constantly fought for against government orders which would marginalize and devalue its educational importance. There are threats, too, to this curriculum in the possible imposition of alien modes of assessment: modes which may carry arbitrary, ethnocentric or élitist standards, or which may draw boundaries between aspects which should remain integral.

For those who offer the curriculum of art and design to classroom learners, these features cannot fail to complicate their teaching. No teacher is an island; antipathetic contextual pressures reach into classrooms in multiple and subtle ways. Being inwardly at war with many of the current official directions is bound to make for mixed messages, conveying dissonance and fragmentation.

If hostile government pressures act to undermine teachers' sense of integrity, this can also sometimes happen through aspects of the curriculum itself. For art and design specialists, the meaning of their subject may itself introduce problems for their teaching. Those who define their curriculum exclusively in terms of Fine Art would represent an extreme case. But for a much larger number, there are inevitable personal limits, boundaries of tradition, of culture, of style or medium, which make it hard to teach with equal conviction across the wide sphere which represents the art and design curriculum. These inescapable personal limitations permeate teachers' relations with their pupils, whose differential sociocultural identities, personal responses and levels of skill endorse or stand apart from their own private sympathies. Of course, our usual educational accounts, generalized and impersonal as they are, gloss over such highly personal and rather uncomfortable aspects. But if we are serious in seeking to practise experiential modes, we must surely acknowledge and address them.

Pupils' relations with the art and design curriculum are of course no less complex than those of their teachers. And unlike traditional modes of learning, experiential methods expose rather than disguise these complexities. This is because in these methods the personal identity of the learner is not incidental, but salient. It becomes impossible to ignore the very different positions towards art and design of pupils from middle- or working-class homes, from Muslim or from Judaeo-Christian religious traditions, from multi-ethnic or Home Counties backgrounds. Nor does this curriculum mean the same for boys as for girls. Like other school subjects, art and design is highly gendered, representing, perhaps, an island of 'masculine' craft within a sea of artistic 'femininity'.

Experience of school learning, especially at secondary level, must also affect pupils' engagement with art and design. The call for an intuitive and feeling response can hardly square with the passive and affectless receptivity demanded in other spheres of learning, and perhaps dominating many earlier years of schooling. Selective forms of organization, currently gaining ground, make their own explicit differentiations between pupils, with often fateful implications for art and design. For someone ascribed low educational status, this curriculum may come to belong to another, alien and unreachable cultural world. This situation cannot but affect pupils' relations with their teacher: relations which are as differentiated within a classroom as the mix of identities within it. At its broadest, experiential learning involves four aspects.

INTEGRATION

In contrast with traditional forms of learning, it is integrative. Rather than presenting separate pieces of skill or knowledge, to be added gradually to the pile, it asks learners to link their classroom experience, in the here and now, to other aspects of what they personally know. Instead of leaving their out-of-school lives beyond the door, pupils are invited actively to draw upon them – to bring their lived understandings to bear upon what they are doing and seeing.

For some learners this is easier than for others. Some pupils have lived in contexts that are socially and culturally close to the curriculum world. But for others there is a vast gulf. Home and neighbourhood may seem miles apart from the lesson in art and design; nothing in personal experience relates in any obvious way to the material, the tasks, the language. The teacher, whose world this is, may appear equally remote, equally alien. Yet bridges can sometimes be built. Teachers' personal knowledge of and respect for their pupils' backgrounds and positions may enable them to make links: to present the curriculum in terms and modes which resonate in those young people's lived experience. When this happens, the lesson is transformed; art and design becomes something personally meaningful, personally accessible, a sphere in which real engagement can confidently occur.

PERSONAL LEARNING

The personal character of experiential learning also represents an obvious contrast with traditional approaches, which take both the modes and the substance of learning as standardized. But what is seen and felt is seen and felt uniquely; by its very nature, experience is subjective, private, idiosyncratic. For teachers of art and design, this is taken for granted. Art is necessarily and deeply personal; both creativity and appreciation are rooted in inner life, in individual response, feeling and impulse.

Yet, as many teachers discover, eliciting genuinely personal responses within classroom contexts may prove difficult. It is not only that such an invitation goes against the grain of the relentlessly impersonal instruction to which many pupils have become inured. It is also that responding personally involves certain risks. To express one's true feelings towards a piece of sculpture, or a museum collection, is highly exposing. You could be holding up your ignorance, or your judgement, to contempt or ridicule. To dare to follow your own ideas in a making task could also be perilous; it would be safer to stick with a well-worn and uninteresting line. Offering impersonal and highly guarded responses may in such circumstances seem the only possible course.

Responding personally is likely to be particularly threatening for pupils whose backgrounds are culturally remote from the world of school. Only the establishment of a sense of trust, on the part of the teacher, may gradually overcome this reluctance, and enable children and young people to feel confidence in their own personal feelings and reactions.

EVALUATIVE STANCE

Evaluating one's own learning means assuming a certain authority towards the learning task: stepping back from the curriculum in order to judge it, to decide for oneself how personally meaningful, how useful, how valid it seems. These judgements necessarily entail looking critically at one's own part in the learning, achieving some sense of one's own strengths and weaknesses in that part of the curriculum. All this is of course absolutely fundamental in art and design education. The informed eye, the intelligent hand: these can only be achieved through prolonged work in art and design, in which personal judgements of value are constantly and actively applied and developed.

But for most young people, their regular classroom work has been of a very different order. Though self-assessment has introduced principles of respect for pupils' own evaluations, this philosophy is implicitly contradicted by much else that is dominant in educational practice. This means that for those working in traditionally run schools, art and design teachers may be faced with the task of developing and nurturing their own distinctive classroom culture.

REFLECTION

If young people are truly to come to know, the uncritical assimilation of information and the unthinking application of skills are not enough. Pupils need to think for themselves, deeply and personally, about what they are hearing, seeing, doing. This can be achieved only through the development, over time, of a personal vocabulary, for without being able to express perceptions for oneself, it is impossible to think about them.

Of all curriculum areas, it is art and design for which this issue is the most central, the most basic. Making things is educationally relevant only if young people can bring to bear upon their making the same frame of reference within which they are also learning to see the wider world of designed objects. Conversely, visual appreciation remains irrelevant unless it draws upon intuitive and unverbalized responses of feeling and association. Both sorts of learning involve linking what is conscious and articulate with what is as yet implicit and unavailable to reflection.

This process is far from being easy or simple. For many young people, their educational experience never allows them to achieve it: to build bridges between what they can say, on the one hand, and what they know in their bones, on the other. So school knowledge remains didactic and irrelevant, rather than being integral with real-life knowledge, infused with personal concerns and personal agency.

One of the major goals in art and design education is the attainment of visual literacy. This term makes particularly explicit the development of a special kind of articulateness. Visual literacy must involve more than the simple acquisition of a new, specialized vocabulary, allowing a glib and facile use of impressive-sounding aesthetic language. If it is to be personally meaningful, visual literacy has to be anchored in what is deeply felt and understood, at the level of lived rather than analysed experience.

Reaching intuitive and inarticulate levels of awareness surely cannot happen all at once. Making available to ourselves what we most deeply understand – coming to know what we really know – is likely to take time, and to entail more than one stage. In achieving visual literacy, young people probably have to begin with second-hand formulations: the verbalizations available from teachers and texts, from the media and popular culture generally. These verbalizations provide a rough, ready-made set of tools with which to begin to explore the unknown landscape of inner reality. Only later, after some experience of using this impersonal and standardized kind of literacy, may it become possible to invest it with something of one's own intuitive feeling, to begin to develop a truly personal literacy of visual response. What is involved in this is, in Roger Poole's eloquent phrase (1972), the achievement of deep subjectivity.

Most school knowledge is quickly forgotten. Only when the curriculum becomes linked with what young people themselves most deeply care about can classroom work inform and enrich their lives. Of all educational approaches, experiential methods offer the greatest hope for learning which is genuinely, personally meaningful. And of all curriculum areas, it is surely art and design in which such methods sit most closely with its own goals and values.

REFERENCES

Kelly, G.A. (1955) *The Psychology of Personal Constructs*. New York: Norton.
Poole, R. (1972) *Towards Deep Subjectivity*. Harmondsworth: Penguin.
Rogers, C. (1983) *Freedom to Learn for the Eighties*. London: Charles E. Merrill.

Chapter 3

Making Art and Critical Literacy: A Reciprocal Relationship

Michael Buchanan

GROUNDS FOR DEBATE

An apparent segregation, in the National Curriculum Order for Art (DES, 1992a), between the activities of investigating and making on the one hand, and knowledge and understanding on the other, has brought into question the relationship between them and the relative weight which should be accorded them in teaching art and design. After considerable controversy about the number, titles and scope of the Attainment Targets, the Secretary of State for Education deemed that art 'should remain essentially practical' and that 'the first practical target ... for investigating and making in the case of art, should carry twice the weight of the second' (DES, 1992b). The Secretary of State's observation that 'the emphasis will be on doing' seemed intent on perpetuating much past practice in art and design education which had been concerned with the acquisition of practical skills, reference to the work of others and the history of art playing very much a subsidiary, even peripheral, role.

A contradiction exists, however. The National Curriculum Programmes of Study specifically require pupils to make connections between their knowledge of art and artists and their own work. While placing his emphasis on making and doing, the Secretary of State also emphasized that 'it is not intended that knowledge of the history of art and the practical elements of art should be taught in isolation from each other' (DES, 1992c). So while there is a requirement to integrate the activities of making and learning about art, the fact that two discrete Attainment Targets exist suggests an artificial separation between them for the purposes of planning and assessing the National Curriculum.

Different aspects of the subject had been thoroughly argued some years previously, when grade-related criteria were being planned for the General Certificate of Secondary Education (GCSE) examination (although, in the event, these were not adopted). The working party concerned proposed three distinct but related 'domains':

- *the conceptual domain* – involving the development of pupils' ideas and imagination, their ability to deal with direct experiences and the use of resource material in the forming of concepts and development and refinement of ideas;
- *the productive domain* – relating to pupils' use of the formal elements of art and design and the handling and control of the technical aspects of the subject; and
- *the critical and contextual domain* – including pupils' knowledge and understanding of contexts in which art and design might be produced, their ability to interpret and analyse their own work and that of others, and their capacity to make informed critical judgements, using appropriate vocabulary.

Each of these domains can usefully be described separately for the purposes of curriculum planning, but in the context of pupils' learning, they are inseparable, interactive and mutually dependent. It is argued that all are vital to the creative process, activity in each domain being dependent upon understandings in the other two.

To compound the confusion, uncertainty also remains as to what constitutes acceptable study within the work of artists, craftspersons and designers. For while the National Curriculum Order for Art (DES, 1992a) demands that 'pupils should understand and appreciate art in a variety of genres and styles from a variety of cultures, Western and non-Western' and that Attainment Target 2 is concerned with 'knowledge and understanding of art, craft and design including the history of art and a variety of other artistic traditions', the examples given are drawn predominantly from a mainstream Western European tradition. Stated 'periods' in the Programmes of Study include the 'Classical and Medieval, Renaissance, post-Renaissance, nineteenth century and twentieth century'. While there is tacit acknowledgement of art from culturally diverse traditions, there is an implied undercurrent of the Western European tradition of art history. The Secretary of State claimed that his revision to the draft Order contained 'sensible references to art ... in non-Western traditions, but I have retained the major emphasis on our national and European heritage' (DES, 1992b).

One year after the introduction of the National Curriculum, the Office for Standards in Education (1993) reported that 'some confusion existed about how the content of Attainment Target 2 might be covered'. While finding some examples of encouraging practice, it was stated that:

> a small number of schools ... failed to inter-relate the two Attainment Targets and presented the study of art history as a dull experience. In many of the schools pupils learnt something of art from other cultures, but in general pupils were not given enough opportunities to look into the social or cultural context in which artists, craftworkers or designers had produced their work.
>
> (OFSTED, 1993, p. 10)

The report reveals that 'very few of the schools had provided pupils with a balanced programme of art, craft and design' (p. 9) in their practical work, most emphasizing art activities with some craft and only limited design-based work. The accent of knowledge and understanding in Attainment Target 2 has tended to be on fine art, with less attention given to craft and little at all to other spheres such as design, the built environment, film and print media. This is due, at least in part, to the statements made about 'our national heritage' and 'the history of art', and to the weight given to the Western tradition of art history in the exemplification of the Order.

It is hardly surprising, therefore, that debate exists about what art historical knowledge should be taught; how frequently it should feature in the teaching; how it should be taught; and in what context. What purpose does the history of art serve in a course of study which is 'essentially practical'? When pupils make connections between their own work and that of others, how might this be manifested? What are the skills associated with critical appraisal which we want children to learn?

COMPARATIVE ARGUMENTS IN THREE SUBJECT AREAS

Teachers of art and design are not alone in having to grapple with such questions. In other subject communities, similar considerations prevail. In English lessons, children learn the mechanics of writing and speech – spelling, vocabulary, grammar, syntax and so on – as a prerequisite of *verbal* communication, in much the same way that art and design education offers children a range of practical skills and concepts – a visual language – necessary for *visual* communication. The skill required to manipulate the mechanics is not regarded as an end in itself, however – rather as a vehicle. Furthermore, children's creative writing is not undertaken in a vacuum. It is informed by frequent and systematic exposure to texts, through reading, from which they learn how ideas can be communicated, moods created and controlled, and the needs of different audiences met. The study of a variety of texts – such as imaginative stories, descriptions, poems, advertisements and reports – allows an understanding of such concepts as expression, pace, style and genre to develop, which enriches the simple mechanics of writing.

The skills of critical appraisal of texts are actively taught: children are not expected simply to learn the titles and authors of books, but to consider, for example, how an author conveys ideas through the use of particular words in a deliberate sentence construction. Structured reading of texts requires high-level skills of analysis and criticism to be developed and employed. It would be an impoverished English curriculum which made no reference, or only partial reference, to the breadth and diversity of existing literature, including fiction and non-fiction, prose and poetry, narrative, description and report – from different cultures, times and social contexts.

In many respects, the parallels between learning in English and in art and design are striking. The acts of creative writing and making art are both concerned with conveying feeling, meaning and response to the perceived world, using a particular language, with its attendant set of codes, conventions and grammar. Writing and art-making are not simply concerned with the utilitarian skill of construction. The potter Alison Britton (1991) writes:

> I notice that finishing a piece of writing gives me an acute thrill. I think it is the sense of hitting the target that is satisfying – capturing something . . . the expression in sharply approximate language of a sequence of ideas . . . I think of words as an invisible material; manipulating punctuation is like focussing the attention on certain points in the painted surface of a pot. (Chapter 1)

Britton's analogy reveals a commonality between drafting (and redrafting) text – an activity central to English language teaching – and the notion of 'crafting' in art and design. Drafting text is a process of writing, reflecting and modifying, shaping a form of words which captures, as precisely as possible, intended expression. Crafting a piece of art or design work requires a similar refinement of ideas over time, in synthesis with the materials employed, in order to arrive at a satisfactory resolution – both of intention and of visual form. To craft a piece of art work is a disciplined and intellectually rigorous endeavour.

A further affinity lies in the fact that both English and art have their 'literature' to act as a stimulus and a comparative model. In both cases, the 'text' (visual or verbal) emanates from a particular historical or contemporary context, from a certain culture; and the reason for its production has determined its form and content. In the National Curriculum Order for English, the Programme of Study for Reading at Key Stage 2 demands that teachers and pupils 'should discuss texts which make imaginative use of English – literature, advertising, songs etc. – in order to bring out the ways in which the choice of words affects the impression given by the text' (DES, 1990, p. 31).

There are both similarities and differences between the 'literatures' of the two subjects. Kress and van Leeuwen (1992) write:

> Language and visual communication are very different. Yet they are part of the same culture and it is ultimately the culture that limits what can and what cannot be meant. So very often they can express the same meanings, be it in very different ways ... This is not to say that everything that can be expressed verbally can also be expressed visually and vice versa. Different periods, different cultures, and different social contexts within the same culture and period, can assign different roles to the verbal and the visual, give them different jobs to do, and they can also value them differently, assign them a different importance in the semiotic scheme of things. (pp. 102–3)

Insights into the cultural and social context, the chosen form and the range of possible meanings conveyed are achieved by close study of the 'grammar' of visual and verbal representation. Such understandings not only help with the interpretation and enjoyment of the work itself, but will, in turn, inform the pupils' own work by enlarging their visual vocabulary and literary language. Particular teaching styles are implied, in which sufficient opportunity is created for critical appraisal and analysis, as an integral part of the process of making and doing.

The Language in the National Curriculum (LINC) project describes the concept of 'literary language' as follows:

> 'Literary language' encourages particular forms of reading. Sometimes the reader is oblivious of this language, lost in the fictional world which the language has conjured; at other times, as with most poetry, the reader is deliberately impeded, made conscious of the *polysemic* (having more than one meaning) possibilities of language. In the end, it may be helpful to define 'literary language' in a deliberately circular way, as a language which both prompts and requires a certain kind of reading – reading that is engrossed, attentive, aesthetically responsive, alert to interpretative possibilities, and tolerant where necessary of oddity, complexity, ambiguity and postponement. To read texts in such a way is to read them as literature.
>
> (LINC, 1992, p. 103)

This responsive and analytical form of reading 'literary language' is analogous to 'reading' of visual imagery. To substitute 'visual language' in the above quotation would suggest something of the value and purpose of critical literacy in the art and design curriculum, and the positive effect of such awareness on children's capacity to undertake the practical dimension of the subject. Given the potential benefit, one wonders why for so long the art and design education community should have failed to take full account of its own 'literature'. Only now is it debating how best to relate to it. One might reasonably question why much work in schools, in the name of critical studies, is little more than pastiche; and why the skills of critical literacy – the ability to 'read' images and decode meanings and intentions – are not clearly understood and often not taught explicitly.

By way of comparison, the use of sources in history teaching and the development of skills of investigation – how to ask the kind of questions which release information held within artefacts – together form a nucleus around which the subject's content is built. The teaching of generic critical and investigative skills is focused upon the use of historical objects and documents. Many such artefacts are works of art, craft and design – fragments of pottery, historical portraits or household objects, for example. Their potency for learning is dependent on the teacher's ability to encourage children to interact with the artefact – to 'interrogate', assess and decode it. The following statements are pertinent in this regard:

> When we look at something we do not always 'see' it or learn from it. Visual skills are not simply the ability to convert what we see into an acceptable drawing or work of art. They enable us to observe and understand and judge what we see and to elicit ideas and information from non-verbal sources. Learning to see is a sophisticated skill that requires conscious effort to develop.

> Relating to objects may come more easily to some than others but you cannot assume it is an innate ability and, just like reading and map work, it has to be taught. Learning from objects takes time and practice.

> (Durbin *et al.*, 1990, p. 18)

Religious education employs similar study of religious artefacts as they are often the physical manifestation of abstract religious ideas and faith systems. Questions are asked of these artefacts in order that information can be discovered relating to beliefs, values, ideas, symbols, rituals and conventions. Not only do art and design educators have something to learn from the teaching methodology used in analysing religious artefacts, but the objects themselves are also of interest as, in most cultures other than the Western European, religious artefacts are the art objects of those communities. A religious artefact can be used as:

- a visual aid;
- a 'contextual map' – where the artefact provides a living framework or context for understanding and remembering aspects of a particular religion;
- the 'world in a grain of sand' approach – where the artefact is closely examined in order to understand the values and beliefs of the community which uses it and where parallels are sought in the lives of those people carrying out the investigation.

> (London Borough of Redbridge, 1992, p. 29)

In these examples from English, history and religious education, a range of sources – texts, historical objects and religious artefacts – form an integral part of the teaching, specifically being used to develop skills of questioning, decoding, critical appraisal and evaluation. They are interrogated to reveal meaning, values and beliefs. Yet this kind of teaching and learning is a relatively rare occurrence in art and design lessons. All too often, art and design objects – paintings and drawings, items of craft and designed artefacts and products – are used superficially to examine technique or style rather than meaning and content. Children learn to paint like Van Gogh yet know nothing about the meanings he tried to communicate or the context within which he worked; they make pastiches of Egyptian art without insights into its symbolic, ritualistic and representational meanings.

To do so is to do an injustice to the complexity of the work, the whole being greater than the sum of the materials, techniques and formal conventions employed in its manufacture. Suzanne Langer (1953) describes the concept of a work of art as being a 'created thing', the content of which is illusory and only imaginatively present, but bound in physical form. Discussing Leonardo's *Last Supper*, she writes:

> The picture is, indeed, not the paint on the wall, but the illusion which Leonardo created by means of paint on damp plaster. The paint, unhappily, has largely disappeared; but there is enough left to sustain the illusion, so the picture is still there. If time obliterates that last feint pigmentation, the work of art will have disappeared, no matter how well anyone may know and remember its vital import – the harmonies of feeling it revealed. The artist's work is the making of the emotive symbol; this making involves varying degrees of craftsmanship, or technique. (p. 387)

FEATURES OF THE MAKING PROCESS

The activity of making in art and design clearly involves more than merely applying technical skill to material, as craftsman and writer David Pye described: 'No conductor can make a bad orchestra play well. The quality of the concert does not depend wholly on the score and the quality of our environment does not depend on its design' (1968, p. 5).

Technical accomplishment is not sufficient. That children in schools can make an accurately registered print or satisfactorily join two slabs of clay is not inherently valuable. What is important is that they master such skills in order that they might use them as a vehicle for communicating ideas, meanings, feelings and perceptions. The purpose is the communication of ideas; the means are the material and the skill with which it is handled. Yet a substantial amount of art-making and design activity in schools is concerned with the technical as the principal objective of the teaching. What differentiates mere technical skill from the creative act of making art is that art and design imagery necessarily involves the exploration and articulation of personal responses. These are plainly cerebral and aesthetic concerns. The Assessment of Performance Unit (1983), attempting to define aesthetic development, claims that:

> An important characteristic of the concept of the aesthetic is that, unlike so many aspects of the curriculum, it is not concerned with means to ends. When one makes an aesthetic judgement ... one is not appraising the phenomenon in question in terms of its possible success in attaining some purpose outside itself. (p. 2)

Examining day-to-day classroom practice with this perspective can help clarify the distinction between an activity and its purpose (separating means from ends). To take one example, the underlying *purpose* of recording from observation might be defined as being concerned with learning to look, in an active and engaged way, and communicating information effectively, rather than simply achieving accurate representation. The skill of looking (and registering what is seen) is one that needs to be practised and cultivated. As John Berger writes in his book, *Ways of Seeing*: 'Seeing ... is not a question of mechanically reacting to stimuli. We only see what we look at. To look is an act of choice. As a result of this act, we see what is brought within our reach' (1972, p. 8). Different ways of seeing, Berger asserts, influence both the ways in which images are read and the way in which images are constructed:

> The way we see things is affected by what we know or what we believe. Every image embodies a way of seeing... The photographer's way of seeing is reflected in his choice of subject. The painter's way of seeing is reconstituted by the marks he makes on the canvas or paper. Yet, although every image embodies a way of seeing, our perception or appreciation of an image depends also upon our way of seeing. (pp. 8, 10)

The skills of looking and seeing, therefore, are important outcomes of a recording activity. In this example, the capacity to see is the 'end'; drawing is the 'means'.

Correspondingly, the motive for handling formal elements of art and design (e.g. texture, colour, tone) might be seen to lie in the need to convey feeling and mood; learning constructional techniques (e.g. in ceramic work) allows ideas and personality to be articulated in physical and visual form, giving vitality and force to the work. Bernard Leach (1940) writes:

> It seems reasonable to expect that beauty will emerge from a fusion of the individual character and culture of the potter with the nature of his materials – clay, pigment, glaze – and his management of the fire, and that consequently we may hope to find in good pots those innate qualities which we most admire in people. It is for this reason that I consider the mood, or nature, of a pot to be of first importance. (p. 18)

The formal elements of art and design are, then, the syntax of the subject. Each is a feature of the visual language, part of its grammar. The grammar can be learnt, but the learning can be witnessed only when it is used.

This is not to diminish the teaching of technical skills. The appropriate use of materials and processes demands that knowledge and confidence be fostered through instruction, experimentation and practice. It is a prerequisite of visual communication. Fulfilment and satisfaction can be gained from making something well, from overcoming technical obstacles: from learning craftsmanship. Nevertheless, the acquisition of making skills is not the prime purpose of art and design education; such skills are needed solely in order to enable pupils to explore and express their visual perceptions and inner feelings.

The Assessment of Performance Unit (1983) establishes a complementary relationship between what it terms 'handling skills', 'discriminatory skills' and the "skills of discourse'. It claims that:

> There is a distinction between technical competence and having something to say. Technical competence, although essential, is also only a necessary condition. Moreover, too rigid an emphasis on the learning of technical skills may have the unfortunate consequence of inhibiting or destroying potential, since these skills are means, not ends. (p. 8)

If effective making of art, craft and design requires both technical skill and having ideas worth communicating, teaching and learning in art and design need to be organized in such a way that the whole range of pupils' art-making skills is developed. It is clearly inappropriate to teach practical skills in isolation. The skills of execution depend for their quality on many other experiences: experimentation, observation, recording, research, critical judgement, discourse, visualization, modelling and so on. This kind of art-making demands different kinds of 'preparation', to use Gentle's terminology:

> first, that of preparing all the external means to enable art making to take place, such things as the preparation of materials, recording stimuli through drawing and notes and organising the work space. Secondly, the preparation of the inner conditions which direct and sustain the endeavour, such things as the imaginative association with other art makers, responses to the phenomena of nature, feelings of self worth and recognition of place in the continuity and tradition of an art form.
>
> (1990, p. 270)

Eisner (1972) suggests four factors which appear to be important in what he terms the 'productive realm of artistic learning':

1. Skill in the management of material.
2. Skill in perceiving the qualitative relationships among those forms produced in the work itself, among forms seen in the environment, and among forms seen as mental images.
3. Skill in inventing forms that satisfy the producer within the limits of the material with which he is working.
4. Skill in creating spatial order, aesthetic order and expressive power.

(pp. 79–80)

These references all suggest a multidimensional art and design curriculum, in which making has a pivotal yet wholly dependent part to play. Classroom activities are called for which relate practical making experiences to visual investigation; to thinking about and developing ideas; and to reflection, critical analysis and evaluative judgement. This relationship between aspects of the subject which are interdependent and mutually supportive might best be described diagrammatically, as in Figure 3.1.

Making art and design depends on the interaction between each of the four contributory factors in the diagram. The use of materials, tools and processes can be effective only when matched with understanding and control of the visual elements. These in turn, need ideas as a *raison d'être*. Ideas derive from perception, imagination and experience. Experiences are shaped and filtered by individual, family, class, culture and group contexts, by the environment outside school and so on. A considered approach to the teaching of art and design, which hopes to lead to effective making, must therefore take account of each factor by providing rich opportunities in which all of them can be stimulated, extended and challenged. There is a relationship between them which is reciprocal and generative.

Evidence can be drawn from the field of psychology to support the claim that children's most lasting learning experiences are those which they undertake experientially. It can be concluded, then, that their practical engagement with materials and processes is not only informed by but also informs their 'reading' of visual imagery. They are better able to interpret, appreciate and evaluate the work of others for

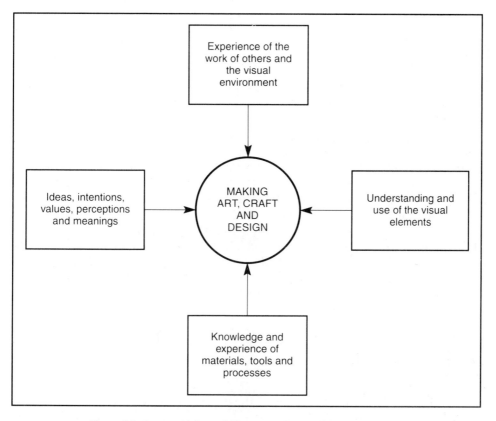

Figure 3.1 *Aspects of the multidimensional art and design curriculum*

the very reason that they have had comparable, active practical experiences. Personal identification with the difficulties, challenges and discipline of art-making makes relevant the work of artists, craftspeople and designers. Connections between personal practical experience and the work of others is characteristic of first-hand, experiential learning. Critical study provides knowledge and insight and gives access to meaning and ideas. It enlarges the possibilities of the practical activity. Equally, involvement in the practical activity sharpens the critical focus, advancing the reading and appreciation of the labour of others.

Working in this interactive way, pupils will be directly involved with the exploration of ideas, values, beliefs and principles, experimentation with ideas and meanings, discussion about art concepts and products, and reflection on experience. These activities are the principal stimulus for ideas, responses and images which have personal meanings. The conclusion that an increased amount of pupils' work should be based on their own (and their cultural and social group's) concerns and preoccupations, sometimes referred to as issues-based work, rather than the present reliance on representational, skills-based work, is inevitable. Such activities demand openness, on the part of the teacher, to those issues which are of concern and interest to pupils. They require a type of teaching which provides rich, varied, topical stimulus, first-hand experience, opportunities for independent working, regular and informed dialogue in the classroom and frequent reference to the work of artists, craftspeople and designers.

CRITICAL LITERACY

Classroom discussion about art, both the pupils' own work and the art of others, involves the consideration of content and intention, as well as of form and style; and the intrinsic relationship between these dimensions. Study of the *content and intentions* of art work exposes how meanings are constructed and conveyed, and offers insights into the context in which work is produced. More practised analysis of context explores the fact that meanings are not fixed, but are culturally, socially and class-bound. Equally valid sets of meanings might be constructed, in response to a given stimulus, by different cultural or social groups.

Just as the making process is time-related, in that intentions change with the accidental and fortuitous interaction of materials, so too the meanings of an art work can change over time. One cannot take in a work of art in one glance – its form and intricacies are revealed progressively through continuing observation and analysis. Its meaning unfolds through sustained looking; and meanings change when interpreted in the light of new information and further experience. The passing of time and familiarity with the artefact also conspire to change our frames of reference, and therefore our capacity to recognize plural meanings and complex intentions.

Examination of *form and style*, on the other hand, involves analysis of the 'grammar' of visual language: how formal elements are organized to stimulate particular aesthetic or emotional responses. Recognizing codes and conventions offers access to the culture of historical context within which the work was produced, and encourages associations to be made with other known images, symbols and meanings. Analysis of the relationship between content, intention, form and style reveals how the choice of form and its organization directly affects, positively or adversely, the ideas transmitted and the range of interpretations possible. The development of understanding of the dynamic relationship between form and content, and the potential for its control, lies at the heart of visual literacy.

In this respect, the analogy with English teaching clearly still pertains. Deciding whether to convey ideas in the form of a poem, story or report is, to a significant degree, attempting to determine something of the intended response. Each form of linguistic construction offers its own opportunities and constraints with regard to pace, drama, texture and formality. In the same way, a decision is made as to whether a painting, print or collage is the most appropriate form for conveying particular ideas, the decision being further refined by choice of colour, composition, materials, scale, codes and symbols employed. The effect of such choices is learnt not by practical experience alone, but by reflecting upon such experience. This reflection can be private or public; and focused on the pupil's own work or on the work of others, in a variety of forms and with different kinds of content. The key factor is regular and systematic exposure to reflective and analytical activities designed to develop critical literacy.

In the classroom, certain demands are placed on the teacher: notably the skill of effective questioning, allowing pupils to interrogate works of art, craft and design, and creating opportunities for the extensive use of language. Some teachers, already hard pressed for time in an overcrowded curriculum, consider such activities a diversion from the central, practical task. It is argued that classroom discussion and critical analysis is a time-consuming luxury. But without such opportunities, the quality of making is impoverished because ideas are not formed as fully as they might be, influences are not exploited and potential stimulus is ignored.

Edwards and Mercer (1987) suggest something of the value of classroom dialogue:

> Apes and monkeys pass on information and learn habits through observing each other's actions; what they do not do is share knowledge by symbolising it out of context. They do not discuss, compare notes, exchange views or negotiate understandings of what they have done or seen. When two people communicate, there is a real possibility that by pooling their experiences they achieve a new level of understanding beyond that which either had before. (p. 3)

Edwards and Mercer make reference to the work of the Russian developmental psychologist, L. S. Vygotsky (1897–1934):

> Vygotsky was proposing that children's understanding is shaped not only through adaptive encounters with the physical world but through interactions between people in relation to that world – a world not merely physical and apprehended by the senses, but cultural, meaningful and significant, and made so principally by language. (p. 20)

Without critical models and the opportunity to consider them properly, the resultant work of pupils might well be technically accomplished but will almost certainly be pedestrian, lacking personal meaning or involvement: making in a vacuum. Time spent on critical activity has a direct and beneficial influence on the richness of pupils' practical outcomes. It is, therefore, a sound investment as the quality of pupils' responses is directly related to the quality of stimulus they receive.

It might be useful to consider the nature of critical skills, in order to plan teaching objectives more precisely. The generic term 'critical studies' is often described as having three elements: the historical, the contextual and the critical. Each has different characteristics and a different role within the process of learning about and making art and design. Furthermore, each can be described in terms of both skills and knowledge. The art work in question might be drawn from a historical or contemporary source, from a familiar or less familiar culture or social context. The skills of evaluation, appraisal and criticism can equally well be applied to pupils' own work, especially when such activity is located in a wider cultural context.

Historical knowledge is sometimes disparaged as dry, decontextualized and academic, particularly when the history of art is presented as a simple, linear and inevitable chronology. But the ability to locate artists and their works in time, in relation to historical events and periods, might well aid understanding of the work, the conditions under which it was produced, its purpose and something of the nature of influence. It is undeniably helpful to know, for example, that the work of the Italian Futurists was undertaken at a time of rapid industrial and mechanical advancement and invention, and that their preoccupations with the machine age and speed were eventually moderated by experiencing the brutality of the First World War. Many historical portraits are statements of class, status and wealth: in other words, they are a social history of a dominant culture and class rather than accurate representations of reality. They are of their time.

Dyson (1989) makes a case for strategic introduction to historical knowledge, not so much as an end to be attained as a locating point for wider understanding:

> What has become in this country the traditional structure for art-historical studies is likely to make far more sense to the pupil ultimately needing to adopt it if it has been approached from the standpoint of early and frequent looking with no necessity to learn and remember names, dates and locations. What is important, though, is that a sense of human shaping, of chronology, of location, and of cultural inflection can be gained, almost by contagion; a realisation that an art object is the work of human hand and mind, the evidence of a particular moment of history, the product of a certain geographical region and the expression of a culture. (p. 128)

If used analytically and evaluatively, works of art, craft and design can provide insights into the nature of culture. It is regrettable that too often such work is chosen and held up as representative of establishment good taste and a superior culture. When working with art, craft and design objects, it is necessary to be keenly aware of the plurality of society; that terms such as 'our culture' and 'our heritage' are misnomers for a dominant culture. Inevitably, one is forced to question, when employing art images and artefacts from distinct cultural sources, how proper regard can be paid to the culture in which it originated, and appropriate value assigned to the work, without personal knowledge and experience of that culture. Consciousness is needed of the dangers of superficiality and tokenism. To treat art, craft and design objects from less familiar cultural sources with respect and sensitivity and, in turn, to elicit pertinent meanings from them, some basic knowledge of the work's context is helpful. More importantly, though, it is a question of attitude and approach. Several questions need to be asked: 'Am I looking at this object from an appropriate perspective? To what extent am I judging it by personal criteria, based on values which are not shared by the culture which produced it? Am I likely to challenge or reinforce the stereotypes of the dominant majority by using the object in the way I propose?'

Handling historical and contextual information – and developing understanding of cultural traditions – might be problematic for some teachers in contemporary, pluralistic society. Such experience, however, is a prerequisite to pupils' awareness of what shapes a culture and how cultures manifest themselves. David Pascall, former Chairman of the National Curriculum Council, in a speech at the Royal Society of Arts, stated that:

> The culture of a society is defined by its political and social history, its religious and moral beliefs, and its intellectual and artistic traditions ... Each of us is the child of history. Our modes of thought and feeling are defined by the culture in which we live. An important role of education should be to ensure that every child growing up in Britain, irrespective of their religion or the community in which they live, is taught about key traditions and influences within this heritage – both because such traditions are profoundly important in their own right and because this teaching will develop that intelligent perspective on the past, present and future upon which our democracy, ultimately, depends.
>
> (Pascall, 1992)

Contextual understanding, as distinct from historical knowledge, is central to the meaningful interpretation of much art and design. To move beyond the merely superficial, it is important to understand that, for example, Russian Constructivism was a product of the political and social conditions prevalent in Russia at the time. Effective analysis of the work is dependent on discussion taking place about the reality of this political and social context. Similarly, the study of much Christian religious art would lack meaning unless it were accompanied by an awareness of the authority of the Church at the time it was created: both its power and influence in people's everyday lives and its importance as a patron of art, craft and design.

If understanding of artists' work has significant potential to influence pupils' practical work, one needs to consider how reference might be made to it in pupils' practical activity. It could be argued that to use artists' work as stimulus for pupils' own work might simply encourage plagiarism. On the other hand, to use artists' work only as comparative information after pupils have concluded their own imagery is to fail to exploit the work's potential for stimulus and imaginative extension. A class which visited a museum to study, say, a variety of masks from a range of cultures, and in doing so learnt something about their role in ritual and traditions in manufacture, would be better placed to make masks themselves which had personal significance, cultural empathy and meaningful connection.

The distinction between influence and pastiche is a material one. The National Curriculum expectation of 'connection' requires close scrutiny. If pupils' making is to be enriched as a result of suitably challenging examination of others' work, in what form might such enrichment be seen? An influence might be direct: the way in which a sky is painted to evoke mood, for example, after analysing the technique of a number of painters; or an awakened interest in pattern after study of Indonesian textiles. The influence might, however, be more indirect, and therefore less explicit: for example, a broader concept of what it is possible to communicate using the media of art and design, an awareness of those life themes which have preoccupied artists throughout time, extended cultural and cross-cultural horizons, or greater understanding of the psychological power of the visual image. Many of these understandings can be identified only in their synthesis, evidenced over time.

Influence is not, however, pastiche. Thirty variants on a Tamara de Lempicka painting do not constitute critical study. To paint in the style of an artist might help develop some technical control but is unlikely to reveal much about the work's meanings or context, the artist's intentions or its effect. Opportunities for more substantial understandings would be missed.

When children gain meaningful insight into the work of others, the impact is likely to be more personal and deep-rooted. It has even been claimed (Taylor, 1986) that it can be a life-changing experience. At the very least, if their experience has been well structured and supported, pupils perceive the world slightly differently; the nature of their expression changes; and their range of visual ideas and concepts evolves. Often, the evidence of such shifts is transient and intangible. It is impossible to legislate for such changes.

DEVELOPING CRITICAL SKILLS

Enhancing pupils' ability to be critical requires not only enough time to be allocated to evaluative activity in which judgements are made, discussed and modified, but also the creation of a suitably supportive learning environment in which the expression of personal feelings, points of view, tentative judgements and emotional responses is socially acceptable and safe. This is equally true in the museum and gallery as in the more familiar environment of the classroom, and with the living artist as well as with the artefact. Revisiting ideas, themes and contexts is needed to practise and extend the use of relevant vocabulary and to refine the quality, depth and rigour of evaluative judgements. The skills of investigation need to be taught overtly, actively and at first hand. Investigative skills include those of questioning, appraising, hypothesizing, observing, deducing, comparing and classifying. Many of these skills are, of course, taught in the history curriculum too and will already be familiar to the pupils.

The development of critical literacy is wholly dependent on exercising the skills of evaluation and appraisal. Critical literacy is concerned with being able to judge, being able to read the visual language employed, understanding codes, symbols and images, and comparing and relating visual information with personal experience. It has to do with making considered and informed responses to ideas, the visual environment and cultural tradition.

Evaluation, in these circumstances, is significantly more than expressing personal preference. Implicit is the exercise of ascribing value to the work. The classroom activity needs necessarily to involve consideration of what is meant by value and to whom the work has value. A particular work might have value to one person or to one society, but not to others. Monetary value might be an indicator but is not, perhaps, the most reliable criterion of quality. The value of an object might change over time, or vary in different contexts. Something might have unique value to the individual, because of the particular associations made between it and personal experience. No value is fixed, in the same way that meanings are subject to infinite interpretation. Yet art, craft and design work is imbued with personal, aesthetic, social, cultural, and sometimes political and religious, values which need to be explored if the meaning and consequence of the work is to be properly revealed.

Appraisal, on the other hand, suggests that criteria exist against which qualitative judgements can be made. To appraise effectively means developing, and possibly agreeing, the criteria by which the work is to be judged: identifying which characteristics are the important signals of quality or value in the context of a given investigation. Again, these criteria need not always be the same; and the judgements made might well change when viewed from a different standpoint.

Critical skills develop over time, with practice and support. Progression in the learning involves systematically gaining access to an increasingly wide range of visual sources, of greater complexity. When introducing pupils to an unfamiliar piece of work it can be helpful to use a structured approach involving strategic phases of questioning, each of which, in turn, involves the pupil more deeply in the work. Such an approach might comprise three levels of questions and activities, in relation to:

- information;
- description; and
- interpretation.

The first of these levels – concerned with factual information – involves sharing what is known about the artist or the work. Often, this is little. Sometimes the broad period or geographical location can be deduced from visual clues, as can information about the materials and processes employed. Information can be gleaned by making connections with similar examples seen previously; employing analogy and metaphor in discussion is a useful tool in this regard. Many teachers, however, faced with lack of specific art historical knowledge (dating, often, from deficiencies in their own training), are discouraged from using works from particular artists, cultures or periods. Rather than being an insuperable hurdle, the lack of knowledge can be a spur to further and potentially rewarding activity. Bowden (1989) writes of his research into teachers' and children's use of original works of art:

> Whilst it is to a certain extent true that complicated analyses of works of art are often made by critics and reviewers, the teacher needs to emphasise – in order to encourage debate – that the uninitiated can express valid views without 'expert' knowledge. The view that art criticism is solely the province of people of learning has done much to inhibit the average person's enjoyment of art. (p. 83)

The second level of questioning – description – requires close observation, analysis and the precise use of language. Things are noticed which at first glance were not immediately apparent. It allows pupils to classify, compare and draw parallels between different types of visual information. This form of questioning encourages inquisitiveness and curiosity. Developing understandings of art, craft and design requires an ability to interrogate the work: describing it in fine detail allows the territory to be mapped, and its landmarks and signposts to be found.

Inevitably, such questioning leads to the third, interpretative phase and questions such as: Why was that included? Why is the person sitting in that way? What do you think they are looking at? Why might they be sad? What do you think has just happened? What might be about to happen? This category of activity requires the use of deduction and the formulation and testing of hypotheses. It involves not just recognizing but being able to read artistic codes and conventions, drawing on personal experience, and arriving at conclusions about meanings.

For purposes of curriculum planning, these three levels of experience can be categorized as knowing, decoding and exploring. Knowing concerns the factual; decoding demands a recognition of visual language; and exploring prompts personal, emotional and aesthetic response. The latter two obviate the need for a substantial body of knowledge before engaging with the work – asking effective questions is the key skill.

A number of educators have suggested other frameworks. Taylor's four 'fundamental areas', 'process – form – content – mood', represent the basis of a helpful teaching strategy. In detail, these areas are:

1. The techniques, processes and methods involved in the making of the work.
2. The formal qualities of the work; its arrangement into shapes, its form, the colour scheme employed, etc.

3. Its content in terms of subject matter; its significance, how the artist has accumulated the information, etc.
4. The mood, atmosphere or feeling evoked by the work.

(Taylor, 1986, p. 181)

The following structure of activity, by way of comparison, is drawn from a religious education text:

a) Investigating – the close examination of the artefact through using the senses in order to describe and then make deductions about what the artefact is, its possible uses, meaning and value etc. This process is sometimes called the 'puzzling' stage;
b) Supplementing – the investigator cannot empirically discover all that there is to be known (you can count the 99 beads on a Muslim set of prayer beads, for example, but you cannot deduce anything about the significance of the number 99 within Islam) and therefore extra information is needed;
c) Personalising – the process by which links are made between what you have discovered about the artefact and its world and your own world. In order to do this, a leap of imagination is often required.

(London Borough of Redbridge, 1992, p. 30)

This last phase of personalizing has particular pertinence in an art and design context: it recalls the National Curriculum requirement that pupils should make connections between their knowledge and understanding of art and design and their own work: the ability to personalize, and apply in practical ways, their wider experience.

Dyson (1989) proposes the use of techniques of comparison and classification, found widely in art history teaching in higher education, in order that pupils might make connections between perception and personal experience. He suggests that the introduction of artefacts, images and visual experiences should be progressive; from the familiar to the less familiar, from the simple to the more complex:

Inviting students to seek similarities and differences in related images is an effective means of compelling them to look and to think (p. 129) . . . The vital property of such examples will be their capacity to bridge pupils' existing awareness and their ultimate understanding of particular art objects. (p. 128)

He offers the following categories of comparison:

1. A comparison of reproductions of art objects with visual records of experiences familiar to pupils, or with every-day objects.
2. A comparison of different art objects with similar subject matter (or different buildings erected for a similar purpose).
3. A comparison of pupils' own work in art with appropriate art objects.
4. A comparison of artefacts of different periods.
5. A comparison of various products of a particular period: choice not restricted to art objects, nor even to visual material.
6. A comparison of art objects of a given School or period.

(pp. 130–31)

It is clear that teachers and pupils can legitimately use works of art, craft and design in different ways for a variety of purposes. They can be used as historical sources in the pursuit of knowledge and as extensions of cultural horizons. They can be used analytically to learn about form and process – how the work was constructed, visually and practically. And the works can be used evaluatively, to elicit from them interpretations of meanings, ideas, beliefs and personal, social and cultural values.

A varied range of teaching approaches, determined by pupils' needs, is proposed. At times, art and design work will be used as stimulus to open up the range of possibilities and to provide a meaningful context for the activity. On other occasions, the work might be employed as a comparative model, being introduced to pupils on an individual basis during the process of making, perhaps as a way of overcoming obstacles or extending horizons. In different circumstances, reference to artists' or designers' work might conclude a practical activity, reinforcing and valuing the learning that pupils have achieved by providing professional, adult examples which have dealt with similar concerns.

That critical study should necessarily be manifested in pupils' practical activity is, however, contentious and the subject of current debate. Among others, Thistlewood (1993) questions the nature of critical studies in the National Curriculum for Art, which, he claims, suggests:

> (1) that it is a 'discipline within a discipline' (it has no role outside the context of art and design), and (2) it is a servant discipline. The interests it serves are those of 'making' or practice. It may be appropriate now to consider whether critical studies may become an independent subject, studied equally for its illuminative capacity in relation to practice, or for the benefit of its own inherent knowledge systems. (p. 305)

Thistlewood establishes two arguments ('new heresies') which challenge some prevalent assumptions: first, that critical studies 'should not necessarily inform the practice of art and design'; and, second, that 'art and design practice may then be undertaken principally for the benefit of informing critical studies'. He acknowledges that 'while each significantly enhances the other, each may also stand alone. They are both serving and served in their mutual relationship' (p. 311).

The beneficial effect of critical awareness on pupils' art-making is well documented in case study; and direct engagement with making processes enhances pupils' capabilities to read and appreciate the work of others, as has been described. How valid, then, is critical activity which does not relate, in this reflexive way, to practical activity: in other words, can accomplished criticism be achieved without making? In the professional world, after all, film critics are not expected also to be film-makers, or literary critics to be writers. Indeed, it is not expected that football fans are also players. The different perceptions and needs of informed audience and active participant are well rehearsed. They have to do with the difference between appreciation and action.

To be undertaken effectively, both require the application of skills; equally, both are enhanced by some knowledge and understanding. In schools, such skills, knowledge and understanding are most fruitfully generated by direct experience and action. In the case of critical skills, the making experience might offer one, albeit not the only, vehicle for experiential learning.

What is being described is the concept of reciprocity: a reflexive curriculum, in which different 'domains' of the subject have both discrete purposes and contributory roles, to their mutual profit.

THE CENTRALITY OF LANGUAGE

High-quality dialogue, prompted and supported by the teacher, is pivotal in the process of analysis, reflection, comparison and evaluation. Over time and with practice, pupils develop confidence in expressing ideas and emotions, their views and judgements become more incisive and their critical vocabulary becomes more extensive. In turn, their ability to decode art and construct meanings flourishes. They become better prepared to codify their own work and communicate increasingly complex ideas and meanings. Classroom dialogue both promotes pupils' insights and provides vital evidence of their understandings. Pupils' explanations make accessible the conceptual connections they make. The role of the teacher in promoting the extensive, demanding use of language cannot be underestimated.

The joint purposes of language use are summarized by Edwards and Mercer (1987, p. 20): 'The role of language in the development of understanding is thus characterised in two ways. First, it provides a medium for teaching and learning. Second, it is one of the materials from which the child constructs a way of thinking.'

Many educationalists have made the case for learning through language. Among the most eminent, Louis Arnaud Reid (1986) argues that language allows abstract concepts to be expressed in concrete terms which have meaning to others. He explores how knowledge, in a conventional sense, is tied up with statements: how 'conceptual thinking' is 'inseparable from its linguistic expression' (p. 6).

Reid also argues that while discursive language is used to express concrete experience and analytical thinking, so too a language must be found to communicate personal experience, sensations and feelings. For the latter, Reid turns to the media of the arts. In doing so, he establishes a reciprocal relationship between language as a way of communicating analytical insight and art-making as a means of expressing personal response to perception. Thus languages, visual and verbal, are proposed as interdependent and complementary.

Good art and design teaching embraces language as a prominent component of the curriculum experience. Indeed, art and design teachers are often cited as being particularly able to generate high-quality and varied use of language in their classrooms. The potential of language, however, might not yet be fully exploited, for as Taylor (1986) points out:

> The emphasis on practical work frequently leads to perfunctory lesson introductions in which the emphasis is on giving and clarifying instructions, followed by practical work extending almost to the bell with just enough time left to clear up for the next lesson. In these circumstances, the one-to-one talk characteristic of art lessons is often of an essentially technical nature. (p. 283)

Hughes (1993) argues the value of 'transferable skills of verbal discourse, analysis and speculation', within philosophical, critical and historical frameworks, and suggests that 'we must use and introduce young people to whatever framework of discourse is appropriate and teach them techniques for doing this' (p. 285).

Hughes refers to Creber (1990), who suggests that 'our task is to energise perception by exercising it', and goes on to describe Creber's standpoint: 'He eschews formula teaching of the kind that often now masquerades as critical study, encouraging art teachers like their English colleagues to make confident use of language and consider what looking at things can do to our thinking' (Hughes, 1993, p. 286).

Numerous references to language in the National Curriculum Order for art – for example, the use of the words 'discuss', 'talk about', 'explain' and 'review' – substantiate its crucial role in both critical study and pupils' practical work. In an earlier paper, Hughes writes: 'If critical studies is to develop and prosper in the curriculum it will ultimately rely as much upon modes of verbal expression and discourse as upon practical art-making' (1989, p. 80).

CREATIVITY, ARTISTIC LEARNING AND THE TEACHING OF ART AND DESIGN

Art and design education is concerned, fundamentally, with creativity: developing the capacity for it and learning to appreciate its manifestations. Peter Abbs (1989) writes:

> One of the terms essential to any understanding of education must be that of creativity. The word has come to denote a disposition of mind which is experimental, engaged, a particular kind of teaching and learning where the results cannot be comprehended in advance of the process. Isn't the educated mind the creative mind? (p. 1)

Just as the concept of creativity is founded upon a nexus of intellectual, perceptual, conceptual and sensory experience, so too must teaching and learning experiences be designed to reflect this mutuality, and to enhance it. Abbs carefully distinguishes between this notion of creativity and previous associations the word might have had with 'originality', which he sees as the subverting of conventions, with 'being different', and with iconoclasm. The task of teachers of art and design is to maximize opportunities for creative thought and action: developing art-making activities which represent more than simply the acquisition of practical skills; and encouraging forms of critical study which foster understanding and creative reasoning and avoid sterile knowledge-gathering.

As Taylor (1986) claims: 'Genuinely expressive work on any appreciable scale would appear to arise most frequently out of circumstances in which insight, awareness and understanding are also fostered. It is here, then, that the truly central ground of art education should be located' (p. 281). It is unreasonable to expect children to develop 'insight, awareness and understanding' by osmosis, by mere confrontation with practical experience. It is necessary to establish the means by which experience is captured and considered: particularly the establishment of structured, guided yet open-ended activities and versatile teaching.

What is needed is an art and design curriculum equally concerned with learning about the formal elements of art (predominantly through practical engagement with them) *and* with the reflective consideration of personal response and feeling. Both, in equal part, shape the way in which the world is read, and create the particular 'frame of reference' through which experience is interpreted. Sadly, many claims for art and design education are not matched by the teaching or content provided. The different orthodoxies of making and, more recently, critical studies sometimes obscure the lack of a conceptual framework for the curriculum offered. To caricature, practical art-making becomes skill acquisition, critical study a superficial and plagiaristic history of art.

Eisner (1972) offers the following concept of 'artistic learning':

> Artistic learning is not a single type of learning. Artistic learning deals with the development of abilities to create art forms; it deals with the development of powers of aesthetic perception, and it deals with the ability to understand art as a cultural phenomenon. Thus, an understanding of artistic learning requires us to attend to how people learn to create visual forms having aesthetic and expressive character, to how people learn to see visual forms in art and in nature, and to how understanding of art occurs. (p. 65)

When adequate attention is given to these three aspects, their reciprocal benefit can be realized. The potential result for pupils is thoughtful and skilled making, visual awareness and critical and cultural literacy. To consider the practical and critical domains of the subject separately is to deconstruct, artificially, the iterative creative process.

REFERENCES

Abbs, P. (1989) *A is for Aesthetic: Essays on Creative and Aesthetic Education*. Lewes: Falmer Press.

Assessment of Performance Unit (1983) *Aesthetic Development*. London: APU.

Berger, J. (1972) *Ways of Seeing*. London: BBC/Penguin.

Bowden, J. (1989) Talking about artworks: the verbal dilemma. In Thistlewood, D. (ed.), *Critical Studies in Art and Design Education*. Harlow: National Society for Education in Art and Design/Longman.

Britton, A. (1991) The manipulation of skill on the outer limits of function. In *Beyond the Dovetail: Craft, Skill and Imagination* (exhibition catalogue). London: Crafts Council.

Creber, P. (1990) *Thinking through English*. Milton Keynes: Open University Press.

Department of Education and Science (DES) (1990) *English in the National Curriculum (No. 2)*. London: HMSO.

Department of Education and Science (DES) (1992a) *Art in the National Curriculum (England)*. London: HMSO.

Department of Education and Science (DES) (1992b) Press release, 10 March.

Department of Education and Science (DES) (1992c) Letter from A.E.D. Chamier, Schools 3 Branch, to 'All those to be consulted under Section 20(5) of the Education Reform Act 1988', 27 January.

Durbin, G., Morris, S., and Wilkinson, S. (1990) *A Teacher's Guide to Learning from Objects*. London: English Heritage.

Dyson, A. (1989) Art history in schools: a comprehensive strategy. In Thistlewood, D. (ed.), *Critical Studies in Art and Design Education*. Harlow: National Society for Education in Art and Design/Longman.

Edwards, D., and Mercer, N. (1987) *Common Knowledge: The Development of Understanding in the Classroom*. London and New York: Routledge.

Eisner, E.W. (1972) *Educating Artistic Vision*. New York: Macmillan.

Gentle, K. (1990) Art making for individuals. *Journal of Art and Design Education* **9**(3), 263–75.

Hughes, A. (1989) The copy, the parody and the pastiche: observations on practical approaches to critical studies. In Thistlewood, D. (ed.), *Critical Studies in Art and Design Education*. Harlow: National Society for Education in Art and Design/Longman.

Hughes, A. (1993) Don't judge pianists by their hair. *Journal of Art and Design Education* **12**(3), 279–89.

Kress, G., and van Leeuwen, T. (1992) Structures of visual representation. *Journal of Literary Semantics* **21**(2), 92–117.

Langer, S. (1953) *Feeling and Form: A Theory of Art.* London: Routledge and Kegan Paul.

Language in the National Curriculum (LINC) (1992) Reading the world. In *The Reading Repertoire: Materials for Professional Development.*

Leach, B. (1940) *A Potter's Book.* London: Faber and Faber.

London Borough of Redbridge (1992) Using religious artefacts educationally: an overview. In *Religious Artefacts: Information, Ideas and Examples.*

Office for Standards in Education (OFSTED) (1993) *Art – Key Stages 1, 2 and 3 – First Year, 1992–93. The implementation of the curricular requirements of the Education Reform Act.* A report from the Office of Her Majesty's Chief Inspector of Schools. London: HMSO.

Pascall, David (1992) The cultural dimension in education. Text of a speech given at the Royal Society of Arts, National Foundation for Arts Education, London, 20 November.

Pye, D. (1968) *The Nature and Art of Workmanship.* Cambridge: Cambridge University Press.

Reid, L.A. (1986) *Ways of Understanding and Education.* London: Heinemann.

Taylor, R. (1986) *Educating for Art: Critical Response and Development.* Harlow: SCDC/ Longman.

Thistlewood, D. (1993) Curricular development in critical studies. *Journal of Art and Design Education* **12**(3), 305–16.

Chapter 4

'Race', Gender and a Touch of Class

Robert Ferguson

The purpose of this chapter is to explore some possibilities for teaching about representation. This is not an issue which is unusual for the teacher of art or design. The approach to be adopted, however, is one concerned particularly with representations of issues relating to race, gender and class in the mass media. The context for this emphasis is that of a world in which, on the one hand, a celebration of cultural diversity in the mass media may be observed. On the other, it may be noted that the representation of issues relating to race, gender and class are (as they always have been) problematic and worthy of serious study. For confirmation of the former, it is helpful to turn to theorists of the media such as Fiske (1989) and Willis (1990) who wish to celebrate the vibrant energy of media representations of the world. The latter case is based upon a recognition that the very same world is at the same time one where all kinds of representational abuse take place. In relation to this position, Masterman (1985) and Price (1993) offer a generally more critical and appreciative approach to the media and media studies.

People live in a time of celebration and concern, of pleasure and of pain related to the mass media. It might be argued that any serious educational engagement with the visual and audio-visual must negotiate its way through the tensions and contradictions which media representations offer daily. The main purpose of education in relation to media representations should be neither to praise nor to condemn. The main purpose should be to identify the ways in which meanings are constructed in media texts, and the ways in which those meanings are negotiated by different audiences in different contexts.

This involves teachers, lecturers, students and pupils in a process of analysis and reflection. It also requires an engagement with theories of representation and society and with a concept of practical work which is productive at the same time as it is analytic.

The presence of media representations in our lives is not an added extra but a component part of existence. Educators ignore these representations at their peril. But this does not mean that the mass media should be treated as a singular, gigantic ogre of the iconic. Nor does it require teachers to see their role as that of adopting a civilizing mission directed at those pitiful pupils who actually enjoy watching television or playing video games. Those teachers who have already made up their minds about the media either as a great evil or as a liberating source of endless representational pleasure should not engage with this chapter further. Such teachers can only hope to act as a kind of talking guidebook, whose activities may sometimes be informative, but will never be educational. To condemn the media as agents of barbarism and enemies of civilization is as unwise as insisting that the media provide a true source of liberation from domination and an alienating existence. Educational activity has to be both more demanding and more circumspect. This is particularly the case in the field of art and design education. Controversy and multiple interpretation of texts is essential to the educational process, whether one is analysing the work of Caravaggio, Warhol, Scorsese or Liberace.

ON PRAISE AND CONDEMNATION

The history of media studies, inasmuch as it exists, is peppered with references to debates about élitism and the fears of the intelligentsia that the forces of barbarism are at the gates, as Storey (1993) demonstrates. Consequently, as Masterman (1985) argues, many educational approaches to the mass media have required a *protective* pedagogy, and sometimes an outright condemnation of the mass media. This type of approach is questionable as an adequate response to the presence and importance in everyday life of media representations. It is also fundamentally flawed because it simply does not work. Neither school nor college pupils are ready to be preached at about the evils of the mass media. Nor are they likely to turn with ease and willingness to the culture of the educators.

It is extraordinary that, as the end of the twentieth century approaches, so many politicians still believe that it is possible to force pupils to develop *good taste* by prescribing the type of texts they should read; the type of music to which they should listen; the type of images they should respect. They forget that the context in which this is attempted is one where large numbers of young people face long-term unemployment, live in run-down communities, or have watched as their own families disintegrate under the pressures of economic and social change. The one thing that all these young people *will* engage with in some way or another is the mass media. They will all watch television, hear some radio, read some magazines and newspapers. A small minority of them may go on to study the *conventional* academic subjects in more depth. The majority will live in and through the mass media. This is not to suggest that the present situation will never change, or that change is undesirable. What is important is that the educational process is related to the world in which pupils live – not to the one inhabited or imagined by those who prescribe and proscribe on behalf of those whom they would police and control.

WHY 'RACE', GENDER AND CLASS?

The choice of the three general areas for study in this chapter is a deliberate attempt to hold on to an agenda which is in danger of dissolving in a postmodern miasma.

A former art teacher, Sarap (1988) provides a useful introduction to postmodernism. It is not claimed that these three categories are the only important fields for critical investigation in the classroom. Nor is it suggested that they should be studied as discrete areas. What is argued is that, almost at the end of the twentieth century, with or without the comfort of grand narratives, power relations in society are alive and well. Lyotard (1984) has suggested that with the breakdown of the Enlightenment tradition there are no longer totalities or grand narratives to which one may turn in times of philosophical or other crises. Hebdige (1988) has provided a lively overview of the debates which Lyotard has engendered, and Norris (1990) has constructed a useful antidote to a less than rigorous approach to the concept of postmodernism.

Power relationships, then, need to be studied as significant dimensions of people's daily lives, but they are also (and crucially for the art and design teacher) represented in a multitude of ways, whether in the news, feature films, television dramas, documentaries, newspapers, comics, magazines, music videos, computer games – the list could go on. Representations of relationships of 'race', class and gender are also sites of struggle, from page three of the *Sun* newspaper in the UK, renowned for its daily bare-breasted woman accompanied by an inane caption, to comic book champions of the people like Judge Dredd; from *Vogue* to *Elle*.

This multitude of representations should not be collapsed into a false unity. The mass media cater for many audiences and their messages are just as often subtle and sophisticated as they are crass and simplistic. The role of teachers and pupils is to identify where and how media messages utilize a range of signifying practices; to what end and in whose interests.

Emphasis will be given in this chapter to representations of issues relating to 'race', but the separation out of 'race', gender and class is more of an analytic convenience than a lived reality. Throughout the chapter, the term 'race' is placed in inverted commas, following the suggestion by Donald and Rattansi (1992) that 'no persuasive empirical case has been made for ascribing common physiological, intellectual or moral capacities or characteristics to individuals on the basis of skin colour or physiognomy' (p. 1).

THE CONSTRUCTION OF MEANING

The ways in which the media construct their meanings are not unknown to children and young people. It has been shown in some detail by Hodge and Tripp (1988) that the decoding of something as apparently simple as an animated cartoon requires sophisticated intellectual skills. The general and sometimes specialist knowledge of aspects of media representation which is possessed by many pupils has been commented on in a large number of books and prefaces (see Buckingham, 1990; Masterman, 1985; and Hart, 1991). This is usually offered because the writers wish to maintain, at the very least, a liberal position in relation to the education of the young. What is often absent from the (patronizing) praise heaped upon those pupils who 'know more about the mass media than their teachers' is that such knowledge is likely to be fragmented, informal, partial, commonsensical, and usually pleasurable.

A media studies approach to this knowledge recognizes the validity of the media experience of pupils, but also wishes to introduce them to some of the more formal ways in which analysts have tried to *make sense* of media representations. The main aim, as already indicated, is not to praise or condemn, but to *understand*. Subsidiary aims may include discussion and debate about what is of merit and value or what is questionable in a whole range of media representations. Discrimination is not something which needs to be taught. It is something which is an essential component of the development of understanding. The development of understanding is the business of the teacher.

In this chapter it will not be possible to cover as wide a range of representations as a general education requires. The principles upon which analysis might proceed, however, are usable across a range of media and representations. It is the present purpose to concentrate on a small number of examples to illustrate some key points.

It is likely that many teachers of art and design will see themselves as concerned most with visual (and possibly tactile) education. There comes a point of potential frustration when such teachers are asked to be as specific as possible about the ways in which the media signify their meaning. It is one thing to teach a pupil about the preparation of a plate for etching, or the processes by which a video or film is edited. It is quite another thing to ask precisely how a film or an etching offer up their meaning, or to be as precise as possible about what that meaning might be.

Part of the appeal of the visual arts has been that they encompass a sense of mystery, of a brushing against the unknown or indescribable. While there may be occasions when such rhetoric can be invoked, these should be the exception rather than the norm. For the rest of the time, the teacher of art and design should be prepared to consider the ways in which media representations confirm or deny existing relations of power and subordination in our society. This is not suggested as a full-time commitment to militancy. It is, rather, a recognition that the understanding and analysis of power relationships is a necessary underpinning for the development of a complex and continuous engagement with the media. The development of understanding in relation to the media is as much about a politics of vision as it is about the development of taste and culture. There is a social and a political dimension to the teaching of art and design which has been denied or evaded for too long. Art and society cannot and should not be separated.

In order to make some sense of the meaning which a media message transmits, it is necessary to develop skills of analysis. These skills should be based, in part, upon the utilization of existing analytical methodologies adapted for the classroom at the appropriate level. This suggestion derives from the work of Bruner (1966), who has argued that it should be possible to present any argument in an intellectually coherent way to an audience of any age.

The advantages of acquiring analytical skills are numerous. They allow certain ground rules to be established in relation to the study of the media, and they avoid the endless pendulum swings between opinions about particular media representations. The understanding and implementation of a particular methodology are also a means of developing a sense of intellectual rigour alongside an awareness of the genuine excitement and relevance which an informed analysis of media messages can produce.

Analysis is not some abstract and esoteric activity designed to give weight to a nebulous concept of *Art*. It is a means of clarifying why messages are as they are, in whose interests such messages may work, and why the student may decide that such messages are or are not of personal interest and relevance. It is also a means of bringing the concept of pleasure into focus as something which is based on more than a simplistic conception of taste.

There are two potential disadvantages to an analytical approach to media messages. The first is that what starts its existence as a stimulating and suggestive analytical methodology can end up in the classroom as an arid, formulaic and often drearily implemented pedagogy. The second is that teachers and pupils may feel that analysis is too dry and intellectualizing as an activity for creative subjects.

The first point is valid and can be tackled only if teachers and pupils work together to ensure that theoretical and methodological concepts and principles are never turned into empty formulae to be parroted on request; as the endless distillation of the work of Roland Barthes (1977) on advertising and popular culture has become in some schools. There has to be a useful and productive tension upheld between the need to recognize complexity in many theoretical approaches to the media, and the need to ensure that pupils are not lost in pretentious abstraction.

The second point clearly relates to the first. There is often a reluctance on the part of teachers to involve themselves and their pupils in theoretical debate. Such stereotypical teachers sneer at theory and pride themselves on their down-to-earth approach to education. This is sometimes made paradoxically complex by the art and design teacher who manages to combine a down-to-earth approach to the technicalities of the creative process (how to register a lino-block or load a camera) with a pseudo-spiritual discourse about the meaning and purpose of art. What is being argued here does not deny mystery or the unknown, but it is based upon a pedagogy where the unknown is what is left after exhaustive analysis and debate.

Careful analysis does not deny spirituality in art or unfashionable concepts such as beauty. It demands more knowledge about them, but combined with knowledge of what has been referred to earlier as a politics of vision. The analytical approach is not prescriptive or proscriptive. It is, rather, concerned with extending knowledge and understanding. Decisions about what constitutes the worthwhile, the pleasurable and the suspect must ultimately be taken by the pupil. It is the teacher's role to provide information, analytical skills and the arena for debate.

In the remainder of this chapter, the discussion will focus on media representations which highlight just some of the key issues in media analysis. There is no attempt to offer a methodology for teaching. It is suggested that the teacher of art and design should adapt or develop approaches to teaching where these issues can be incorporated *over time*. Beginning to teach about media representations is no more susceptible to the one-off lesson than was anti-racist or anti-sexist teaching. It has to be said that a great deal of the harm done in the name of these once worthy educational fields was caused by an attempt to reduce complexity to fit the constraints of the school timetable. When combined with missionary zeal it was a lethal brew. What is argued here is the need for a revised pedagogy, but one which nevertheless holds on to certain fundamental concerns about 'race' and gender relations in society.

The recognition of the importance of mass media representations does not imply the abandonment of all previous practice. It does, however, require the willingness to acknowledge tensions and contradictions in understandings of all media representations, and a determination to incorporate a politics of vision within the sphere of teaching. Analysis, deconstruction and the identification of how discourses operate are regarded as practical activities. They require both pupils and teachers to get off their intellectual backsides and rethink their positions in relation to the media. They also require both pupils and teachers to reappraise and constantly question the relationship between all communications media and society.

Anyone for tennis?

The first example to be discussed comes from a documentary made by the now defunct Thames Television in the early 1980s, entitled *Small World*. The programme in question is about the exploitation of women in appalling factory conditions in what are designated as 'export-processing zones'. The section to which attention is drawn is unusual because it shows someone voicing in one interview ideologically based judgements on all the issues which are suggested by the title of this chapter.

The speaker is D.A.N. Osborne, who was at the time President of International Sports. The sequence shows him seated at a desk, intercut with footage of the factory and the women at work producing tennis balls. It is immediately preceded by a spokesperson for the Marcos government, who points out that 'we' have never been particularly worried by that ogre of the multinational. He says, 'We've been happy. They've been happy.' The 'we' to whom he refers, however, is not likely to include the women working in the factory. Mr Osborne then speaks:

1. Well Dunlop in its overseas activities certainly has its own manufacturing and trading companies all the way around the world. It was a considered decision to come to the Philippines to make tennis balls in the same way as we make them in any part of the world, with the same materials, the same processing plant. Just the location that's different.

2. Well in the mid 1970s we were looking for capacity to make tennis balls, and of course in an export-processing zone import/export are going to be free of all duties, which helps and also cuts a lot of red tape that can exist in foreign countries.

3. We run a three-shift system here. We work six days a week because that is normal here. (...) From the company point of view, if you build a profit centre and not a loss centre, you've fulfilled your company's objective.

4. Under the laws of the Philippines, striking is not allowed in certain classes of industry and the export-processing zone is one of them.

5. The thing you've got to be careful about in talking is saying oh you're exploi..., you've come here to exploit the natives, you see. Well that isn't really true, um, because we're only an employer amongst many. It's probably true to say that their happiness, their willingness, uh, to do things for fun or even in work, their mental age is probably lower than Europe is. Or perhaps even the rest of Asia.

6. But make no mistake, you know, you get some very clever children and there's some very clever people here indeed. And I don't mean that in a nasty sense.

This remarkable interview is now over fifteen years old. As such it works as a suitable reminder that both representation and understanding have histories. Mr Osborne learned his wisdom and the ethics of business from someone, and he, in turn, is passing it on to those who would listen. A key concept in the study and understanding of media representations has to be that of *history*. This is particularly important as we study the imagery of advertising, but it is also related to our understanding of images generated in the more conventional world of Art (see, for instance, Dabydeen, 1985; Gilman, 1992; and Richards, 1986).

There is a coherent implied discourse informing the statements made by Mr Osborne. The concept of implicature is very helpful when considering certain aspects of discourse. According to Fowler (1986), an implicature 'is a proposition emerging from something that is said, but not actually stated in the words uttered, nor logically derivable from them. It must therefore be a product of the relationship between the utterance and the context; and a vital part of context would be the knowledge and motives of speaker and addressee' (p. 106).

It is possible, through an educational involvement with the text, to reconstruct Osborne's discourse. In paragraph 1 it is stated that there is no need to be concerned about the quality of the tennis balls produced in the Philippines. It is suggested that there is here an implicit discourse about the potential unreliability of 'foreigners' to produce a product which is up to British standards. There is a reassurance that there is no need to worry because the plant and materials used here are the same as anywhere else. So, by the way, is the management. The hint that women of the Philippines might be the only variation in the otherwise stable relations of production is taken up again in paragraph 5.

The reasonableness with which it is suggested that there are certain classes of industry where striking is not allowed is linked to the argument about removing 'duties' and cutting red tape. There is no mention here of the poor conditions under which the women work and the meagreness of the wages which they earn. The emphasis is all on the quality of the product and the potential benefit to the consumer. Mr Osborne is not, however, at ease with his own argument and he counsels the viewer not to judge him or Dunlop too harshly. The racism floats to the surface of his discourse as he allows himself to mention 'the natives', whom he insists he is not exploiting. The logic here is breathtaking in its ineptitude. Mr Osborne is not 'exploiting the natives' because he is only one employer amongst many. QED.

In paragraphs 5 and 6 a discourse is offered which still informs many western understandings of 'foreigners'; of the Other. The reason that it is all right to make them work in conditions which no one in the 'civilized' West would accept is that they are just happy all the time and also mentally retarded. But Mr Osborne would not want to be misunderstood. They have some lovely children. He does not want to be 'nasty'.

This is the benevolent racism which has taken over from the arrogance of the empire-builder. Women of the Philippines can be patronized and exploited because they are women and because they are Filipinas. They can be designated as child-like in their adulthood. They can be exported as servants to all parts of the world using the same rationalization. They are just so happy and they breed such pretty children.

The representative from the Marcos government who was not troubled by the ogre of the multinational might not be so easy to insult with impunity, because he is someone with whom Mr Osborne has to do business. Mental retardation is then reserved for women of colour, and women from the working class. A key discourse of popular racism is virtually complete. The whites have to watch over and protect those simple-minded, happy working-class women.

There are many lessons to be learned here. The obscenity of white 'liberal' racism is only the most obvious. It is the history of representation which is of importance to the art and design teacher. This same history is important when considering the conditions under which many of today's products are manufactured – from trainers to computer components. But it is also important when considering the tradition of benevolent racism which has allowed advertising imagery to represent certain peoples as 'sweet' – as long as they do not pick up arms and seek their liberation. Once this occurs the happy native becomes the fiendish oriental.

Discourses are invoked for specific occasions. Imagery is manufactured or utilized to give substance to the discourse. The teacher of art and design has to be prepared to move across to the study of written and oral language use as well as engaging with the languages of the visual. One has only to consider the narrative power of Conrad's *Heart of Darkness* or the pictorial eloquence of the painting by Paul Friedrich Meyerheim entitled *The Savages* in Pieterse (1992) to understand the historical and ideological underpinning of so much of Mr Osborne's discourse. His words are precious in a ghoulish way. In his naivety, he gives explicit form to a discourse which is usually reserved for the afternoon tea party or cocktails before dinner.

What about a bottle of exotic beer?

The study of individual advertisements can be a valuable and important means of developing analytical skills. It is also something which encourages pupils to develop their ability to describe with accuracy, and to evaluate and debate the relationship between text, imagery and audience.

Much of the earlier classroom-based media study of advertisements was modelled upon a version of Barthes' (1977) brilliant analysis of an advertisement for Panzani pasta in a French magazine. The problem with such work, however, was that it was not so easy to transfer it into the classroom context. Either the work was unsatisfactory because neither pupil nor teacher could bring such a wide range of reference and understanding to bear upon the 'text', or the approach taken oversimplified semiotics. If this happened, the lesson was little more than an exercise in spotting somewhat mechanically the (unproblematic) denotations and connotations of the various components of the advertisement. Everything just *meant* something.

A well-prepared and enthusiastic teacher was once observed to lose his confidence as his introduction to image analysis was taken over by a group of girls who were way ahead of him. In small groups, they were provided with examples of advertising from colour supplements and asked to carry out a simple semiotic (the teacher did not use the word) analysis. They not only understood what the teacher wanted, but finished the whole activity within about ten minutes. There was little more that either he or they could say. The palm tree meant exoticism; the cigar meant success; the raised chin meant confidence. It was all so easy and really rather obvious. It seemed that the girls were surprised that the teacher had difficulty recognizing such things!

The situation just described is somewhat extreme. Sometimes pupils are just plain bored by having to look hard at images. Sometimes they can become enthusiastic. There are two points to note here. The first is that any work which involves precise description and the careful articulation of implied or explicit meaning is of educational value in its own right. The search for precise expression is the business of art and design teachers and their pupils. Language development is about the use of images as well as the use of words, but it is through words that the use of images is justified or rejected. The second point to note is that it *is* important that pupils at school or students in further or higher education should have experience of basic image analysis. As with so many other educational activities, however, the basics should lay a foundation – not become an end in themselves. There is a tendency, especially at the General Certificate of Secondary Education (GCSE) level, to oversimplify the process of making meaning and the process of understanding meaning. With these caveats in mind, attention is now turned to a possible approach to the analysis of an advertisement for a Dutch beer.

The advertisement in unassuming, comprised of simply a man with a bottle of beer on a tray. The brand of the beer is the only written message. But there is clearly more to the advertisement than this description would suggest. The beer is in a conventional brown glass bottle. The tray is unremarkable. The man, however, is somewhat different. He is an exotic 'Other'. This is signified first by the fact that he is wearing a turban. He is facing the potential customer, though he does not have the power of the look. That is because his eyes are in the shadow which covers much of his face, serving only to highlight the form of the cheeks and nose.

There is mystery in this graphic rendition. To be served a bottle of beer by this man is, to state a well-known thesis informing the study of advertising, to be offered more than just a beer. The advertisement does not promise that the viewers may become like the man if they buy the beer. This is a common advertising strategy, but one which is not appropriate in this case. What customers are offered is the possibility of *associating* with the man. This association is, of course, imaginary. It may take the form of an (imaginary) excitement which this exoticized figure bestows upon the beer through the mere association of the beer with a turban and a shaded face. Behind this, in turn, there may be a history of exploration, travel, adventure – or colonialism, exploitation and racism if another discourse is adopted. These two discourses are poised in delicate opposition to one another in the simple and direct appeal of the advertisement. What holds this mysterious waiter in check is the very product which he is there to advertise. By placing the product on a tray between the viewer and the figure, the former is given licence to study, to brood over, to take strength or pleasure from a figure who in another context might prove less mysterious and more threatening.

The history of advertising abounds with examples of exotic figures who are serving, carrying loads or bearing gifts for the (mainly white) customer (see Pieterse, 1992). Probably the most famous exoticized bearers of gifts are the three wise men in the Nativity story. All these representations offer either reassurance or excitement.

There is another dimension to representations of the exotic, which is also present in the beer advertisement. This is the dimension of sexuality. The mysterious figure can also be read as 'full of Eastern promise', to borrow a slogan from the manufacturers of a chocolate bar. The sexuality associated with people who are constructed as 'Other' is both attractive and repulsive at the same time. For this reason, reading the sexuality in an exotic representation is what would have been described in a seaside postcard as 'naughty but nice'.

There is, however, a representational hair's breadth which separates certain advertising imagery from overt racist propaganda. Take away the product, the bottle of beer, and there is a challenge in that eyeless stare. The nameless figure can quickly take his place as a character in numerous adventure stories – as a potential threat. Such a possibility is communicated in numerous books, films, television dramas and comics. Orientals are not to be trusted. This is not to suggest that *all* representations of people seen as foreign or exotic are racist. What is being argued is that the general discourses through which advertising imagery has operated have tended towards racism. Some years ago the British National Front used a simple but heavily racialized image of three turbaned males for a very different purpose than that of the beer advertisement. There was a warning under the image which suggested that these figures were after 'our' jobs, 'our' homes, 'our' country.

The representation of exoticism is, then, both complex and problematic. It is not something which can be dealt with quickly or glibly. Teaching about such representation is, it is argued, very important, but it requires much more engagement and study than has been acknowledged in the past. It may be that the way to understand representations of this kind is to approach them 'obliquely'. This means that semiotics is of very limited use if it is dependent *only* on existing knowledge – whoever happens to be the pupil. It is pointless asking someone who has little knowledge of Britain's imperialist past what is 'meant' by an image of Britannia portrayed having a cup of tea while servile exotic Others stand in the background carrying decorative cartons of tea. (For an excellent source of visual material concerned with imperialism and advertising, see Opie, 1985.) Meaning here has to be informed by a knowledge of history as well as a knowledge of certain conventions in graphic and typographic design. This, in turn, requires both teacher and student to engage in study as well as discussion, for which the work of Blonsky (1985) is particularly relevant.

Burglary, blackness and business

The next example to be discussed is an advertisement which is a full page from the *Guardian* newspaper on 27 December 1988. It is for a charity called 'The Prince's Youth Business Trust'. The brief descriptive analysis offered here is intended to illustrate the way in which character traits may be attributed to people by forms of insidious argument. It is also an example which does not make any explicit reference to history or the Empire. What it does do is to pick up on an accompanying discourse to that which sees black people, among others, as exotic or servants. This other discourse could probably be traced back to the time of the Empire, but is drawn upon whenever patronization of exotic Others gives way to distrust. In this discourse, black people (or Jews or the Irish or some other chosen exemplar according to the needs of history) are seen as potential thieves.

The young man represented here is looking directly at the reader. He is asked a question which might seem innocuous in another context. But Sydney's answer triggers a whole range of prejudicial judgements with which the reader is then entertained. Burglary seems like a 'natural' choice for Sydney, for as the narrative under the image informs the reader, he is part of the vicious circle of deprivation and law-breaking which results from inner-city living conditions. He is also, in the implicit discourse which provides the core content of the advertisement, simply a young black man. This implicit discourse tells readers what they are always already expected to know – that young black men are (potential) thieves.

On reading the whole text, it becomes clear that Sydney has gone into business, with the help of the 'Prince's Youth Business Trust', and that he is selling burglar alarms. The reader is informed that Sydney was 'given' an accountant, whose name we are told is Sabash Patel. The only possible reason for naming the accountant would seem to be the desire to impress the reader with a name which accentuates the multiculturalism of the Trust. But whether the whole story with its 'happy ending' is read or not, the central motif of the narrative remains unchanged. It is one of a host of discourses about black people which are learned socially but very often perceived as 'natural', as common sense.

The range of media representations mentioned here could be considerably extended, and could include such popular television as Terry Wogan programmes or *The Cosby Show*. (A scholarly and very readable account of research into the possible racism in *The Cosby Show* can be found in Jhally and Lewis, 1992.) In each of these it is possible to find examples of more or less refined, more or less patronizing, racist attitudes. Whether or not such representations are planned and intentional is not the main issue. They are significant because they form the overall ideological setting in which pupils, both black and white, have to locate themselves. They are significant because they inform the attitudes and interpretations of society and eventually the world of all school pupils. This does not mean that everyone believes every piece of prejudicial or xenophobic material which they come across on television or read in the newspaper. But it does mean that such material has to be kept under constant review in order to avoid complacency or the naturalization of prejudicial judgements. The representation of black people as servants or decorative additions to the Court in the work of painters of undoubted repute such as Velasquez or Rembrandt need to be discussed in this way.

Studying the real thing

A recent documentary series on British television looked in some detail at the ways in which advertising operates. (It should be noted here that the recent change in copyright law now makes it possible for schools to show general broadcast material upon payment of a relatively small annual fee.) A significant moment in the representation of issues concerned with race and gender came when two very well-known advertisements for Coca-Cola were shown. The first dates from the late 1960s and shows a large number of young people from various places and cultures seen at first from an aerial shot and then from just below their eye level as the camera glides past them. They are all looking off into the distance and singing about wanting to buy the world a Coke to the melody of a popular song of the time. The breadth of the camera's vision gives stature to the representation. It is about the universality of Coca-Cola. It is also about the representation of diverse cultures and peoples. They are very carefully presented in forms of national dress or costume, thus retaining their exoticism and the appeal of bright colours and patterns. These drinkers of Coca-Cola are not our neighbours. They are still exotic Others, held in melodic place by a white woman who commands the main lines of the song in close-up. She is an earth mother who resembles the figure of Mama Cass, the lead singer in a very popular group of the 1960s called 'The Mamas and the Papas'. This is a representation of multiculturalism with everyone in his/her place. It is the advertisers' aesthetic of communitarianism. It is also a fine example of the importance of understanding the historical context in which imagery/advertising is produced. The Vietnam War was at its height. Young people were showing signs of rebelliousness in many countries. But the multicultural world shown in this advertisement is one where solidarity is in the bottle of Coke rather than the espousal of one or another cause.

By the 1980s advertisements had become somewhat more sophisticated. The multi-racial world of Coca-Cola has moved now to an indoor setting where one young white girl begins the latest Coca-Cola song as she sits alone in what appears to be a council chamber. She is then joined by more and more young people whose appearance suggests that they may inhabit the same multicultural society. No more folk costumes. The sentiments now are about more than just simply loving each other and wanting to buy the world a Coke. They are now in the era of doubt and hope. The white child sings:

> I am the future of the world
> I am the hope of my nation
> I am tomorrow's people
> I am the new inspiration

She is then joined by more and more children from different ethnic and cultural backgrounds. They sing and smile and they speak of a common humanity:

> And we've got a song to sing to you
> And we've got a message to bring to you
> Please let there be
> For you and for me
> A tomorrow (tomorrow)
> If we all can agree
> There'll be sweet harmony
> Tomorrow (tomorrow)

There is a politics of vision in this advertisement and it is one which asks of viewers as consumers a will to peace and 'sweet harmony'. It also contains a somewhat tautologous argument. But the key point, whether viewers drink Coca-Cola or wear Benetton, is that they will remain aware of the existence of these two giants. Along with their aspirations for a better world, they are persuaded in different ways that they should remember the names of the manufacturers and their products:

> And we all will be there
> Coca-Cola to share
> Feeling so real and so true
> Promise us tomorrow
> And we'll build a better world for you.

United colours in a disunited world

The advertising campaign associated with Benetton is the one with which the present discussion will conclude in making a case for the teacher of art and design to become involved in the study of mass media representations. *Ducking the Issue* (Channel 4, 1993) featured Oliviero Toscani, the campaign photographer for Benetton. The programme is excellent material for analysis, but the purpose here is to concentrate on the arguments which seem to be being put forward by Toscani, by representatives of the advertising profession and by pupils from Acland Burghley school in London. These will also be compared with certain tendencies in media research and media education.

Some of the most perceptive writing and research about discourse and semiotics – for example, Williams (1989) and Voloshinov (1986) – has pointed out that in any given society there is likely to be a struggle over the meaning of certain concepts or signifiers. In the world of advertising and the field of media studies more widely, this struggle is of great educational relevance.

The argument put forward by Toscani has an abrasiveness which could encourage thought and reflection. He suggests that, in the conventional (Christian) religious context, the Church used imagery to sell itself. It had its own 'supermodels' in the form of saints. The Church, he argues, hired all the best artists and had the courage to let those artists express themselves freely. The churches of today are the multi-national companies. For Toscani, these companies have a great responsibility and potential above and beyond that of selling their products. They might also use their advertising campaigns to communicate messages which are not directly related to the product, but which may be associated through their quality and seriousness with the product they are vending. So, for instance, he suggests that Fiat might sell their cars through an advertising campaign linked to representations of issues around drugs. (He does not stipulate which ones, but it is fair to assume that he would be unlikely to include either tobacco or alcohol in his campaign.) Such a campaign, according to this logic, would make customers think twice before they bought any car other than a Fiat!

Toscani suggests that the large corporations often lie to their customers in their advertisements. He suggests they are 'telling us lies like in a sukh in Marrakech'. He then laughs, catches himself, and says, 'No, actually in Marrakech they are actually more serious than a big company. Those street vendors are actually much more serious. At least they show you the product and say, sir, would you like to buy this.' This may be read as the statement of one who is trying to retreat from recognition of his own racism, or as a genuine attempt to mount a critique of the conventions of contemporary advertising. Either way, it does highlight the importance of considering what the advertisers are up to.

The position of the advertising executives seems to be quite clear. Adam Lury suggests in the programme that 'advertising has an enormous responsibility in terms of shaping and leading society'. He speaks for the new and sophisticated advertising professional. He suggests that 'all media manipulates (sic) and to single out advertising is distinctly unfair'.

The school pupils who speak in the programme are also concerned that the media may be attempting to manipulate audience response. In the face of a somewhat aggressive approach by Toscani over his (and Benetton's) image of the angelic white youth and the young black child with hair plaited to look like horns, some of the pupils insist that it is offensive and likely to bolster racism. Toscani insists that it takes courage to use the kind of imagery he chooses – including a deathbed scene, a newly born baby which is still connected to its umbilical cord and a dead victim of street violence. He says it is about Benetton making the buying public think. The reason the Benetton advertising campaign has been explored here is that it raises issues which are central to any contemporary educational process.

The relationship between the economic and the aesthetic is particularly delicate in relation to advertising. Either the whole Benetton campaign is a cynical confidence trick, or it is a genuine attempt to develop what might be called 'concerned customers'. It may even be both at the same time. Debate and discussion over the nature of advertising and advertising campaigns requires the assembly of data, the mounting of arguments and the development of methodologies for analysing design processes. It is also a sector of the total media output where representations of issues concerning 'race', gender and class are susceptible to careful investigation.

It is important to set the concern of the advertising professional about the social responsibility of advertisers against certain approaches of the media studies educators. Many educators emphasize correctly the failure of 'effects' media research to prove all the negative effects which advertising is supposed to have on children. Perhaps what is necessary is to concentrate instead on the ways in which pupils can develop their capacities for independent thought on these issues.

It has been argued in this chapter that there is a strong case for the teacher of art and design to work with and through mass media representations, and that the study of 'race', gender and class is one appropriate focal point for the 1990s. It has been suggested that such teaching requires a long-term commitment from both teacher and students, and that teaching about media representations should avoid formulaic or simplistic modes of analysis – whether laudatory or condemnatory. Finally, it has been suggested that the study of media representations can develop skills of analysis, language use and the ability to interlink different strands of intellectual enquiry in a manner both productive and relevant.

REFERENCES

Barthes, R. (1977) The rhetoric of the image. In *Image, Music, Text* (trans. Stephen Heath). London: Fontana.
Blonsky, M. (ed.) (1985) *On Signs*. Oxford: Basil Blackwell.

Bruner, J. (1966) *Towards a Theory of Instruction*. Cambridge, Mass.: Harvard University Press.

Buckingham, D. (1990) *Watching Media Learning: Making Sense of Media Education*. London: Falmer Press.

Dabydeen, D. (1985) *Hogarth's Blacks: Images of Blacks in Eighteenth Century English Art*. Kingston-upon-Thames: Manchester University Press.

Donald, J., and Rattansi, A. (eds) (1992) *'Race', Culture and Difference*. London: Sage/Open University Press.

Fiske, J. (1989) *Understanding Popular Culture*. London: Unwin Hyman.

Fowler, R. (1986) *Linguistic Criticism*. Oxford: Oxford University Press.

Gilman, S. (1992) 'Black bodies, white bodies: towards an iconography of female sexuality in late nineteenth century art, medicine and culture', in Donald and Rattansi (1992).

Hart, A. (1991) *Understanding the Media*. London: Routledge.

Hebdige, D. (1988) *Hiding in the Light*. London: Comedia.

Hodge, B., and Tripp, D. (1988) *Children and Television: A Semiotic Approach*. Cambridge: Polity Press.

Jhally, S., and Lewis, J. (1992) *Enlightened Racism: 'The Cosby Show', Audiences and the Myth of the American Dream*. Oxford: Westview Press.

Lyotard, J.F. (1984) *The Postmodern Condition*. Minneapolis: University of Minnesota Press.

Masterman, L. (1985) *Teaching the Media*. London: Comedia.

Norris, C. (1990) *What's Wrong With Postmodernism*. Hemel Hempstead: Harvester Wheatsheaf.

Opie, R. (1985) *Rule Britannia: Trading on the British Image*. London: Viking.

Pieterse, J. (1992) *White on Black: Images of Africa and Blacks in Western Popular Culture*. London: Yale University Press.

Price, S. (1993) *Media Studies*. London: Pitman.

Richards, J. (1986) 'Boy's Own Empire: feature films and imperialism in the 1930s'. In MacKenzie, J. (ed.), *Imperialism and Popular Culture*. Manchester: Manchester University Press.

Sarap, M. (1988) *Post-Structuralism and Postmodernism: An Introductory Guide*. London: Harvester Wheatsheaf.

Storey, J. (1993) *Cultural Theory and Popular Culture*. London: Harvester Wheatsheaf.

Voloshinov, V. (1986) *Marxism and the Philosophy of Language* (first published 1929). London: Harvard University Press.

Williams, R. (1989) *The Politics of Modernism: Against the New Conformists*. London: Verso.

Willis, P. (1990) *Common Culture*. Milton Keynes: Open University Press.

Chapter 5

Objects of Desire: By Design

Kate Schofield

The purpose of this chapter is to promote the idea that design as an ideology is an under-researched area within the field of art and design education. As a mode of cultural representation, the interpretation of designed artefacts has largely been ignored by scholarly critics. Indeed, the questioning of this ideological system rarely appears in books about design or design journals; nor does it feature to any great extent in exhibitions of design. Books about design are for the most part concerned with the designer, the superficial, the material from which objects are made and the surface 'gloss' of designed artefacts: what they are called, their appearance and function. What an artefact is called and how it is used can be subsumed with little mental agility. After all, it may be thought that if a chair is made to the right height, is reasonably comfortable and is not unpleasant to handle or awkward to sit upon then it can be dismissed as an object fulfilling its purpose. It is perceived as being ergonomically successful and may short-circuit further investigations. Its visual appearance is a question of equal interest and one that has attracted and continues to attract a great deal of attention.

For the most part, writing about design tends to focus on the aesthetics of artefacts, bibliographies of designers' work, chronological histories, and overviews of technical advances. However, what a designed object might 'mean' and how it may be analysed and used for the teaching of art and design has largely been ignored by educationalists and those concerned with design and designed objects, such as museum curators. This is not to say that the meaning of material culture in general has avoided scrutiny. Those working within the field of cultural history – for example, Willis (1990), Hebdige (1988) and Williamson (1990) – have made significant contributions. In particular, the place of consumerism in contemporary society has been well documented. Featherstone (1983) makes the point that 'consumer culture points to the impact of mass consumption on everyday life which has led to the gearing of social activities around the accumulation and consumption of an ever-increasing range of goods and experiences' (p. 4).

Fine art has been subjected to extensive theoretical and critical analysis. Aspects such as contexts, significance, meaning and values in art are propounded by a number of critics. Through the formulation and use of certain frameworks of analysis, perceptions of fine art have been challenged and definitions stretched. Design has for the most part escaped this critical bombardment, although why a designed artefact, carrying within it a summation of historical knowledge and meaning which is unique and significant, has so far succumbed to such little critical analysis is surprising. Perhaps it is because the nature of design is primarily functional that it has been taken for granted for so long. In a general sense, critiques and theories of art seek to make sense of what comes under the general paradigm of conceptual ideas, aesthetics and human expression. For example, expression, dialogue and narrative, representation, formalism and gender have all been encompassed and examined within different frameworks operating in the arena of fine art. It is suggested that design too may be analysed, using frameworks which may be useful in a pedagogical situation.

The subject of design, arguably, occupies a place between art and industry. On the one hand, the very essence and nature of art is that it is some act of self-expression which may or may not manifest itself as a visible or tangible object or objects. Industry, on the other hand, is concerned with the mechanics of manufacture, marketing and the sociological aspects and economics of mass production; of which mass-produced designed artefacts are an essential part. The common denominator of these two areas – art and industry – is design, which as both a noun and a verb has become subsumed within the area of the 'visual arts'. A designed object emanates from a designer's creative thinking, or more accurately a type of problem-solving, and is necessarily different from the conception and act of making art. Designers accept the imposition of finding solutions to briefs set either by themselves or else by clients who request something special for a particular usage or context. Ideally, artists have no such external restrictions, such as function or cost, to contemplate. For artists, any invention and its possible manifestations usually carry no bounds, other than those set by themselves, and may adhere to no conventions, although this may be disputed within certain cultures where it may be said that certain rules apply. For example, a Muslim artist will have the restriction of being forbidden to represent a human figure. The 'message' intended by the artist is necessarily different to that proposed by the designer, although through interpretation the meaning might be the same in certain circumstances. It is suggested that a designed object may be called 'art' or perceived as art when seen in particular contexts. This is an area to which further reference will be made.

The intention now is to examine ways of perceiving mass-produced objects which fall into a special category, objects which are commonly known as 'designer objects'. Such objects – for example, kettles made by the Italian manufacturer Alessi, or chairs designed by the Frenchman Philippe Starck – have a certain status. The first example demonstrates that it is the company name, Alessi, which by promotion has made their objects special. *The Times*, in an article about kitchen gadgets, reinforces this popularist appeal: 'Cubist-shaped Moka machines and sleek architect-designed Alessi coffee makers owe their popularity to the Italian tradition of raising homely devices to the status of cult objects' (23 October 1993). The second example illustrates how, through promotion and marketing, the name of the designer, Philippe Starck, calls attention to the commercial object. Promotion of goods has the effect of lionizing a designer as well as promoting brand-names and styles where uses of language and advertising are as potent as the objects for sale. This semantic evidence acts as a stimulus to the perceiver and can carry a very definite and powerful message. It is suggested that all 'designer objects' carry coded and esoteric messages. Such objects, in turn, may be consciously promoted to become familiar cult objects through advertising and promotion. There are many examples. Haug (1986) states:

> The means of establishing this monopolistic situation is to elevate the commodity to the status of brand-name. All available aesthetic devices are employed to further this end. The decisive factor, however, is the concentration into one named character of the aesthetic, visual and verbal communications contained in the styling of the commodity. (p. 25)

Consumers of manufactured objects have, it seems, become increasingly status-conscious and more responsive to visual criteria. The wish for attention is conspicuous and the need for constant change is transposed to and becomes the need for a new purchase. Williamson (1990) suggests that a fetish for the object is a human desire: 'Consuming products does give a thrill, a sense of both belonging and being different, changing normality with the excitement of the unusual' (p. 13). A 'designer object' might be the catalyst to manifest expression of status – aesthetic expression from the world of the commodity. In the words of Pierre Martineau, 'The automobile tells us who we are and what we think we want to be ... it is a portable symbol of our personality and our position ... the clearest way we have of telling people our exact position' (Packard, 1981, p. 50). Mass-produced designer artefacts, such as a Starck 'Fluocaril' toothbrush, or a kettle designed by Aldo Rossi and manufactured and promoted by Alessi, have, it is suggested, become vehicles through which communication occurs. The longing for, day dreaming about, purchasing and possession of, for example, an Olympus 'Mju' camera, can inform others about the owner's status, values, personality and place in society. Following the purchase and 'use' of these 'designer objects', pleasurable dramas can be imagined and enacted. In addition, 'designer objects' such as those mentioned above have been promoted to become something *extra*-ordinary by inclusion in design museums and art gallery collections. This, it is suggested, places them in a special category, isolated from their usual commercial connotations, and may raise them to become things other than mere functional objects. For these reasons mass-produced 'designer objects' and their place in society warrant further investigation.

Within the arena of design one reason for the neglect of critical thinking might be that, with the advent of the machine and mass production, the designed artefact's *raison d'être* has not so far fallen under branches of enquiry which might normally be applied to art. Human expression, for example, has given way to the machine with all its connotations of mass production. However, a designer's conceptual thinking, which must have come before any realization of a mass-produced object, was undeniably projected on to such products. It is perhaps true to say that only a designer's prototype may be a 'valid' product. This is the first true representation of a designer's expressiveness, the original formulation of a collection of materials which together form the object. Once mass production and the machine take over the production of the object, that object becomes something different with a different meaning. It is interesting to note that Le Corbusier, speaking of taste and aesthetics in 1925, said:

> So, in the nature of things a cult object has to be mass-produced by machine and is 'designed'. It has to be promoted as one of thousands or at least has to give this impression, as the cachet of identicality provides its power and significance.
>
> (1987, p. 509)

Nearly seventy years after Le Corbusier's remark about a machine-made artefact, it is often the designer who is promoted. Can designer equal cult object? In the past designers have been caught somewhere between art and industry with no clearly defined role. Jollant-Kneebone (1992) recognizes the designer's unique quality:

> that is his capacity to cross-fertilise all logics and to transcend 'verticalities'. He is horizontally, transversally, champion of alternative thinking. He is the one who brings the burst of irrationalism in problem solving ... he is the one who brings pleasure to our lives, and excitement to everything we may acquire or dream of possessing. (p. 509)

The designer has a power to formalize glamour in such a way that reinforces status differences in goods and lifestyles, and the machine carries out this 'image-making' through its aspect of material production. However, Leiss (1983) suggests that: 'This does not imply a "manipulation" of the consumers by image makers: the market place is far too complex to suggest a one-directional flow of influence' (p. 11).

Design as an activity responding to a felt need has been replaced by an imagined image of a particular lifestyle with consumers not necessarily being passive. Their class, gender, education and geographical and age grouping accrete to determine the selection of any artefact that is for sale. Willis (1990) continues: 'Far from being the passive victims of commercialism's juggernaught, the consumer has progressively been recognised as having a substantial and unpredictable decision-making power in the selection and use of cultural commodities' (Introduction).

The discussion will now focus on the idea that brand-names and terms such as 'cult objects' and 'icons of the marketplace' do not relate to an objective content of an object. Recently, Sir Terence Conran stated that 'The history of the world can be documented by the design of objects and the study of these objects gives a clear message about the changes that were taking place in society' (*Sunday Express*, 3 October 1993). If Conran's word 'by' is substituted with the word *through*, and it becomes possible to document the world through the analysis of mass-produced objects, then undoubtedly there is material for critical enquiry. Designer objects are fascinating raw materials through which investigation may be instigated at different levels of intellectual enquiry and within different teaching and learning contexts.

'DESIGNER OBJECTS' WITHIN CONTEXTUAL STUDIES

Contexts for objects

It is necessary to recognize that there are many intellectual pathways through perceptions of artefacts within ontological contexts. Commodity discourse attracts many interpretations and is prone to semiotic and semantic analysis. Cummings (1993) sums this up neatly:

> commodified objects yield easily to the play of semiotic analysis. Inseparable from the

effects of their promotion, seductive in their excess and abandon, it is not surprising a media biased theorizing has accompanied the material excesses of the last decade.
(p. 18)

In order for pupils to consider pragmatically, analyse and make 'use' of objects, appropriate conditions must be created. Research by Schofield (1992) revealed that by working within a carefully constructed framework, students' perceptions of an object change. To own or to be allowed the facility to handle and therefore use an object in its functional capacity – for example, a chair by Mario Belini – would be a desired luxury. Nevertheless to view and investigate the chair within a home, a museum or shop (or handle it under supervision) could be equally useful. Studying the chair from a photograph or slide could also be informative. Each of these situations of use may suggest many different interpretations and therefore elicit definitions. Investigation through the close examination of an object can be extremely worthwhile. The journey from an initial visual encounter of an object through a working involvement to the end of an intense scrutiny can be a stimulating and valuable experience.

It is now suggested that it is only through the study of mass-produced 'designer objects' within different contexts that investigations develop understanding. It is solely by an object having a physical being and by it being perceived within its context that it can evoke responses from its perceiver. An object in its normal circumstances – for example, a swivel chair in an office – will be perceived differently to, hypothetically speaking, the same chair in a desert or on a beach. Although these are extreme examples, it is not the chair that changes but rather the context that changes perceptions of it. Artists play around with this concept: that is, the idea of displacing objects to evoke reactions. The Surrealists, for example, explored the idea of displaced objects in order to evoke a wide range of responses. The study of mass-produced functional objects within differing contexts can give rise to relative and subjective definitions which may be innovative within the arena of contextual studies. This particular avenue may stimulate and aid further investigation; pupils may wish to investigate ways in which the idea of displacement in art and design has been manipulated to surprise, challenge or shock.

Rather more subtle and challenging examples than the ones given above are now proposed. Two contextual areas through which objects may 'travel', having been ejected from their source of commercial production, and to which teachers and students have access, are now considered: commerce and museums and galleries.

Under the aegis of commerce, the first point to consider is that of an object's function and material physicality within its circumscribed and projected promotion as a commodity. At the moment at which the object comes into being through production, it attracts and becomes a passive vehicle of meaning. Through advertising and knowledge it can, and often does, assume meanings for a targeted market. The arena in which this takes place is commerce: in other words, the route from factory to shop to consumer. Shops have become the new sphere for the cultural activity of consuming. The department store, according to Bayley (1989), implies 'commitment to mass consumption, products become commodities'. He suggests that 'such stores revolutionised the process of buying, turning it into a cultural activity' (p. 46).

This commercial effect of commodity-production is a system based upon the demands of consumerism, which in this context may be a conscious attempt to influence and persuade the consumer to select and purchase that which is made irresistible. Design as something responding to a felt need has been replaced by an imagined image of a particular lifestyle, and this continues to be an important selling factor and marketing ploy:

> Whereas 30 years ago consumers were more concerned with a product's function – efficiency, reliability, value-for-money, durability and convenience – today's customers are prepared to pay more for a stylish product as they become more affluent and visually sophisticated.
>
> (Whiteley, 1993, p. 26)

The purchase and possessive ownership of the consumer object is, it appears, a central feature in the economy and in society as a whole. Consumers have become more status-conscious and more responsive to visual criteria. Whether or not an object fulfils a physical need (a new kettle to replace a broken one), or whether it is purchased to fulfil a desire to create a style and portray an image, is debatable and raises a fascinating set of issues for pupils to explore. Possible reasons why such objects are purchased and by whom could be fertile ground for detailed explorations. The purchase and use of an object might be more of a conscious expression of personality than is commonly thought to be the case. An object might be the catalyst which manifests expression of status – aesthetic expression from the world of the commodity. Can an assumption be made, therefore, that a functional commodity such as a Russell Hobbs kettle or a Philippe Starck toothbrush might be purchased or enjoyed for its aesthetic appeal rather than for its *raison d'être*, that of functional practicality? The particular area of function will be examined later in the chapter.

A second area through which an object may travel is that of the context of a museum or gallery. This area too provides a rich and provocative starting point for contextual study. Objects placed in museums and galleries function, and are possibly perceived, in a way different to that of the arena of commerce. Museums can act as powerful tools by projecting on to objects meanings and values which otherwise they would not have. It is suggested that similar objects to those in daily use in the home can look totally different within a museum or gallery. Sponsors and education-alists recognize museums as attractive contexts for the display of mass-produced 'designer objects'. There are precedents for this idea, for as early as 1917 at the Metropolitan Museum in New York, industrial art was placed alongside fine art. Nowadays such institutions as the Design Museum and the Victoria and Albert Museum in London, the Vitra Chair Museum in Germany, the Pompidou Centre in Paris and the Museum of Modern Art in New York select and display mass-produced objects similar to those simultaneously on show for purchase in shops. This poses the question, why are they included in special displays within the walls of very special places – namely museums and galleries?

The different contexts that can affect an object can give ammunition to those opposed to the possible 'elevation' of such everyday artefacts. There are, it appears, inherent risks and dangers in putting a mass-produced object behind glass in a museum. First, it could be said that it can make the object 'special', and second, it may be argued that in this situation the object may be seen as 'art'. For any object to be placed in a museum, certain criteria have to be applied to the object to necessitate its selection and inclusion. This inevitably involves the judgements of a curator whose connoisseurship is special, relative and self-conscious. The collection and display of an object has to be achieved consciously – how it looks, 'feels' and 'reacts' to other objects in close proximity is of prime importance to a curator, and this idea has been used in many ways by teachers. The use of a glass case to 'enshrine' an object is another area which is problematic, not only to curators but also to pupils and adult visitors to a museum. Objects may be perceived as being precious and endowed with status and meaning which in a normal commercial context they may not have. Student teachers of art and design, however, appear to welcome these modes of display as challenging, affording a chance to 'read' functional objects in a different, possibly symbiotic way.

> The attitude of the spectator will be one of seeing the object in isolation – isolated from history and isolated from any real functional value. The object will become 'insubstantive'. And it will effectively mean that the object will become charged with meanings other than the intended one of utility.
>
> (Schofield, 1993, p. 12)

It is not an innovative idea that a mass-produced object seen within a museum context could be called 'art'. Indeed, when Duchamp selected and displayed his first 'readymade' in 1913, the agenda was set for the acceptance of such mass-produced objects as works of art.

It is undisputed that the interaction between the curator's intention and the perception of the museum visitor is one of complex fluidity. For the museum viewer there is a constantly shifting field of procedures and experiences harnessed to a conscious production of values and meanings. A possible shift from utility to the symbolic may require the context of a museum or gallery. Objects can invite ideas, meanings and values in a more focused way within these unusual and prescribed contexts. Objects in glass cases in museums can become resting places for invention and memory where imagination, reminiscence and revelry into nostalgia become part of their language. Pupils, with the careful guidance of teachers, may therefore choose to make reference to objects in museums and galleries.

The study of contexts for advertising and promotion through objects, and the ways and means by which mass-produced objects come to be displayed in museums or galleries, are fruitful starting points for investigation. This contextual approach could be useful for those engaged in the teaching of graphic design, product design, cultural studies, history of art and design, media, gender studies and multicultural studies approached through the broad area of art and design. It is suggested that it is only through such investigations into contexts that any further work can be grounded and extended.

Figure 5.1 illustrates how the two suggested areas of context surround, impinge on and interact with an object, the object itself being the starting point for this investigation and not the perceiver. The diagram shows how it is possible to 'use' an object as an existing material presence for investigation and study.

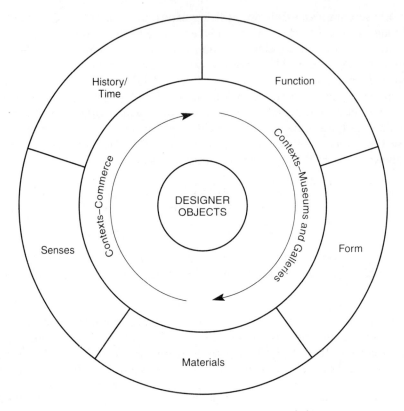

Figure 5.1 *A framework for the investigation of objects*

Domains for the contextual study of mass-produced objects

Moving on from the generality of contexts, further reference to Figure 5.1 is helpful. Research involving both further education students and student teachers of art and design has revealed that there are five domains in which investigations into mass-produced objects can be located. They are:

- history and time;
- function;
- form and style;
- materials;
- senses.

The five outer segments of Figure 5.1 show how such a framework of domains might be applied to mass-produced artefacts once contexts have been explored. As a pedagogical tool, this framework is not prescriptive, but has evolved through the writer's research into some of the more important issues arising from students' perceptions. The five domains were used by students to pose questions and to categorize replies and solutions. The domains should not necessarily be seen as having equal importance. Students' work revealed their use of links with domains other than the one in which they were working. Therefore, it is necessary to make explicit the idea that the domains will interact and no one domain should be seen in isolation.

History and time

It might be true to say that a mass-produced object signifies the time that has elapsed since its creation. This judgement of it and any conclusion reached will be arrived at by more than one route. Scientific and historical methods of calculation and investigation concerning stylistic changes may help elucidate the object for the viewer, but these may or may not be significant to the object. For example, a toaster may have been purchased in the 1940s and for some reason put away in its box and never reopened or consequently used. Theoretically, therefore, the toaster is 'brand new', and yet it is fifty years old and has passed by the action of time into a state of desuetude. Conversely, a training shoe may incur so much wear within, say, a month that it is deemed 'old' and will be discarded. Of course, the shoe is not old, other than being a few weeks or months older than when it left the production line, but it is merely worn and can appear old.

The present tends to be thought of as belonging to those who populate it, and this idea has been a difficult one to address. The date of an object's production might be likened to its birth. The reference point of 'birth' may be ineffectual until the object is perceived by viewers, who necessarily bring to the object their experiences. As with any branch of subjective study, researchers bring their own cultural values, beliefs and dispositions to bear on the activity, in this case perceiving an object. The contextualizing of a chair of the 1950s, for example, will be approached differently by a historian, a design museum curator, a student of art and design, and members of the general public. A historian may see the chair as representing certain sociological changes, the curator as being innovative from a stylistic viewpoint, the student as demonstrating an interesting use of materials and a non-academic as being nostalgic, part of a known context of a home environment, and for these reasons it may well produce emotive responses. A manufacturer, on the other hand, may take the view that the same 1950s chair was a 'best seller' and was therefore a monetary success. Each of these assumptions and facts may appear 'right' or 'wrong' to other viewers of the chair.

Historical developments in styles of chairs may be 'out of step' with, more advanced or retarded than the general perceived culture of society as a whole. Teague (1940) makes a similar comment: 'A single character of design gets expressed in whatever is made at the time and not a chair . . . comes into existence except in a form which harmonises with everything else being made at the time' (p. 207). A factor to be considered in this context is a possibly misleading signal by objects of the time-scale and the 'spirit' of the age in which they are manufactured. Are objects representative of their time or do they merely capture a 'snapshot' of a period? Might it be easier to place an object in today's context rather than to attempt to situate an object from a bygone era into its true historical context? It is possible that there may be too many misleading signals for people to try to contextualize an object they consider to be truly representative of and significant for today.

Another intriguing issue for investigation is the possibility of time inventing meanings. Take, for example, a Bush Bakelite radio produced in the 1940s. If the radio had been contextualized then and is subsequently contextualized again now, it is likely that it will have been perceived differently on each occasion. Through use the radio will not have altered to any great extent, but the viewer will have changed. The same viewer now carries new ideologies and cultural values, and therefore the radio appears different from its prior investigation. Furthermore, this may have little to do with any changes of its context from then to now. This domain poses fascinating research questions because every person is affected by notions of time passing. Research has revealed that perceptions of objects can change over very short periods of time, during the space of a four-week project, for example. At the end of particular project-work concerned with investigation into mass-produced artefacts, further education students admitted that their perceptions of objects had changed significantly (see Schofield, 1992). How pupils manage and work within a project's time-span and how this length of time changes perceptions could be harnessed and fed back to enrich their own contextual studies.

Function

Function is defined here as the specific activity or operation of use. How individuals relate to an object by using it – in other words, handling it, driving it, plugging it in, writing with it, listening to it or cleaning with it – is axiomatic to its use. Function is concerned with an object's physicality and presence within a space and how individuals relate to it. An awareness of physical properties such as temperature, weight, gravity, texture, sound and form, and how these relate to the body, is made explicit through use. The utilization of a kettle, for example, informs the user of its physical being, as well as communicating something more about it. The act of picking up a kettle and filling it, absorbing its weight and tactile qualities and subsequently pouring boiling water from it, is a mundane and quotidian operation. This functional use of a kettle is peremptory and as such may obscure other elements. Nikolaus Pevsner (1946, p. 4) suggests that 'functional objects are essential to start with when embarking on visual education' and that they give out 'something provable' as a foundation. To prove that an object works and how well it achieves this can be subjected to qualitative analysis. How it compares with similar objects may also be a valid area for consideration. However, to investigate function in a vacuum is more difficult and possibly of limited value. The act of boiling a kettle in preparation for making tea involves sensory experience. For the Japanese, making tea is a ritual, while in other cultures it can act as a social metaphor. Separating function from any cultural associations is problematic as the ability of an object to perform a function does not explain its essence. Objects will function only by human intervention, and cultural meanings will be invested by perceivers on seeing and using objects. Personal meanings centred around the functioning of objects will subsequently be invented. This idea, it is suggested, offers fruitful possibilities for investigation by pupils.

Form

Analysis of the function of an object may seem elementary, but the use to which the object is put defines its form or, to be more precise, determines minor variations of form. In his pedagogical ideas centred around the Bauhaus, Walter Gropius put forward the notion that there should be two separate elements to the creation of a design – function and aesthetics. Function should be concerned with practical efficiency, while the designer was permitted to modify the surfaces of machine-made objects by responding to the nature of the object's function.

The now famous theory by Louis Sullivan, writing in 1896 on the relationship of form and function, refined in his later writings to 'form follows function', was an adage taken up by the Bauhaus and one that has, until recently, generally been accepted as meaningful by both designers and architects. In 1928 Willi Lotz stated: 'Objects which are designed not for the sake of appearance but to fulfil their function as well as possible, will arrive at that form which most clearly expresses that function' (Benton and Sharpe, 1975, p. 229). Might it be assumed, therefore, that whenever a mass-produced artefact becomes totally adapted to the purpose for which it was intended, it approaches its ultimate form? This is one where an object, with both the conceptual ideas of the designer and the manifestation by machine, may reach a totally aesthetically pleasing synthesis between form and function.

Generally speaking, for most of this century the idea of function defining form has been significant. Within the context of postmodernist theory, it might be argued that advances in technology have overturned this idea that form should respect the characteristics of materials and the possibilities of the machine. Today designers might be said to hold the key, along with new materials, to creating revolutionary forms where the repertoire of imagery is boundless. Blaich (1990) of the Philips Company, sums up current ideas:

> The new freedom in design as a result of technological advances means that form is no longer dictated by function. Hard rectilinear shapes will continue to give way to soft, sculptural, more ergonomic forms. The past: Form follows Function. The future: Form leads Function. (p. 23)

So, if function once determined form, form might now be said to have an ability to express function with a flexibility that was unthinkable a few years ago. Every successful invasion (modernist design) breeds a resistance movement (postmodernist design of the 1980s and 1990s). This new design strategy encompasses concepts like 'soul' and 'morality' as well as 'poetry'.

The reasons why objects are desired are embedded in the relative associations between function and emotion. According to Starck, 'The design of tomorrow must be, "less to see, more to feel"' (*The Face*, 1993). This opinion suggests that one function of form is to provide meaning. According to Lambert (1993), 'These meanings may be concerned equally and simultaneously with the form's practical uses as with its potential for giving spiritual enrichment' (p. 61).

The excesses of 'high style' and the 'matt black' forms of the 1970s and early 1980s modernist design movements, where forms were pared down to the bare minimum, are disappearing. The formal qualities of 'designer objects' may now contain ironic references and present images less formal than those coined as modernist.

Materials

Today there is a whole new vocabulary of materials which may be used for the manufacture of mass-produced artefacts. Advances in technology and fast changes in the economy of serial production have produced objects 'grown' from these new materials. Metal, glass and plastics, for example, can be stretched to limits previously unknown. Toughened glass is made into tables and welded sheet steel fabricated into comfortable armchairs. Chairs created by Ron Arad, and corrugated card married with aluminium to form chairs designed by Ross Lovegrove, are both challenging and yet ergonomically successful. The old aegis of 'truth to materials' promoted by Pugin and Morris has now been displaced with reference to contemporary 'designer objects' which can be fabricated from any materials. A chair may be made from wood, but it can just as easily be formed from plastic, corrugated card or glass. Thirty-eight or so different plastics are used in the production of objects today, many having the ability to be shaped, contorted and moulded into forms so 'perfect' that even the machine appears to have had no part in their production.

Historically, materials such as wood and metal have been subjected to ever-changing technology, and this idea is one that would bear closer scrutiny. For example, taking a historical perspective on how a chair has attracted alteration and modification as technology has progressed could be a beneficial starting point for pupils and one which could be interdisciplinary. In the eyes of a growing number of consumers and protagonists of the 'green' movement, the misuse of wood, for example, is irresponsible. Unlike glass or most plastics, wood made into objects is not so susceptible to recycling. This pertinent and contemporary issue is one that pupils might approach as prospective artists and designers and as ecologically aware future consumers. Mass-produced objects would make good springboards from which to address the issues of the use and misuse of materials. For example, study of the Zanussi Nexus range of washing machines which can be recycled would illustrate the pressure of the 'green' movement on manufacturers, and how this had been addressed in a range of household goods. Or pupils may consider why it is that some cameras are made to be used once and thrown away. This example of a cardboard box camera says something about today's 'throw away' society as well as the targeting of a particular market, and is another issue that pupils may like to investigate.

The domain of investigation of materials may be approached not only through the material itself – what it stands for and how it can best be used – but in other, more abstract ways. The semantics of the names of materials – for example, wood, glass, plastic and paper, and such brand-names as Bakelite, Styrene and Formica – bear closer investigation. Connotations of the words and their relationship with that of their characteristics generate diverse associations. Characteristics such as flexibility, hardness, softness, brittleness, pliability and absorbency converge with those more akin to visual perception: reflectivity, transparency or redness, for example. Within this semantic lexicon there are words associated with materials and manufacturing processes – riveted, glue, welded, sewn, pressed or moulded. Cummings (1993) suggests that this is an area for consideration:

> The ability to differentiate, to structure meaning as it coalesces around wood products, metals, fabrics and ceramics for instance is not to exclusively bind meaning to their physical attributes, but certainly to recognise affinities adhering to their particular characteristics. (p. 25)

Pupils' use and development of language is very important. Not only is it necessary to acquire a technical vocabulary through art and design lessons, but a development of language for expression and critical evaluation is highly desirable and is a requirement of the National Curriculum for Art (DES, 1992).

Materials are the tangible evidence through which an object is seen and its physicality makes a particular statement. The presence of an object may be seen merely as a body of materials which are known by experience to have certain characteristics. The feel of a kettle, its weight, empty or full, its coldness or method of heat conduction, and the noise it makes, are associative values and can elicit sensory reactions. The choice of materials fused into objects is already a gesture from the designers. The symbiosis of form and idea is expressed by a designer and carried out by machine to become the material quality of the object. Any affinity with the object is bound up with the capacity of the user or perceiver to react to and appreciate the particular characteristics of materials. It is from this reaction that dialogue can be instigated with pupils, or art and design work can be carried out.

Senses

The domain of the senses is a difficult one to address as it can encompass all other areas. As has been shown, history, materials, function and the form an object takes can affect and evoke emotional responses. The thorny question of aesthetics could sit happily within this domain. The *New Shorter Oxford Dictionary* defines aesthetics as 'the science of sensory perception or that which pertains to perception of the senses'.

Design is a very complex subject and it is generally believed that design is simply another word for appearance; the embodiment of aesthetic values in a product. Needless to say, as with painting, a 'designer object' can affect the senses and therefore provoke an aesthetic reaction. Aesthetic awareness consists of the adoption of a particular attitude or standpoint which involves discrimination and judgements on the part of the individual. It is not a matter of individuals recognizing certain *features* of things in the way they discover, for example, the form or the colour of an object, but rather individual perceptions of and responses to an object or activity engaged in, in a way that is special for them. For example, the visual effect of wear on an object, its scratches or discolouring, or the sound of a lid being replaced on a coffee pot, or the tactile sensation when sitting in a chair or car, or a shape being reminiscent of something else (for example, a hairdryer looking like a weapon) may evoke an aesthetic response.

Aesthetic response to a 'designer object' comes from an existing set of organized concepts. To perceive an object is not to see many disorganized fragments and then to mentally reorganize them, but rather to perceive something as an existing comprehensible arrangement which in summation makes sense. This perception relies on the percipient's experiences and any aesthetic response is personal to him/her. It is not only the cultural aspects that are brought to bear on an object, but rather how these are refracted by each percipient's life experience and how this concept can be grasped. How pupils may attempt to harness and represent sensory experience is problematic. Pupils' skills need to be developed to enable them to realize and bring out such feelings. Teachers can help pupils by suggesting ways and means of expressing these feelings visually and verbally in art and design work. In this area of consideration, art and design work is an important way of expressing something about that which is perceived and felt.

Pupils may set about answering questions about mass-produced 'designer objects' as a result of teachers' helping them to raise questions. Formulating a question to be answered is as important as any desired answer. Any definitions and 'answers' are relative and therefore relevant to the enquirer. In other words, it is not only the relative aspects that are brought to bear in investigation of objects and their potential 'meanings', but how these are refracted by each pupil's life experience. As such there can be no closed ends or answers; the diversity of the pupils' experiences will enrich the variety of the responses.

The five domains are offered to provide areas in which potential enquiry might be instigated. How this might be achieved will be open to interpretation by teachers and pupils. It may be thought that the narrative is already built into the object. If this is the case, how best may pupils make sense of it? How is this message perceived? Parsons (1993) summarizes the educational value as follows:

> aesthetics begins with a problem, with something that puzzles us in an encounter either with art works or with talk about art. This is a good way to teach it [aesthetics] to students because the connection with their experience will make it more meaningful. (p. 32)

Emotive and sensory responses to a 'designer object' can be manifested in both verbal and visual ways. Pupils may record and document their sensory reactions by expression of their feelings for the object in question. This could be achieved both through language and by making art and design work which expresses these feelings and which for them has a personal meaning.

In conclusion, design has become more irreverent and challenging and at the same time is in danger of being misunderstood and marginalized in the classroom. With technological achievements it has become a much more flexible activity, opening up new arenas for the designer and in consequence for the consumer. In one context the consumers might be the purchasers of objects, while pupils may also be thought of as consumers of objects, making 'use' of them in the classroom.

Rigidity of past conventions about design, both its rules and ergonomics, can be challenged. It is suggested that the blurred line between functional 'designer objects' and art is fast being erased, and the two are set on an exciting collision course. Any attempt to distinguish between the two may not be helpful in the future as it is likely that it will be difficult to tell whether or not a 'designer object' has any real utilitarian or functional purpose. Is an Alessi kettle, for example, intended primarily as an aesthetic object carrying a suggested intention of use? Its purpose may become one of status, decoration or having a collectable value. This object may be considered as an art object with all the aesthetic values contained therein, while remaining that of being 'kettlelike'. As such it will pass into history assuming meanings as it goes. Of course, its ability to do this is not new, but the fostering of an ability to question and decontextualize objects such as this kettle may be a relatively new idea within the realms of art and design education. It is one with which art and design teachers and pupils may like to grapple.

REFERENCES

Bayley, S. (1989) *Commerce and Culture*. Kent: Penshurst Press.
Benton, T., and Sharpe, D. (1975) *Form and Function*. London: Crosby, Lockwood Staples.
Blaich, R. (1990) In Thompson, R. (ed.), *Review 2*. London: Design Museum.
Cummings, N. (1993) *Reading Things*. London: Chance Books.
Department of Education and Science (DES) (1992) *Art in the National Curriculum (England)*. London: HMSO.
Featherstone, M. (1983) Consumer culture: an introduction. *Theory, Culture and Society* **1**(3), 4–9.
Haug, W. F. (1986) *Critique of Commodity Aesthetics*. Cambridge: Polity Press.
Hebdige, D. (1988) *Hiding in the Light*. London: Routledge.
Jollant-Kneebone, F. (1992) 1940–2000 crafts and industry from divorce to honeymoon. *Royal Society of Arts Journal* **140**(5431), 500–09.
Lambert, S. (1993) *Form Follows Function*. London: Victoria and Albert Museum.
Le Corbusier (1987) *The Decorative Art of Today*. London: Architectural Press.
Leiss, W. (1983) Icons of the marketplace. *Theory, Culture and Society* **1**(3), 10–17.
Packard, V. (1981) *The Hidden Persuaders*. Harmondsworth: Penguin.
Parsons, M. (1993) *Aesthetics and Education*. Champaign: University of Illinois Press.
Pevsner, N. (1946) *Visual Pleasure From Everyday Things*. London: Batsford.
Schofield, K. (1992) Ways of Perceiving Mass-Produced Artefacts with Reference to the Context of a Design Museum. Unpublished MA thesis. Institute of Education, University of London.
Schofield, K. (1993) *Design Museums: A Critical View*. London: Institute of Education.
Teague, W. D. (1940) *Design This Day*. London: Harcourt, Brace.
Whiteley, N. (1993) *Design For Society*. London: Reaktion Books.
Williamson, J. (1990) *Consuming Passions*. London: Marion Boyars.
Willis, P. (1990) *Common Culture*. Milton Keynes: Open University Press.

Chapter 6

Museums and Galleries

John Reeve

> I do not profess to be an 'artist' now, but I do believe that anything is possible!
>
> (Sixth-former after a Royal Academy outreach life class)

> This is the best thing I ever did since I was born.
>
> (Young child in a Museum of Mankind workshop)

Any museum or gallery education officer can provide testimonials to the motivational value of a museum or gallery visit and its impact on work in schools. However, the National Curriculum, changes in the ways schools are funded, and new arrangements for the initial training and professional development of teachers are now forcing museums and galleries towards a much harder-edged evaluation of the experiences and services that they offer. Their collaboration with schools and other organizations is under review. After years of promoting the value of museum and gallery education to teachers, teachers in training and educational policy-makers at all levels, museum and gallery education staff are now being asked to deliver on an unprecedented scale across the whole curriculum at all Key Stages. This is in addition to all the other roles that museum and gallery educators now try to fulfil. There have been no extra resources available from central government for museum education, and resources have often been withdrawn. Some 80 per cent of all museums and galleries do not have any educators.

This chapter explores the background to the current situation and then concentrates on how museums and galleries in partnership with teachers and others have responded to a series of challenges in recent years. These include the development of critical studies, and issues of gender and multiculturalism. The biggest challenge has been, and remains, to counter the static idea of a museum or gallery as enshrining someone else's art history – someone else in the past, some other continent, class or gender, someone else's opinions, 'as if it were a universally valued archive of stable treasures' (*The Arts in Schools*, 1982, p. 12).

BEFORE THE NATIONAL CURRICULUM: MUSEUMS, GALLERIES AND EDUCATION

As Hooper-Greenhill (1991) shows in Part 1 of *Museum and Gallery Education*, the fortunes of education in museums and galleries have always been on a kind of roller-coaster, vulnerable to changes in funding, direction, local government organization and priorities in education. Today's crisis should be seen in that context. Curatorial control of museums and particularly galleries, and the under-resourcing of museum education, have often ensured a gulf between rhetoric and reality in educational provision, with several notable exceptions such as The National Gallery. Education flourished there with the support of Sir Michael Levey as Director (1973–86) and has continued to do so. Alistair Smith, as Head of Exhibitions and Education, and also as a curator, developed direct educational work with schools by budgeting to employ freelance teachers in addition to core staff. He also invested in the production of educational video for adults and schools. He pioneered an incisive type of exhibition that might comprise just two contrasted portraits and a video, or look thematically at the collections; it might also result from an invitation to an artist to make a personal selection. Several artists have been in residence or have worked as associates of the Gallery. They include Paula Rego and Ken Kiff. Most innovative of all, National Gallery educators were themselves invited to put on exhibitions: for example, 'Bodylines' on the human figure. A stream of often slightly disrespectful gallery trails for children and families encouraged others including the British Museum (BM) to follow suit. Holiday attractions have included a magician member of the Gallery's Education Staff, and an art educator appearing in role as Seurat, Gainsborough and other artists.

Popular publications written by National Gallery educators (Peppin *et al.*, 1992; Peppin, 1983; Cassin, 1987; Wolf, 1988) have been aimed at children and adults. Perhaps the most far-sighted of Alistair Smith's projects at the National Gallery was the instigation of the Micro Gallery which eventually opened in the Sainsbury Wing in 1991. This is now also available as *Microsoft Art Gallery* on CD-ROM. CD-ROMs have also been produced by the BM (with Research Machines) on the *Anglo-Saxons*, and by the Tate Gallery (with ICL/Attica) on *Investigating Twentieth Century Art*. Others include *The Design Image Bank* (Design Council/NERIS), and *The Commonwealth Institute Database* (with Systems Simulation).

Elsewhere innovation has often come slowly. Although the British Museum had been founded in 1753 with the admirable intention 'to encourage the study of history, archaeology and art . . . not just for the learned and the curious', it did very little to live up to these ideals in terms of active education until after 1970 (see Reeve, 1988). Similarly, the Victoria and Albert Museum (V & A) was originally intended to be a practical inspiration for artists and designers, but it very soon became a decorative arts museum. Some of its pioneering educational work is described by Marcousé (1961). In the 1980s Sir Roy Strong changed the educational priorities of the museum and only recently has education for schools and colleges been given a new impetus. Today part of the V & A's original educational mission is also being carried out by the Design Council, the Crafts Council and the Design Museum. As well as the V & A, the Photographers Gallery and museums such as the National Museum of Photography, Film and Television in Bradford and the National Portrait Gallery (NPG) are active educationally in the field of photography.

There is still no national policy either on museums or on museum and gallery educational provision, although both are promised. Outside London, many museum and gallery education services began as offshoots of nineteenth- or early twentieth-century civic pride. In the years after 1945, museum and gallery education often followed in the footsteps of educational pioneers like Alec Clegg in the West Riding of Yorkshire. There a schools' loans service was set up as part of an integrated system for resource-based learning that included libraries, works of art, advisers and residential in-service courses for teachers, plus the Clarke Hall Educational Museum in Wakefield. The latter epitomizes the best in museum education formerly funded by Local Education Authorities (LEAs): a period house, lovingly restored and opened only to one, pre-booked school at a time. Charismatic teachers in role as seventeenth-century people demonstrate good practice to other teachers through their work with pupils, including those with disabilities and special needs. The activities include role-play and drama, spinning and weaving, music and dance, art, cooking and gardening, all in a historical context. The planning of visits to Clarke Hall has focused work in primary and secondary schools right across the curriculum, and has involved teachers and museum educators throughout the area. It has also helped to develop museum and gallery skills in countless children.

During the 1980s museum and gallery educators everywhere had to become more rigorous and better organized, in order to be more influential within their institutions and beyond, and latterly to survive. The Group for Educational Services in Museums became more broadly the Group for Education in Museums (GEM), attracting more teachers and advisers, publishers and television producers. Close links developed with television for schools, while an annual training course, a newsletter and the *Journal of Education in Museums* began to disseminate good practice on, for example, evaluation, multicultural education and a greater awareness of activity abroad. GEM has made effective representations to the National Curriculum working parties, ensuring, for example, a place for learning from objects at Key Stages 1 and 2 of the history curriculum. Museum and gallery education officers have served on examination boards, on the original National Curriculum Art Working Party, and on the Advisory Group reviewing the history curriculum for the Schools Curriculum and Assessment Authority (SCAA) in 1994.

THE CURRENT SITUATION

In the current funding crisis, many museum and gallery education services are under threat of major cuts or extinction. More than half of 172 museums surveyed in the summer of 1993 had suffered cuts in education services or expected to. Much of this current crisis is the result of Local Management of Schools (LMS), whereby funding is largely devolved to schools and the former central funding of museum services by Local Education Authorities is no longer possible. As a recent report on museum education warns, some 'services may be restricted to the better off schools and those within walking distance' (Museums Association, 1993, p. 10).

Without such a specific shopping list as for the history curriculum, museum and gallery visits related to the art curriculum have often proved more problematic. It is often difficult to convince headteachers, school governors, parents and even some colleagues that an art visit is essential, especially when it disrupts the timetable. Art has been, and continues to be, the poor relation in this respect: an issue which the revised National Curriculum for Art should address.

Other aspects of this crisis are less easily defined. There is a danger that museums and galleries will prioritize projects that can be more easily funded, are more attractive for sponsors, relate more narrowly to the curriculum, or meet what teachers perceive as their immediate needs. There is already less 'missionary' work in museums and galleries in areas such as multicultural education, which received lip service from central government in the 1980s and 1990s. Museums and galleries provide unique opportunities for the implementation of the school curriculum, but they are not part of the school system. They also have other functions such as lifelong learning, outreach work with the disabled and with ethnic communities, publishing, and input into the planning of galleries and exhibitions. It may be that museums and galleries, like performing arts companies, will have to provide much more direct input into arts education if it continues to receive inadequate space and resources in the school curriculum. This is a situation which has to some extent occurred in the United States.

Museums and galleries in Britain have very different priorities in the 1980s and 1990s. The V & A, with sponsorship, has appointed Education Officers specifically for India and China to work with new galleries. The Tate Gallery, Liverpool, has concentrated particularly on new audiences for contemporary art, on outreach projects with the local community and with prisons, and on the application of information technology. Others have been able to provide a high level of direct teaching as part of their basic mission (e.g. the National Gallery) or with the help of sponsorship (e.g. the Tate Gallery and the Museum of Mankind).

The Trustees of the British Museum decided in the 1970s not to pursue a programme largely of direct teaching, but to concentrate efforts on 'cascading' expertise via teachers, to mount a substantial adult education programme and to provide resources and publications. It would now be extremely difficult to provide in crowded galleries a live input for visits from about 150,000 children a year, a threefold increase in numbers since the introduction of the National Curriculum, largely at Key Stage 2 for both history and art. The overriding priority has been to make the best use of particular expertise. All staff have had to prioritize their direct teaching with groups. For example, initial teacher training and multicultural work with the Japanese and Oriental collections is a particular priority of one post. A colleague has devoted a great deal of time and energy to producing a multimedia programme on the Anglo-Saxons applicable at all levels of the art curriculum as well as for history, technology and English. Another member of the team has specialized in work with the physically and learning disabled (Pearson, 1985, 1989; Attenborough, 1985). A recent project, in museums, on children with learning difficulties has shown the extraordinary impact that museum visits can make (Pearson and Aloysius, 1994).

Volunteers and postgraduate students are trained to help with handling sessions at the BM when they are a priority; elsewhere handling is often an integral part of a museum visit (e.g. Museum of London, the Horniman Museum). The development of publications and other resources as a form of 'distance learning' has become a priority for many museums, especially national institutions.

CRITICAL STUDIES

The influence of the development of critical studies on museum and gallery education during the 1980s has been considerable. In collaboration with museum and gallery educators, art advisers have 'cascaded' the principles of critical studies as articulated by Taylor (1986). The former Inner London Education Authority (ILEA) Art and Design Inspectorate, for example, developed in-service courses in the 1980s that gave teachers time to try out ideas in schools between an initial input from advisers and museum education officers and the follow-up sessions months later. This is a model that might usefully be adopted more often, not least to evaluate the impact of in-service provision. Some of the ILEA work in 1984 is documented in Dyson (1986). On the theme of cities, the case studies range from sixth-form projects on outdoor public art to work on bricks with Key Stage 3 groups (the notorious 'Tate bricks', ancient glazed tiles and terracotta in museums, and Dutch and twentieth-century urban painting showing brickwork by L. S. Lowry, and others). A project in St Albans was based on Roman and medieval structures, designs and technology. Other projects on hair and heads, tigers, lilies, flags and the sea all involved gallery visits; others used slides from museums and galleries. Crucially, all this work was shared by the whole group of teachers and then recorded. Museum and gallery education officers shared in this learning process and helped to disseminate the results. The role of museum and gallery education departments in this kind of information exchange between teachers is greatly underexploited.

The benefits of a long-term relationship between museums, galleries and specific schools are shown in *The Arts in the Primary School* (Taylor and Andrews, 1993) and in the work of the Whitechapel Art Gallery and the Camden Arts Centre (Selwood and Clive, 1992). An inner-city secondary school, Maria Fidelis in the London Borough of Camden, has made regular use of museums and galleries at all levels of its work, resulting in a very confident and critical approach by pupils in deciding what is the best source material for their personal studies within examination courses. Not surprisingly, given these opportunities, sixth-formers from Maria Fidelis were able to respond fully to the challenge of learning how to produce a Japanese woodblock print through all its stages, in just a week at the BM. This is an example of sponsored collaboration between the Museum Education Service and the Artists and Craftspeople in Education (ACE) Project, based in the Centre for Multicultural Studies at the London University Institute of Education. This project with the artist Juginder Lamber was inspired by one of the regularly changing exhibitions of Japanese art in the BM's new galleries, 'Ukiyo-e Paintings'.

The ACE Project works with a range of artists, several of them of Asian background, like Shaheen Merali whose family originated in Gujarat and then moved to Tanzania and finally to Britain. He has worked as a community artist and in the medium of batik to explore, for example, the theme of colonialism in India. Other ACE projects have taken place at Chiswick House (European Arts Festival), in Avon and at the Museum of London (for the 'Peopling of London' exhibition in 1994). At the BM, each week-long, museum-based project begins with an intensive day of drawing in the exhibition, focused by a talk from an education officer. The children's drawings may be enlarged on an overhead projector and transferred to wooden panels for carving, engraved on copper plates or mounted on to wooden blocks prior to cutting for woodblock prints. Each project involves close liaison with the class teacher and other adults – sometimes parents, teachers in training from the Institute of Education and museology students attached to the Museum. Each project is documented and exhibited to bring these 'pilot projects' to a wider audience, as will a forthcoming publication.

The BM and Royal Academy (RA) education teams have collaborated on a number of joint programmes to bring together artists and some of their source material. For the Joshua Reynolds exhibition (Penny, 1986), pupils at the BM explored how, beneath so many of his portraits, is the stance and gesture of a classical sculpture, and how artists were trained from the Renaissance into the twentieth century by drawing from classical sculpture or casts (Haskell and Penny, 1981). Pupils could visit the basement gallery of Roman sculpture to see pieces that Reynolds knew very well, and look at facial types, costume and props, gesture and conventions, and standard subjects – the heroic athlete, the gloomy Greek thinker, the gnarled senator, Venus. The subsequent visit to the RA exhibition was an opportunity to 'clothe' these stereotypes, but also to see how Reynolds developed other ideas and sources.

Collaborative work, with expertise from outside the museum or gallery, is usual now. At the Serpentine Gallery in London, for example, young artists are a regular part of the education work, and this gallery has hosted a number of 'Live Art' projects (see Layzell, 1993). The Barbican and Whitechapel Galleries also use the expertise of artists in their programmes (*In and Out of the Gallery*, 1993). Over a third of museum and gallery educators in Britain are now part-time, and about a quarter have temporary contracts. The core staff may therefore develop a new kind of entrepreneurial role, particularly in the changing world of in-service training (INSET) provision for teachers. Inspectors of schools have reported favourably on the quality of INSET provided by museums: some national museums may provide INSET for 1,000 or more teachers a year. The National Gallery, with Birkbeck College (University of London), is running term-long evening courses for primary and secondary teachers on the Renaissance and on 'Tradition and Modernity' (European art, 1750–1900). On Saturdays, four-week and six-week courses for teachers include 'Eye Openers', which aim to examine important paintings in wider contexts.

THE INTEGRATED CURRICULUM?

Mason (1988) explores the idea that art and design education should be more integrated into the secondary curriculum, as it frequently is in the primary school. If museums and their exhibitions are to speak more profitably with several voices, instead of offering a naive and numbing attempt at 'neutrality', schools using galleries and museums will benefit from a variety of teacher and pupil skills in responding. Some of the most successful visits to the Addis Gallery of Islamic art at the BM have been jointly organized by teachers of art and religious education. History teachers working on the Islamic options for Key Stage 3 History would benefit from similar collaboration. Collaboration also reduces the amount of research to be done by the individual teacher, when using other specialist colleagues or museum education officers. Museum education officers can fruitfully be used for the discussion and feed-back at the end of a visit, as well as to provide focus and impact at the beginning. A collaborative visit also helps to avoid teaching Islamic art as just another database of value-free patterns and shapes. A cross-curricular approach also benefited the 'Skeleton at the Feast – The Day of the Dead Festival in Mexico' exhibition at the Museum of Mankind, 1991–3, which was extensively used by art and design teachers at all levels, by art colleges and by primary teachers.

The National Curriculum for History aims to present the 'cultural and aesthetic' dimension, but this seems to evaporate as pupils approach the twentieth century at Key Stage 3. There should also be more collaboration with the art curriculum at examination levels. Most history, textbooks still use works of art merely as illustration rather than as evidence to be critically assessed. History and art and design teachers could also profitably work together with their language colleagues. The creative writing initiatives taken, for example, by Frances Sword at the Fitzwilliam Museum, Cambridge, or by Pat Adams at the Tate Gallery, should be a natural part of museum and gallery work at all levels, enhancing functional as well as creative writing and talking (see Benton and Benton, 1990).

With the marginalization of drama and dance in many schools and the collapse of much theatre-in-education for financial reasons, it is especially important that a cross-curricular 'whole arts' approach does not disappear: it remains one of the most successful ways of using museums, galleries and historic houses and sites. The shared, concrete experience, especially in a dramatic context, can yield remarkable results, as many 'living history' projects show, whether English Heritage or the Young National Trust Theatre. Actors are used in role at the Science Museum, the Museum of the Moving Image, and the Geffrye Museum. Role-play is a technique successfully implemented in the 'Palestinian Costume' and 'Paradise' exhibitions at the Museum of Mankind.

Music is another area for collaboration with art and design. In the 1980s the British Museum Education Service worked with Kent Opera, combining drama and music, history and the classics, contemporary and historical issues. Sixth-formers joined adults for workshops on the theme of war based on Tippett's opera *King Priam*, followed the story line of the Trojan Wars through illustrations on Greek vases and sculpture throughout the Museum, then attended sponsored evening performances at the Royal Opera House. Key Stage 2 and 3 groups came for workshops on Mozart's *The Magic Flute*, some of them playing in an *ad hoc* band to accompany the singers, some using the galleries as source material for design of costumes, make-up and staging, and some to research gesture and movement. For the contemporary opera, *A Night at the Chinese Opera* by Judith Weir, each group of sixth-form and college art or theatre design students was given specific technical data for the theatre where it was to be performed, a cassette of musical extracts and the libretto. They were given briefings by a company designer, and by a museum educator on Chinese design sources for them to research in the Museum. The opera designers visited each group during the project to advise on their work, and an impromptu exhibition was arranged of all the stage models and costume designs where the students could hear the comments of the production's designer, director and composer. They later visited the theatre, went backstage and attended a performance. Of course, such intensive and expensive projects depend heavily on sponsorship or awards.

With the Royal Opera House Education Department, the BM has recently worked with six Suffolk schools, primary and secondary, on an ambitious opera project based on the Anglo-Saxon epic *Beowulf.* This was related both to the history and the art and design curriculum, including visits to a special exhibition at the British Museum, and to Suffolk as the home of the ship burial discovered at Sutton Hoo, finds from which are in the Museum. Music, drama, art and design all benefited enormously from the collaboration of the different age groups involved, and from the expertise of professional composer, designer, producer and choreographer.

One result of the National Curriculum for History and Art that is already tangible on museum visits is the greater confidence of pupils and teachers, and a sharper focus and purpose to their visits. Secondary art and design teachers need to build overtly on the skills and knowledge developed at Key Stage 2, such as the enthusiasm for the art of Egypt or Benin, or a familiarity with looking critically at Tudor portraits or Victorian photographs, or at buildings, objects and textiles. One approach might be to develop more whole-school in-service training based on the use of museums and galleries, at secondary level (as at primary level), rather than training by subject departments as at present.

Cross-curricular projects on initial teacher training courses are now more problematic. The new structures make less likely the sort of projects described by Mason (1988) with her students, or the intensive options on museums and galleries available at Brighton Polytechnic or the Institute of Education in the 1980s. Trainee art and design teachers at the Institute took part automatically in a five-day course on museums and galleries, with the Tate, National Gallery, BM and V & A (Paine, 1985, 1989). Each student was helped to plan a visit and was observed bringing a teaching practice group to one of the museums or galleries, often by other students as well as by staff, and this was followed by shared feed-back and reflection. Today many of the issues that were formerly touched on during initial training are dealt with either partially or hurriedly by in-service courses or in far greater depth through an MA course such as the Museums, Galleries and Education MA, initiated in 1993 jointly by the Institute of Education, Art and Design Department, the BM and V & A Education Services. Another new course on Art Gallery and Art Museum Education began in the autumn of 1993 at Birkbeck College, University of London.

GENDER ISSUES

Lay back, keep quiet, and think of what made Britain so great is the title of a painting by the black artist Sonia Boyce (1986), in the Arts Council Collection. Multiculturalism, feminism and political debate come together in works like this, where each panel 'represents' a segment of the British Empire tangled with the stems of black rose bushes. This picture appeared in the controversial exhibition, 'The Other Story' at the Hayward Gallery (Araeen, 1990; Poovayer Smith, 1991); and in the display 'Moving into View' at the Royal Festival Hall in 1993, as an exploration of 'questions of identity', teamed with Maud Sulter, recently an artist of residence at the Tate Gallery, Liverpool.

Remembering to mention Gwen John or Mary Cassatt occasionally in art lessons is clearly not an adequate response to gender issues. Many art gallery educators now offer special programmes and resources on women painters, designers, sitters and patrons. The 'Visualising Masculinities' exhibition at the Tate Gallery (December 92–June 93) aimed 'to explore the complex ways in which masculine identities have been depicted since the mid-19th century'. Pupils attended workshops on 'Images of Men'. A school visit to the NPG in summer 1992 involved pupils on a project entitled 'Modern Madonna', which required them to debate their individual viewpoints about the position of women at the end of the twentieth century.

The BM Education Service began to work on women's history in the classical world when women appeared as a topic in a classics syllabus for 16- to 18-year-olds. The Greek literary record is often scathing about women or ignores them altogether: the evidence of Greek vase paintings shows the range of their activities. In ancient Egypt, upper-class women sit demurely with their husbands except when ruling as queens in the Nubian Kingdom of Meroe (see the Egypt and Africa Gallery, BM), and take on a much stronger individuality and sense of power only in Roman Egypt.

The BM Education Service has produced resources for teachers on prehistoric, classical and medieval women using the permanent displays. The prehistoric resource contrasts the highly slanted evidence (exaggeratedly buxom or anorexic, from prehistoric Norfolk or Cycladic Greece) with a similarly slanted sample of contemporary female images taken from advertisements (sleek perfection, mostly scantily clad). Several study days have been held with Women's Heritage and Museums (WHAM) focusing on women in South America and the Islamic world, and as patrons and producers of art in medieval Britain. British Museum Press has published titles on women's history, including a critical look at the evidence on Greek vases (Johns, 1990). Hindu goddesses and how they are depicted and described (benign, powerful, sometimes terrifying) are discussed and illustrated in Blurton (1992), and this makes an excellent focus for work in the Museum's Hotung Gallery, contrasting male and female in religious art. In Buddhist art, the compassionate aspects of the Buddha become progressively feminized in the Far East.

Work on women's history, particularly in social history museums, is discussed by Gaby Porter (1988, 1991), a curator in the Manchester Museum of Science and Technology. At the V & A, Shireen Akbar of the Education Department has been very active in the past with the Bangladeshi community in developing exhibitions at the Whitechapel Art Gallery, and at the V & A she has initiated a remarkable textile project with mainly Asian women throughout the country, to culminate in a large Mogul-style tent of which each panel is a statement by a group of women about their lives.

Pointon (1994) introduces feminist art history for students and suggests further reading, such as Pollock and Parker (1981) and Cherry (1993). Bryson *et al.* (1991) has an essay on 'Women, art and power' by Nochlin, followed by rejoinders from two other women art historians. Textiles in particular have been downgraded by art historians, and this is brought out by Parker (1984) and Callen (1980); see also Harris (1993). For women in design history, see, for example, Judy Attfield (1989). Gill Saunders, a curator at the V & A, organized an innovatory exhibition there on the nude in art with an accompanying book (Saunders, 1989). Other areas of women's history and literature can be explored through Ruthven (1990) and Larrington (1992).

MULTICULTURALISM

You can no longer define, Sir, classify or categorise me. I'm no longer your bloody objects in the British Museum. I'm here right in front of you, in the flesh and blood of a modern artist. If you want to talk about me, let us talk. BUT NO MORE OF YOUR PRIMITIVIST RUBBISH.

(Araeen, 1987, p. 18)

That was Rasheed Araeen reacting to the notorious exhibition in 1984 at the Museum of Modern Art in New York, ' "Primitivism" in 20th-Century Art' (Rubin, 1984). Museum and gallery educators can avoid this kind of critical response by:

- making sure that artists, performers and teachers from the cultures put 'on show' take a large part in the exhibition education programme (this is the policy at many museums now);
- avoiding generalized, historical 'connoisseur' treatments of other cultures ('Treasures', 'Splendours', 'Masterpieces', etc.); and
- dealing with the contemporary wherever possible as well as the art of the past.

It has recently been observed of the National Curriculum for Art that 'the Programmes of Study suggested reveal a marked concern for pupils' knowledge of British national heritage and Eurocentric artistic traditions' (Selwood and Clive, 1992, p. 3). Museums in particular are in a strong position to help counter this imbalance, as the National Curriculum Art Working Group acknowledged, 'enabling complex and difficult issues to be addressed through direct contact with artefacts'. The Geffrye Museum in East London, for example, collaborated on the *Black Contribution to History* (1988), exploring the museum collections in an anti-racist framework.

Work with Jacob Epstein's non-European art collection in Walsall Museum and Art Gallery is illustrated in Hughes *et al.* (1990). A Maori stone carving prompted questions from one pupil about 'restitution of cultural property'. Another showed a totem-pole worn by wind and rain, as 'a metaphor for the erosion of native lifestyles by western expansionism'.

From the museum and gallery perspective, the main danger is in using 'non-European' source material as an enormous coffee table book to be flicked through. Any mask or flowery tile will therefore 'do' for the art and design curriculum, and knowing about the context of the object can be seen as an optional bonus if there is time. This is clearly unacceptable: no one believes that any altarpiece in the National Gallery will 'do', or that knowledge of Rembrandt or David Hockney is some kind of optional extra. Resources with a critical 'window shopping' approach to multicultural collections can be both stimulating and responsible in experienced hands, and in the context of a critical studies programme. Palmer (1988, 1989, 1990) achieves this by juxtaposing images selected from European and non-European culture, past and present, and organized by themes. The BM Education Service booklet for art and design teachers is similarly organized by themes picked out from the art curriculum, cross-referenced to galleries, resources and publications. British Museum Press has published a series of design books, taken from a range of cultures (Wilson, 1983, 1984, 1986, 1988, 1994; Jewell, 1994). The new BBC School Television series *The Art* (1994) also draws on a wide range of sources organized thematically (clothes, food, magic, things, living things), aiming to inspire young people to create their own art.

A museum or gallery can help by presenting non-European art in a variety of contexts. The question of context is of course controversial: is it that of the culture from which they have been severed, the culture that acquired them or the pupils' own culture (Durrans, 1988)? This could mean a Museum of Mankind recreation of an Asante palace; objects marshalled in rows in the Pitt-Rivers Museum, Oxford; or Nigerian or Mexican art seen in isolation as works of art at the Royal Academy or the Hayward Gallery. Recently, the Museum of Mankind has combined all three approaches in the exhibition 'Images of Africa', which presented the collection brought back from Zaire in 1900–9 (Mack, 1990). The implicit purpose of the exhibition was to show how discoveries of highly sophisticated art, developed indigenously in central Africa, knocked on the head the European idea that Africa could produce great art only under outside influence, usually European. The art of Zaire brought back by Torday was very influential on European sculptors and collectors like Epstein.

Pupils following examination courses in art and design picked out masks, textiles and sculpture from this exhibition. To make it more accessible, especially for younger pupils, the Museum of Mankind Education Service developed a self-help activity area in the exhibition, to be used with trained volunteers. This comprised trays of African material for handling and close observation, each with accompanying texts and a slide carousel with notes.

Pupils and students are also frequently sensitized to the art of other cultures through the eyes of modern artists. For art college students and some school groups, BM education staff present the classical tradition of the human figure in sculpture and then the reaction to this in the twentieth century by Picasso and others, particularly Henry Moore, who used the BM collections intensively as a student and throughout his life. His notebooks and commentaries (e.g. Moore, 1977, 1981, with excellent photographs by David Finn) show the impact on him of the scale and grandeur of outdoor Egyptian and Easter Island sculpture, of tension in African, Greek and Egyptian figure sculpture, of the potential of different materials and of the combination of many different museum and other sources with natural forms (Pennine rocks, beach pebbles, flints). For example, the seated king and queen for a hill-top site uses an Egyptian couple as a source and also Cycladic and African sculpture; the helmeted heads use Greek helmets and also an elephant's skull; the enclosed forms were inspired by Polynesian wood-carving. Both Moore and Picasso owned casts of one particular piece now in the Museum of Mankind, and the poet William Empson was also inspired by it to write 'In praise of the British Museum'.

During the Henry Moore exhibition at the Royal Academy (Moore, 1988), pupils and students began their visits by looking at his experiences as a student in the context of either the Museum of Mankind or the BM. After an introductory talk, large drawings in charcoal or pencil were made from different angles of the massive Easter Island head, African and Polynesian or Egyptian and Greek sculpture that interested him. The groups then moved on to the RA exhibition, sometimes to a handling session in a simulation of Moore's studio, and to more large-scale drawing. Some groups were working on a tight examination course brief for a sculptural monument of a hero or heroine using the human figure.

Mason (1988) singles out the exhibition selected and created by the artist Eduardo Paolozzi at the Museum of Mankind, 'Lost Magic Kingdoms'. This was partly nostalgia and autobiography (the 'granny's attic' museum of his youth, his early scrapbooks), but also an attempt to provoke the visitor of whatever age. In this it succeeded: unlike many exhibitions it generated fierce debate, an often underused took in museum and gallery education. The National Gallery, for example, uses a disagreement between a curator and an educator about the relative merits of a painter or painting as the basis for a joint gallery talk. In 'Lost Magic Kingdoms', educator Penny Bateman (anthropologist and formerly a curator) argued in public gallery talks and study days with the author (attempting to represent the artist's point of view) about what Paolozzi was doing. The usually rather reticent public joined in without restraint. A teachers' pack explored generally how European artists have used non-European arts (Paolozzi, 1985; Reeve, 1988; Coombes and Lloyd, 1986).

Mason advocates a more 'anthropological' approach to the arts of other cultures. The anthropologist Layton (1991) deals with concepts of 'primitivism' and (despite the usual absence of artists' biographies) how to approach issues such as style or the creativity of the artist, through case studies on Inuit masks, Nubian houses and Benin royal art. His section on 'Art in Protodynastic Egypt' could be used with the new Early Egypt Gallery at the BM and compared with the related publication (Spencer, 1993).

Curators, particularly of ethnography and non-European art, have been concerned to address multicultural issues in their exhibitions and in redisplaying their galleries, making them especially suitable for art and design projects (see Ames, 1990). Nima Poovayer Smith (1991) describes her work in Bradford. Jane Peirson-Jones has developed an exciting new gallery in Birmingham Museum, and Tony Shelton in Brighton. At the V & A, the curators for China and India have been especially concerned to evaluate public needs including school groups, in researching and displaying the Nehru Gallery of Indian Art and the TT Tsui Gallery of Chinese Art. The Hotung Gallery of Oriental Art at the British Museum is also the result of close collaboration between curators, designers and educators (Rawson, 1992; Blurton, 1992; Reeve, 1994).

In the exhibition 'Traffic Art', at the Museum of Mankind, rickshaw paintings from Bangladesh were looked at as 'art' in one room alongside a more 'ethnographic' approach in an adjacent display showing workshops and the rickshaws themselves. The same paintings recurred in an exhibition on 'Collecting the 20th Century' (Carey, 1991), unusually, alongside examples of German Expressionism, Bauhaus design, Japanese, Chinese, Indian and Islamic prints and paintings, and ethnography such as the remarkable Chinese paper and wire grave goods from Malaysia. The latter simulated a scooter, typewriter and Sony Walkman for the dead, just as the Egyptians took model slaves and ships with them and the ancient Chinese took pottery soldiers, animals, horses, games and food. When the Museum of Mankind returns to Bloomsbury it should be much easier to make these links and to offer the contemporary or more 'popular' end of cultures as a point of access for the art and history student: modern Egypt, Maoist art, contemporary Africa and South America, as well as their predecessors (see Brett, 1986).

METHODOLOGY

> They sit the kids down and talk to them about the paintings – opening them up in a
> very matter of fact way. It's not a lecture, more a sort of active discussion.
>   (a teacher commenting on a National Gallery visit: Selwood and Clive, 1992)

Pointon (1994) offers a methodology for interrogating a work of art, and Hooper-Greenhill (1991) suggests a methodology for looking at objects. Michael Compton (1979) offers a model of clear writing about pictures in 'Looking at Pictures in the Tate Gallery' without using technical language or a deluge of facts. Renée Marcousé (1961) describes her methods of developing in children a critical and expressive vocabulary. National Gallery videos often show a method for looking at a painting, a period, or a problem in art, such as 'Impressionism' or 'The Wilton Diptych'. A BM Education Service video for 'Rembrandt Drawings' looks at the same corpus of his drawings, first biographically and then thematically, and reinforces this in the teachers' pack with a thematic grid for all the drawings. It is often left to an Education Department to problematize an exhibition, make its basic methodology apparent, or suggest alternative structures for interpretation.

Some of the most useful publications on methodology for museum, gallery and site visits have been produced by English Heritage. *A Teacher's Guide to Learning from Objects* (Durbin et al., 1990) includes the almost parodic Canadian strategy, '50 ways to look at a Big Mac Box'. School practice could profitably become more like that of a museum educator: starting from the specific object then moving to the general trend rather than the other way around. Durbin (1993) looks at historic houses, complete or ruined, and shows how to compare them, for example, with a Victorian terraced house. *A Teacher's Guide to using Portraits*, with accompanying slide pack (Morris, 1989), includes exercise on pose, expression and costume together with practical advice and cross-curricular suggestions. It poses questions such as 'Do you trust the message?' Portraits are an especially accessible 'way in' to using art collections.

CONCLUSION

Substance and Shadow, a report for the London Arts Board on the relationship between education and visual arts organizations in London (Selwood and Clive, 1992), offers an update on the current situation. Much of the report is encouraging, with news of artist placements, outreach, collaboration between different types of organization, after-school projects for examination groups (at the Whitechapel Art Gallery and Camden Arts Centre, for example), and cross-curricular projects and resources (such as the resource pack for the Hokusai Exhibition at the Royal

Academy). However, there are a lot of problems still to be addressed. Teachers often feel patronized by arts organizations:

> Resourcing has been on their terms ... We've had this arrogance in a sense that the art world thinks it knows what's best for schools.

> Teachers want to work in partnership with gallery staff. This will grant them more 'ownership' of any materials produced and ensure the development of resources to suit their needs. In the past, collaboration was always very one-sided ...

Museum and gallery educators have to listen more often and more carefully to the views of teachers and other groups, to evaluate more precisely the work they are doing, and to try to plan for the future accordingly. This is all very well in theory, but problems of staffing, budgets and facilities often make it very difficult. While local galleries in London may be underused (according to this report), many major galleries and museums cannot cope with the enormously increased demands upon them. Teachers, therefore, have to rely on in-service courses, teachers' previews of exhibitions, and resources prepared by museum and gallery educators where these are available, in order to plan their own visits. Visits will frequently happen without help from museum or gallery staff on the day. Nearly 75 per cent of the 1,032 school groups who visited 'Monet' at the Royal Academy did so on their own. Exhibitions of Monet, Warhol, Pop Art or Leonardo have been very popular with teachers; exhibitions of Australian, Japanese, Indian or African art, much less so.

As a result of LMS and the absence of advisory services in many LEA's, new relationships have to be forged directly with schools for in-service work and for planning visits and projects. New organizations, such as LAADE (London Association for Art and Design Education) and NAGE (National Association for Gallery Education), cannot be expected to take over the whole responsibility formerly discharged by advisers and teachers' centres. Attitudes and relationships are changing rapidly: museum and gallery work has become much more sharply focused since the introduction of the National Curriculum. It is still necessary to answer the often justified criticism that 'The overwhelming impression of education in museums is one of confusion' (Maton-Howarth, 1990, p. 188).

Two further reports have been published in spring 1994. The first is *Art, Feat and Mystery* (Binch and Kennedy, 1994), a follow-up from the London Arts Board to *Substance and Shadow* (Selwood and Clive, 1992), looking at the next phase of collaboration between schools, museums and galleries. *Art in Schools* (The Arts Council) documents successful projects by artists working in schools. They help us see how far we are successfully addressing the criticism made by Laurie Peake of Camden Arts Centre (in Selwood and Clive, 1992), that 'there is a false sense of security and a general stodginess about art education ... There's a need for doubt, risk, experiment ... a more holistic approach ... Arts bodies should establish models of good practice outside formal education, as well as inside it' (p. 15).

REFERENCES

Ames, M. (1990) Cultural empowerment and museums: opening up anthropology through collaboration. In Pearce, S. (ed.), *Objects of Knowledge*. London: Athlone Press.

Araeen, R. (1987) From Primitivism to ethnic arts. *Third Text* **1** (autumn), pp. 1–22.

Araeen, R. (1990) *The Other Story*. London: Hayward Gallery.

Arts and Schools (1990) London: COI for DES/OAL.

Attenborough, R. (1985) *Arts and Disabled People*. London: Bedford Square Press.

Attfield, J. (1989) *Feminist Critiques of Design*. In Walker, J. (ed.), *Design History and the History of Design*. London: Pluto Press.

Benton, M. and Benton, P. (1990) *Double Vision*. London: Hodder and Stoughton.

Binch, N., and Kennedy, M. (1994) *Art, Feat and Mystery: Links Between Schools, Galleries, Museums and Artists*. London: London Arts Board/LAADE/NAGE.

Blank Contribution to History (1988) London: CUES/Geffrye Museum.

Blurton, R. (1992) *Hindu Art*. London: British Museum Press.

Brett, G. (1986) *Through Our Own Eyes: Popular Art and Modern History*. London: Gay Men's Press.

Callen, A. (1980) *Women of the Arts and Crafts Movement 1870–1914*. London: Astragal (a reprint of *Angel in the Studio*).

Carey, F. (ed.) (1991) *Collecting the 20th Century*. London: British Museum Press.

Cassin, M. (1987) *More than Meets the Eye*. London: National Gallery.

Cherry, D. (1993) *Painting Women*. London: Routledge.

Compton, M. (1979) *Looking at Pictures in the Tate Gallery*. London: Tate Gallery.

Coombes, A., and Lloyd, J. (1986) Lost and found at the Museum of Mankind. *Art History*, December, pp. 540–5.

Durbin, G. (1993) *A Teacher's Guide to Using Historic Houses*. London: English Heritage.

Durbin, G., Morris, S., and Wilkinson, S. (1990) *The Teacher's Guide to Learning from Objects*. London: English Heritage.

Durrans, B. (1988) The future of the Other. In Lumley, R. (ed.), *Museum Time-Machine*. London: Routledge.

Dyson, A. (1986) *Art History and Criticism in Schools*. London: Institute of Education/AAH/ILEA.

Harris, J. (ed.) (1993) *5000 Years of Textiles*. London: British Museum Press.

Haskell, F., and Penny, N. (1981) *Taste and the Antique*. New Haven: Yale University Press.

Hooper-Greenhill, E. (1991) *Museum and Gallery Education*. Leicester: Leicester University Press.

Hughes, A., Stanley, N., and Smith, J. (1990) *The Art Machine*. Glasgow: Glasgow Museums and Art Galleries.

In and Out of the Gallery (1993) London: London Arts Board/NAGE/LAADE.

Jackson, T. (1989) Researching the community: modern art and the new audience. In Hooper-Greenhill, E. (ed.), *Initiatives in Museum Education*. Leicester: University Dept of Museum Studies.

Jewell, R. (1994) *African Designs*. London: British Museum Press.

Johns, C. (1990) *Sex or Symbol?*. London: British Museum Press.

Larrington, C. (1992) *The Feminist Companion to Mythology*. London: Pandora.

Layton, R. (1991) *The Anthropology of Art*, 2nd edn. Cambridge: Cambridge University Press.

Layzell, R. (1993) *Live Art*. London: The Arts Council.

Mack, J. (1990) *Emil Torday and the Art of the Congo, 1900–1909*. London: British Museum Press.

Marcousé, R. (1961) *The Listening Eye*. London: HMSO.

Mason, R. (1988) *Art Education and Multiculturalism*. London: Croom Helm.

Maton-Howarth, M. (1990) Knowing Objects through an Alternative Learning System. In Pearce, S. (ed.), *Objects of Knowledge*. London: The Athlone Press.

Moore, H. (1977) *The Drawings of Henry Moore*. London: Tate Gallery.

Moore, H. (1981) *Henry Moore at the British Museum*. London: British Museum Press.

Moore, H. (1988) *Henry Moore*. London: Royal Academy.

Morris, S. (1989) *A Teacher's Guide to Using Portraits*. London: English Heritage.

Museums Association (1993) *Responding to Change*. London: Museums Associations Annual Report.

Newsom, B. Y., and Silver, A. Z. (eds) (1978) *The Art Museum as Educator*. Berkeley: University of California Press.

Nixon, J. 91985) *Guide to Multicultural Education*. Oxford: Basil Blackwell.

Paine, S. (1985) The art museum as classroom in the training of art and design teachers. *Journal of Education in Museums* **6**, 15–19.

Paine, S. (1989) Museums as resources in the education and training of teachers. In Hooper-Greenhill, E. (ed.), *Initiatives in Museum Education*. Leicester: University Dept of Museum Studies.

Palmer, F. (1988) *Themes and Projects in Art and Design*. Harlow: Longman.

Palmer, F. (1989) *Visual Elements of Art and Design*. Harlow: Longman.

Palmer, F. (1990) *Art and Design in Context*. Harlow: Longman.

Paolozzi, E. (1985) *Lost Magic Kingdom*. London: British Museum Press.

Parker, R. (1984) *The Subversive Stitch*. London: Women's Press.

Pearson, A. (1985) *Arts for Everyone*. London: Carnegie UK Trust.

Pearson, A. (1989) Museum education and disability. In Hooper-Greenhill, E. (ed.), *Initiatives in Museum Education*. Leicester: University Dept of Museum Studies.

Pearson, A., and Aloysius, C. (1994) *Museums and Children with Learning Difficulties: The Big Foot*. London: British Museum Press.

Penny, N. (ed.) (1986) *Reynolds*. London: Royal Academy.

Peppin, A. (1983) *The National Gallery Children's Book*. London: National Gallery.

Peppin, A., Smith, R., and Turner, A. (1992) *Approaches to Art*. London: Ginn.

Pointon, M. (1994) *History of Art: A Student's Handbook*, 3rd edn. London: Routledge.

Pollock, G., and Parker, R. (1981) *Old Mistresses: Women, Art and Ideology*. London: Routledge.

Poovayer Smith, N. (1991) Exhibitions and Audiences. In Kavanagh, G. (ed.), *Museum Languages*. Leicester: Leicester University Press.

Porter, G. (1988) Putting Your House in Order. In Lumley, R. (ed.), *Museum Time-Machine*. London: Routledge.

Porter, G. (1991) Partial Truths. In Kavanagh, G. (ed.), *Museum Languages*. Leicester: Leicester University Press.

Rawson, J. (1992) *The British Museum Book of Chinese Art*. London: British Museum Press.

Reeve, J. (1988) The British Museum. In Stephens, M. (ed.), *Culture, Education and the State*. London: Routledge.

Reeve, J. (1994) Review of the Hotung Gallery. In Pearce, S. (ed.), *Museums and the Appropriation of Culture*. London: Athlone Press.

Rubin (1984) *'Primitivism' in 20th Century Art*. New York: Museum of Modern Art.

Ruthven, K. K. (1990) *Feminist Literary Studies: An Introduction*. Cambridge: Canto.

Saunders, G. (1989) *The Nude: A Perspective*. London: Icon.

Selwood, S., and Clive, S. (1992) *Substance and Shadow*. London: London Arts Board.

Spencer, J. (1993) *Early Egypt*. London: British Museum Press.

Taylor, R. (1986) *Educating for Art*. Harlow: Longman.

Taylor, R., and Andrews, G. (1993) *The Arts in the Primary School*. London: Falmer Press.

The Arts in Schools (1982) London: Calouste Gulbenkian Foundation.

Wilson, E. (1983, 1984, 1986, 1988, 1994) *Early Medieval Designs: North American Indian Designs; Ancient Egyptian Designs; Islamic Designs; 8,000 Years of Ornament*. London: British Museum Press.

Wolf, F. (1988) *Myths and Legends: Paintings in the National Gallery*. London: National Gallery.

Chapter 7

Using Contemporary Art

Lucy Dawe Lane

As the twentieth century closes, contemporary art offers a plethora of possibilities. In this situation of pluralism, itself a sign of health as much as of fragmentation, this chapter will suggest how to make positive use of any aspect of contemporary practice in schools; how to plunder it for all it is worth, which is a great deal. The purpose of this chapter is threefold:

- to propose reasons why contemporary art is an important and unique resource to support the implementation of the National Curriculum for Art;
- to identify key issues with which contemporary artists are concerned and to explore ways in which broad curricular themes can link to these issues; and
- to suggest ways in which teachers of art and design can update their subject knowledge and identify resources available to them.

WHY CONTEMPORARY ART?

For many people the very notion of contemporary art spells difficulty, and excites anxiety, even anger. Teachers of art and design have every reason to use established collections of historical and modern art, as they present tried and tested examples of quality, seminal works, readable histories. The contemporary, however, has yet to be fixed, judged, categorized. Walk into an exhibition of new work, and the visitor is in uncharted territory. Posterity has yet to sift it all into something altogether more manageable. It is the intention here to argue that the difficulties that contemporary art at first presents and which usually preclude the use of contemporary art in schools are also the reasons why it is a challenge worth taking on. Art needs to be exposed to young people as often as possible, and art is deliberately made the passive side of the equation. It is time to train active audiences to read and enjoy the visual languages that are made available to them. If people only realized, art is at their disposal.

Art requires audiences for survival, or at least to become part of common visual currency. At the Whitechapel Art Gallery it is a daily occurrence that pupils from the neighbouring schools, among other visitors, will come in and furnish mute art objects with diverse and often startlingly sophisticated readings of their own making. This is the power that future audiences have. Art objects are purpose-built for receiving meanings by those who use them. Currently artists are making works which actually need audiences to take on an active role in completing them by finding potential meanings in them. Art is made to be treated with critical rigour, rather than swallowed whole. What is more, it does not bite back.

Teachers of art and design have a responsibility to ensure that art made today has a role to play as part of the day-to-day lives of all pupils. It is not yet known which of the objects made today will ultimately be most evocative of the end of this century, but an example like *House*, made by Rachel Whiteread in 1993, is already part of a collective memory bank. This is not because it was preserved, or placed in a museum, but because so many people saw it, read about it, watched it on television; because it entered the minds of many people, and therefore, in a way, still exists. The public had as important a role to play in the creation of that sculpture's significance as did the critics, dealers and councillors who fought over the span of its brief existence.

ART AND THE PRESENT

The most compelling reason for including contemporary art in the secondary school curriculum is that it reflects on current cultures. Either self-consciously, or in spite of itself, art is a product of its own times and can be approached as familiar ground which is going to reflect some of the concerns, interest and experiences of pupils, simply because that experience is of the late twentieth century. This truism sets the scene for enabling pupils to feel a sense of ownership over this material in a way which they may not feel for historical objects. Moreover, the many cultures which art objects can be said to reflect and invoke today mean that the study of art can provide an arena for developing an awareness of cultural difference, issues of imperialism between cultures, sexual difference and so on. How pupils situate themselves in contemporary debates on any subject from environmental issues to fashion can be picked up and used to woo them into a direct involvement with visual art.

The clumsy argument for matching cultural groups to relevant art objects by using such criteria as gender and race has, one hopes, long been replaced by the desire for individuals to develop a finely honed sense of their own 'place'. They also need to be given a wide enough sense of various cultural perspectives to be able to choose the avenues along which they wish to travel in the future. Again, a great advantage of contemporary work is that it addresses directly some of the issues and dilemmas of difference, of cultural heritage; whereas art of the past can speak only of its own time, and the perspectives which it reflects need to be recreated in order to understand it.

ART AND ART HISTORY

To pursue the issue of teaching art history, the work of a contemporary artist can provide an ideal introduction to an area of study, by revealing in very deep and often very personal ways how art objects and cultures of the past can feed directly into the creative processes of today. Artists are themselves the most exacting and critical of art history scholars, mining the past both visually and ideologically, but also re-evaluating it, even reinventing it. Their gaze does not stop with art objects either, but casts a contemporary consciousness and visual sense over the ideas and objects of social and political histories, and of anthropology, the history of science, and medicine. The list is as long as the number of disciplines history encompasses. It is important that pupils are able to appreciate the variety of research that artists might undertake in order to create their work, and that the discipline of art is far from hermetic.

ART AND THE FUTURE

Having briefly explored the reasons why some artists today provide a route into art history, it is also worth mentioning that many also have a unique role to play in shaping the future. Despite the tiredness of the very concept of an 'avant-garde' in today's permissive climate, it is nevertheless true that artists are defining the future visual environment and the visual languages that will operate. It only has to be mentioned how ubiquitous early twentieth-century fine art images now are in advertising, in the cinema, in fashion and so on. Even though it plays with the notion of exclusiveness by appearing to single out only those who are enough in the know to buy the product, the recent 'Picasseau' campaign by advertisers of Perrier, using a Cubist-style bottle, relied on recognition for the message to work. What at first caused outrage and confusion becomes an accepted and understood language to be used in a relatively casual and undemanding context. There is every reason to think that this process will continue, so that art being made now will become part of the visual vocabulary of many more people in the future than it reaches currently.

LEARNING VISUAL LANGUAGES

What can teachers do in the meantime? Do they wait for the art of today to become assimilated before using it in school, or do they try to bridge the gap, and negotiate the difficulty, the unreadability, of new works of art? If art is a language or a group of languages which use visual rather than verbal signs, then an analogy with language learning may be appropriate for discussing how to proceed with art.

While there is an argument for beginning by learning rules of grammar and declensions of nouns, verbs etc., there is also a case for learning through immersion in the spoken language, for plunging right in. The idea of listening to language/ looking at art as a constant activity alongside practising the speaking/making for one's self is useful. In this model the idea of keeping pupils away from art objects for fear of their being too complex just does not stand up. Taking part in a conversation can be the best way to get interested enough to want to learn the rules.

Having mentioned rules, it is also worth bearing in mind that artists today are intensely involved in a debate about visual grammar. The early twentieth century saw new rules being forged for the use of visual language. Since then the pace of change has increased such that currently there can be very many different conversations going on, each with a separate agenda. There are some artists working within genres such as landscape painting, whereas for others the redefinition of landscape, and of the place of painting, happened many moons ago. The result is that artists as diverse as Richard Long and Michael Andrews can both be said to be contemporary landscape artists, but their mind-sets and methodologies are almost totally exclusive to one another, perhaps like dialects of the same parent language. There are even returns to earlier forms and ideas, such as neo-Expressionism and neo-Conceptualism, so that the problem which art and design teachers set for themselves is not merely to include in their teaching reference to the many new visual ideas which are currently being forged, but also to make sense of how complex the organic whole is to these raw shoots at the extremities.

BROADENING IDEAS ABOUT ART

It is vital to introduce into schools some sense of the changing relationship between skills and ideas in the making of art, and how these are fused together with a different emphasis according to the intentions of the artist. Intentions might vary at different historical moments and in different cultural contexts. Again, it is important to grasp that today there is no one orthodoxy in these matters, so the breadth of available variations within contemporary practice presents an inclusive and somewhat confusing picture to young people. The issue of skill and talent is one which affects everyone, and the current openness with which artists use any method and explore any material at their disposal to put across ideas, rather than rely on innate or cultivated practical skills, is surely a welcome environment in which to encourage pupils to negotiate as well as to develop their own manual abilities. There are several areas in which it is possible to succeed in art, and the National Curriculum happily bears this out, with attention being paid to understanding art, to investigate skills and to the quality of ideas, as well as to the finished product. But how will pupils feel about this, when most are engaged in their own struggle to fulfil their expectations, in terms of drawing skills, for example?

One of the most common reactions to a contemporary art object is that the artist has made a deficient object, one which seems to exhibit a lack of ability. This lack might be either in the area of physical skill, or in the ability to make an object which is at once comprehensible to the viewer. The idea that this could be deliberate, as part of a strategy to focus on aspects other than the display of talent, or indeed a decision to make something which does not reveal any recognized patterns of thought, cannot at first be entertained.

It is important to investigate the reasons why a change has taken place in artists' attitudes towards demonstrating skill, and to discuss what skill actually represents in a post-industrial society. Is a preoccupation with, and questioning of, manual skill in fine art a reflection of a similar ambivalence in attitudes towards technologies which have taken over most manual activities? To question an artist's use of industrial techniques to make objects, for example, is a bit like saying that mathematicians should not use calculators. Behind the shift in aims away from the demonstration of skill lies the decline of academy-style art training which was the norm in the last century, and which was eventually replaced by the Bauhaus model. The goals shifted at that time to embrace creativity and invention, rather than the imitation of models found in nature, and the exploration of the formal possibilities of each medium took precedence over traditional subjects.

When looking at a work of art it is important to remember that the artist has deliberated on every aspect of its physical appearance and that, rather than looking for mistakes, the aim is to find clues to the artist's intentions. Gauging the intentions and deliberations of the artist must therefore be seen as one essential step in the process of reading works of art. It does not follow that viewers should agree with the artist's proposed meanings entirely. Rather, they might consider the art object a crossing over, a confluence of ideas, both those of the artist and their own. In this case the artist's input is only one part of the work.

Artists are perhaps only united by the necessity to define and analyse their own practice; by a consciousness of their position, which means that to paint is to decide to paint as a deliberate move in the continuing and lively debate about the status of painting. It is possible to do almost anything, as no area of object-making need stand outside aesthetic consideration. It is not possible, however, for artists to do anything meaningful without considering, even if choosing then to disregard, the context of current visual and theoretical debate. The implications of this statement for the implementation of the National Curriculum for Art are far-reaching.

THE VALUE OF ORIGINALITY

It is useful to recognize a dual standard in society today towards originality. On the one hand, the constant creation of demand for the new in fashion, in technological inventions, in the design of cars and washing machines, etc. is what drives capitalism. On the other hand, there is deep suspicion towards anything which is unrecognizable and defies expectations. Whereas the ideal of individualism is deeply rooted in people's consciousness, and consumerism offers genuine possibilities for self-expression, these possibilities are within strictly defined limits. Underlying the market there has to be some degree of conformity, because it is a mass market.

However, young people are naturally inventive with the materials at their disposal, especially in terms of combining available options in, for example, street fashion to produce their own styles. There is much here that can be harnessed to generate an understanding of how artists work and think. They too are open to experimenting with materials, and have an eclectic visual approach to existing objects. It is essential to give pupils a sense of the relationship between the professional artist's approach to everyday experiences, and their own, so that they can begin to practise various ideas for themselves, and do so with an awareness that, whether or not they will themselves become artists, these skills are all beneficial in their own right.

Most people would think of practical skills in various media if asked what it is that artists do. Lateral thinking, problem-setting and solving, investigative skills, creative drive, perseverance, the ability to work alone, or to collaborate with other specialists who have complementary skills; this might sound like a list of personal skills for any number of jobs. Over the past thirty years, the transferable skills learnt during an art school training have formed some of the most influential and original people at work today, in fields as diverse as pop music and banking.

WHICH CONTEMPORARY ART?

Having discussed arguments for the use of contemporary art, broad topic headings are used in order to focus upon examples of projects with artists and secondary schools undertaken by the Whitechapel Art Gallery. Reference is also made to a wider selection of artists' work where appropriate to the topic headings. It is intended that these topics will reveal how varied the approaches and products of individual artists can be on a single theme, and that teachers will see how to match or to complement their own pupils' existing interests and experiences through a considered choice of contemporary art for study.

ART AND THE ENVIRONMENT

The depth with which artists consider their visual surroundings, and the diverse ways in which this feeds their work, will, on viewing that work, or working alongside an artist, promote a similar seriousness about investigative and documentary activities in school.

Consider the city. Artists today find aesthetic interest in almost any aspect of the made environment, whether it be the spectacular, such as the new environment of London Docklands, which has already been the site of many projects and commissions, or the commonplace, such as the featureless interiors of public buildings recorded meticulously by the painter Paul Winstanley. The city as a total system, as explored by Julian Opie, or the city as a conglomeration of individually seen and experienced textures and incidents, is an endless mine of visual ideas.

While many artists work in studios in inner-city areas, where rents are cheap, artists have also used the urban environment to create a setting for showing their work, rather than choosing to exhibit in pristine galleries. The Freeze exhibition of 1988, organized by then art student Damien Hirst, in a disused warehouse in Wapping, is a now famous example. Artists are drawn to make site-specific works in urban and suburban settings, often by drawing out existing qualities of a space, and altering them only minimally. They might be attracted either by the everyday ordinariness of the place, or by its almost exotic qualities of decay.

Some work is virtually invisible, such as Cornelia Parker's temporary sculpture in a Limehouse church spire, which was impossible to see from the street. In contrast, other public art works, whether permanent or temporary, can completely alter their surroundings by dominating the space they occupy. It is this aspect of contemporary art that often reaches the press and public beyond art circles, and quite often because the work does not meet with public approval or expectations. Festivals or large-scale projects such as the Tyne International, Edge, or Television and South West Arts, include a variety of works in public spaces both urban and rural, and would provide an excellent study for local schools.

The opposites of the city in environmental terms, such as a desert or an Arctic wasteland, preoccupy artists for different reasons. Christo's large-scale artworks such as *Wrapped Coast* exploit the scale and drama of uninhabited spaces, whereas Ian McKeever's journeys to hostile and uninhabited places result in paintings which take account of not only the large-scale formations of landscapes, but also the minutiae of rock formations.

There is now a tradition of work which uses natural materials in rural and wild places, to make works which are temporary, and often result only in verbal or photographic productions. Richard Long, Ian Hamilton Finlay and David Nash represent just some of the very individual ways in which this type of work first developed in Britain. The idea of a walk, or a sculpture built with ice, being a work of art might seem odd at first, but when art is seen as an activity, with certain intentions planned and then carried out by artists, rather than having a lasting product, the range of possibilities is extended.

Pupils appreciate the moral position that much of this art represents in terms of not using materials to produce yet more objects, but merely to move materials around for a while, to create equally stunning visual or conceptual results. Again, the idea that art can exist only temporarily, especially if it is only ever seen by the artist who made it, provides challenging philosophical problems to explore. These ideas can be investigated by making ephemeral works in school, and experimenting with natural materials (the simpler the better: artist Andy Goldsworthy has made rain sculpture by lying down on hard ground the moment the rain starts, and revealing a dry image of his body, which lasts only a few minutes before being covered by more rain).

A project undertaken by artist Kate Allen with special educational needs pupils at Stormont House School in London in 1991 combined two extremes of environment by creating a hybrid: an urban rain forest, made largely from scrap materials. Following the principles of her own working methods, the project created an archaeological record of objects found by pupils, from shoes to safety pins, and set them into cardboard boxes using differently coloured layers of plaster. Into these blocks of plaster were set lengths of wood to form the supports for exotic foliage, and fauna, again made from found materials. The impact of these 'trees', when brought together in a display at the Whitechapel Art Gallery, was stunning.

Another project relied on a formula for collecting materials. Artist Jordan Baseman led a series of three Saturday GCSE workshops at the Whitechapel Art Gallery during an exhibition of contemporary Japanese art, and spent a total of five days continuing the work at Central Foundation Girls' School. The exhibition as a whole concentrated on the high technology available to artists today, such as LEDs and computerized photomontage. Shinro Ohtake's work was, in contrast, quite low-tech in techniques and therefore made an excellent choice for practical investigation. Jordan asked participants to collect a diary of rubbish over the winter holiday. This resulted in a huge diversity of material and methods of collection. Furnished with black plastic sacks, pupils returned in January with an extraordinary array of magazine clippings, in Bengali and in English, Christmas decorations, bus tickets, meal wrappings, etc.

Inspired by the diaries documenting worldwide travel made by Ohtake, the pupils made fascinating books. Some had three-dimensional objects incorporated in them; all had a wry and iconoclastic slant to them, and a refined sense of combining and cross-fertilizing materials from the different cultures encountered as a natural part of their holiday. During the workshops it was decided that they would fax Ohtake in Japan, and as a result, he replied and sent participants small collages and then colour photocopied notebooks with their names on the front. This sort of matter-of-fact and yet very real involvement with artists succeeded in both cases in closing the gap between the artists' true concerns and the everyday experience of pupils, by providing carefully prepared routes into the concepts behind the work, and room for personal contributions within the framework of the project.

ART AND TECHNOLOGY

As with contrasting environmental topics, looking at technologies has high- and low-tech aspects in artistic practice. An important issue for schools is to demarcate visual art practice from the study of technology *per se*. This chapter is concerned only with the creative harnessing of technology by artists, for their own very distinct contribution to present-day society. Bill Viola is an American artist whose approach to video and computer technologies lies not is what the machines can do, but in what he can do with them. His interest goes beyond a love affair with technology for its own sake. This attitude can be found among many other artists who will often ignore the technical finesse or logical extremes of a medium, and use them at a very unsophisticated level because the focus of their interest is elsewhere.

The same could be said of painting as of computer graphics, in that the medium has to be fully grasped technically, before this kind of approach is truly a choice rather than just a necessity. But very welcome it can be to teachers who are daunted by the prospect of starting a video project because the school possesses no equipment – in which case a very effective course could run using any home players and camcorders that might be borrowed. The inspiration of an artist during a short residency can often spur a teacher into extending into a new medium by plunging in and starting with an artistic aim, which the technology has to be made to serve.

Creating a still life on video, for example, which requires a fixed position for the camera, and frees all members of a group to explore ways of introducing different materials and objects into the picture, could be a useful first step to using video visually rather than as a narrative medium. In early 1994, artist Shona Illingworth made a short film on the theme of fire and water with Bengali women and girls living close to the Whitechapel Art Gallery. The theme naturally provided action through time, and allowed the group to introduce other materials which they associated with these elements. In this project, as with most successful work planned and undertaken by the Gallery, the principle of 'less is more' when setting the content resulted in a corresponding richness and coherence in the finished work.

Contemporary artists use an array of industrial techniques and materials in their work. One of the most memorable pieces of work made in recent years is Richard

Wilson's *20 : 50*, originally shown at Matt's Gallery in 1987, and now the property of Saatchi Galleries. The work is composed of a room which appears to be half-filled with sump oil. The material is as precisely calculated in its effect as oil paint, and refers to painting in the way it literally reflects nature (the ceiling above). In contrast of scale, cotton buds, a mass-produced product rather than a raw material of industry, have been used by artist Caroline Russell. She uses such existing products, together with display techniques and industrially produced finishes, in order to comment directly on the process of display and sale of consumer goods.

What is striking about both these examples is how, once out of context and isolated in a gallery, these materials become extraordinarily beautiful. There is a great challenge and also a great deal of enjoyment to be had in discovering and sharing the aesthetic qualities of everyday objects. Projects which simply modify the context, or even create a special context, for looking at certain objects and materials are well within the reach of every art and design department, and such art practice has a distinguished history.

The meanings which found objects, artefacts and materials can generate are diverse. Picasso used existing objects for their anthropomorphic or zoomorphic qualities, most famously the bicycle saddle and handle bars becoming a bull's head. In contrast Ange Leccia, a Parisian artist, uses portable cassette players and television sets, and displays them, often on top of their boxes, and in the same symmetrical formations that are seen in shop windows. They represent themselves, and are placed in art galleries for the viewer to contemplate their meaning. The context requires that they are perceived differently. It may be that, when looking to buy something in a shop, the emphasis is on differentiation: what distinguishes one model from another, both functionally and aesthetically. The artist presents half a dozen of the same kind, and dwells on the generic type, which stands for all ghetto blasters everywhere.

Introducing practical projects using existing objects or materials might be profitable only when those chosen have some resonance with the pupils concerned. Designer training shoes, for example, need not be relegated for ever to be a subject for still-life drawing. They could be used as found objects to trigger further work which examines their significance. For example, everyone understands about aesthetic value and material cost when the object in question is a real part of their own lexicon of values. Making work which explores this would involve tackling one of the most thorny issues of all: art and money.

ART AS COMMODITY

One of the most significant developments of this century has been the decision at various times, by artists, to stop making saleable objects, or even stop making objects at all. Resulting work includes performance art, conceptual work and installations. Some of these works set out to protest against the fetishization of art objects and the market value they represent, when to artists their value lies in the ideas they contain and the aesthetic pleasure they generate. Nevertheless many seminal works which attempt to defy market forces very often end up being tied to them, because their importance to the intellectual development of art ensures their place in public and private collections, even if what is held there is simply a document.

What exactly is taking place when someone buys a work of art? Are they buying an object, an idea or an experience? They may be collecting art in order to have unlimited access to it; to furnish their home; to invest money; to impress their friends or colleagues. There are therefore private reasons for wanting to own art, but also ones which are social, to do with projecting an image. Businesses form art collections to enhance their corporate image by association with the arts.

In this context, contemporary art is quite a seasonal buy. The 1980s saw a huge amount of corporate investment in visual art, which represents risk, originality and flair. There were tales of buying in bulk, sight unseen. In times of recession, however, contemporary art is the first victim of belt-tightening and generally suffers more than sounder investments in old masters. It is not just that there is less money around, but that people choose to express themselves differently under these conditions. To buy contemporary art is to make a certain statement, and not necessarily the one to put out when times are conservative. This overview is deliberately wooden and stereotypical in order to demonstrate that, in the case of contemporary art, its cost and the values that people wish to express through it can be inextricably bound to one another, and can be as seemingly subjectively determined as the fluctuations of the stock exchange. The value of contemporary art has to be decided over time, and depends largely on what the art means to people, and what they can use it to mean.

In the school context, any discussion of monetary value in art can always be accompanied by discussion of paying for original ideas, however valueless the materials used. How can a sculpture made of 100 rubber dogs be worth more than one cast in bronze? Looking at the drive for new forms in popular music, and the accompanying machinery of promotion, comparisons could be made in terms of pushing for a new aesthetic, and in the seemingly enormous amounts of money involved. Not many artists are as rich as pop stars, however, even though their work might seem to be attracting large sums of money. It is useful for questions about large price tags to be taken seriously, and to r..ake some calculations as to how many works could be made and successfully sold in a year, and to place that against studio and material costs and so on.

HOW TO USE CONTEMPORARY ART

The aim of this chapter is not only to disperse some of the mythologies surrounding contemporary art, but to show how it can be incorporated into school resources.

Studios

Artists' studios, whether in a complex or single, often have organized openings, sometimes as part of local arts festivals. This presents an excellent opportunity to view work and to get to know the artists. Some offer organized activities for small groups from schools, often as part of their charitable status as a community resource. In other situations there may be artists working from home whom it is possible to contact through lists and slide collections held by Regional Arts Boards. They will also know which artists are interested and experienced in providing educational activities. Building up a long-term relationship with even one artist can have real impact on a school, and bring to life at least one example of art practice.

It would be ideal to find a contrast between a ceramic artist, or printmaker, and a fine artist practising in a very different way, and to compare the two studio environments. One might resemble a workshop, with systematically laid-out tools and equipment; the other might be a clean white space, with very little in it, or be full of a chaotic array of materials and objects, and have masses of unfinished work around. Once back at school, it may be possible to recreate a studio by removing all tables from a room and creating an empty space to work in, to see how the scale and nature of the work made can change due to the circumstances of its production. If all the art produced at school has a school-art feel to it, maybe that is because all art-rooms have an art-room look to them.

Galleries

Starting locally, it is worth getting to know the collections and exhibition spaces in the locality of the school, and any commercial galleries, however small. The main advantage of using local resources, in conjunction with occasional visits to special collections or exhibitions, is that it can make a local resource a regular point of reference. A study of a local collection can reveal much about attitudes to contemporary art if only by its absence, or by the tokenism of one or two tired-looking abstracts. Are they well displayed? What would the pupils do to add to the collection? Would they buy or make work which was interesting because relevant to the locality? Knowledge of how the collection came about would lead to further conclusions about the significance of its contents. Whether it started as a bequest or as a municipal foundation, for example, could have completely different implications for further study.

Public exhibition galleries are a particularly valuable resource, because they provide a cross-section of work being made today, and if the space specializes in showing certain types of work or concentrates on one medium, then it is well worth planning this into the art and design curriculum so that full advantage can be taken of the annual programme. Many museums and galleries offer some kind of support to schools. A full education programme will include teachers' evenings and in-service courses, workshops, tours and talks undertaken by gallery staff and/or artists; some with outreach activities taking place in schools.

If there is little or no activity that answers specific needs, it may be worth trying to cultivate a curator or exhibitions organizer to generate some rapport between school and the venue. While the National Curriculum for Art demands services from galleries and museums, there is not the accompanying commitment from central government or from Local Education Authorities to bear the cost of providing gallery education services. The field has grown enormously over the past ten years, encouraged greatly by funding support and education policy coming from the Arts Council and from Regional Arts Boards. However, many posts and facilities are under threat, due to a lack of funds, and sadly often suffer from a lack of commitment to education from within the institutions themselves.

Secondary sources

The provision of adequate books, slides and reproductions in support of the National Curriculum for Art is very difficult for many schools which lack sufficient funding. For contemporary art, although there are some ravishing books, there are also cheaper resources available from galleries exhibiting new work, such as illustrated leaflets and catalogues, and sometimes slides or postcards.

In addition to these resources, art magazines provide an introduction to issues in contemporary art. There are several on the market, with *Art Monthly, Frieze* and *Modern Painters* providing a survey of available critical positions. Specialist magazines such as *Third Text*, which has a perspective on cultures worldwide, and *Feminist Art News* also give a sense of the different dialogues going on in specific areas of visual art. As well as looking at the criticism, reviews and exhibition announcements that these provide, there is a case for making accessible some copies of *Apollo, Gazette des Beaux Arts* and the *Burlington Magazine*, and also some Sotheby's and Christie's catalogues, to present a picture of the commercial world of art-dealing.

In London there is a bimonthly sheet of all exhibitions in contemporary spaces, both public and commercial. This free leaflet, which is obtainable at most public galleries, is an excellent way of getting an instant overview and update of the contemporary art scene. If pupils have seen the work of a particular artist in an exhibition, they can trace any subsequent shows that include that artist.

In summary, it is essential that pupils in secondary education are given every opportunity to experience the richness of current artistic practice, and have access to an unbiased selection of resources. They are not only potential artists of the future, but should all be considered the audiences for contemporary art, and should be able to negotiate the art world with ease and confidence.

Chapter 8

Human Resources: Artists, Craftspersons, Designers

Lesley Burgess

Over the last 20 years, arts organizations have developed an elaborate network of support structures in order to bring the worlds of practising visual artists into a closer working partnership with educational institutions. National bodies such as the Arts, Crafts and Design Councils, Regional Arts Boards and museums and galleries have developed education policies to support collaborative work in this field. As a result residencies, workshops, studio visits and teacher placement schemes have been introduced.

While recognizing that these developments can make an important contribution to art and design in the school curriculum, they have not been without problems. The experience of the Artists-in-Schools (AiS) programme in America is significant, and its rapid implementation and ensuing problems provide useful comparisons to parallel developments in the United Kingdom.

The involvement of professional artists in education was welcomed with enthusiasm by teachers, and for some time artists enjoyed uncritical acceptance. As their popularity grew, the lack of any evidence to show that they were of long-term educational value caused concern. Clear rationales and effective evaluation systems have since been developed. Nevertheless, the validity and viability of working with practising artists at a time of rapid educational change and financial restraint need to be carefully examined. In the light of the Education Reform Act (1988) and the changing priorities of arts organizations and funding bodies, it is important to identify the most appropriate ways, both pedagogically and financially, of involving professional artists, craftspersons and designers in education. Failing this, the continuation of such schemes is threatened.

BEGINNINGS OF INVOLVEMENT: 'SEE WHAT HAPPENS'

In 1972 the Gulbenkian Foundation set aside £30,000 to develop a scheme to encourage links between professional artists and schools. This scheme was described by Peter Brinson, then director of the Foundation, as an attempt 'to break away from the traditional concept of artist-in-residence and try new things in new ways'. Its aim was modest, he declared, with no other motive than to 'do it and see what happens' (Braden, 1978, p. xi). This initiative signified the state of schemes developed to involve professional visual artists in education – a trend which has continued to evolve. However, it was not unique, since a scheme already developing in America echoed the same sentiment. Nancy Hanks, director of the National Endowment for the Arts (NEA) claimed that the AiS programme, started in 1969, was saying: 'Let's stop talking and writing about how to put the arts meaningfully in our schools, let's just put some live artists in and see what happens' (Hanks, 1971, p. 14).

The motives behind these early 'pilot' schemes were complicated and included securing employment for artists as well as providing a resource for education. It is significant that these initiatives began in the early 1970s. In retrospect they can be seen as a result of the political, social and ideological thinking prevalent in the late 1960s, which engendered notions such as alternative culture, cultural democracy, community arts and de-schooling. It was during this period that artists and critics challenged, even attacked, the institutions of the art world, questioning the role of art in society, and concentrating on new ways of putting art and artists back into social contexts. The sterility of many art forms was being questioned, 'events', 'performances' and 'live art' were taking place outside the traditional context of the gallery. At the same time new approaches to art history were being disseminated.

THE DEVELOPMENT OF AiS IN AMERICA: PANACEA OR PROBLEM?

It has been suggested that the model for artists working in schools had its origins in the United States of America and that initially the United Kingdom followed the received pattern. Certainly, similarities to the early developments in the United Kingdom can be found in schemes in America. However, it is important to note that differences in the two education systems make any direct comparison difficult.

In 1965 the Federal Government passed the Elementary and Secondary Education Act, which engendered the beginnings of partnership between the arts and education. Later, in 1969, the Office of Education sponsored the placement, through the National Endowment for the Arts (NEA), of six visual artists in secondary schools. The programme expanded rapidly, by 1972 including 50 states. Positive responses from schools followed by increased support from the Office of Education indicated to its supporters the success and value of the project.

Not everyone viewed this development with enthusiasm. The NEA saw the project growing from strength to strength and deduced that this was tangible proof of its effectiveness. A number of educationalists had strong reservations. Smith (1977) and Eisner (1974) were outspoken in their criticism of the programme, which they believed to be ill-conceived and ill-considered. Eisner was sceptical about the value of the artist in school *per se*. He claimed:

> The concept of bringing the artist into school is an intriguing one, one which lends itself to good copy. Artists are believed to be interesting people; and as such are viewed by many as an antidote to the bland atmosphere of schools and teachers. (p. 20)

Eisner and others attempted to persuade the NEA to reflect on its approach and to institute a thorough appraisal system of evaluation. These requests went unheeded. Consequently, Eisner produced a vitriolic attack on the programme. In a paper entitled 'Is the artist in the school program really effective?' (1974) he gave the following reasons for his condemnation:

- *Evaluation.* There was no professionally competent evaluation, just a 'slickly designed booklet intended to function as a public relations document'.
- *Funding.* To increase levels of funding so drastically without competent evaluation was not only irresponsible but set a dangerous precedent.
- *Failure.* The AiS programme could provide an excellent opportunity to learn about the ways in which educational improvement could be brought about. To secure understanding about this required careful attention not only to programmes that succeeded but to those that failed as well.
- *Entitlement.* Only 2–3 per cent of the school population benefited from the scheme. To spend such a large percentage of available funds required at the very least some competent assessment of the programme's effectiveness.
- *Thesis.* The implicit and at times explicit thesis in the AiS programme was that 'those who can best teach are those who produce art'. Art teachers and school art programmes were apparently not considered competent to provide a valid art education.

In spite of these criticisms that AiS budget continued to grow: in 1982 a total of five and a half million dollars was allocated to it. However, in the meantime regular school art programmes and teachers of the arts were being reduced in many schools.

The AiS scheme can be seen as a substitute for properly trained and qualified art teachers. For years it inhibited the development of pedagogically sound programmes with built-in continuity and progression. More recently, the promotion and implementation of Discipline Based Arts Education (DBAE) has to some extent redressed the balance, and AiS is now viewed by many educators as a problem for art and design education rather than a panacea. This experience has shown that careful consideration must be given to the role of the professional artist in education; to developing effective strategies which enable artist and teacher to work in partnership. The NEA made the mistake of trying to implement its programme without the formal participation of professional art educators. The approach in the United Kingdom has been more considered and partnership is seen as fundamental to success.

THE DEVELOPMENT OF AiS IN THE UNITED KINGDOM: GENUINE PARTNERSHIP?

In 1973 seven Local Education Authorities (LEAs) accepted an invitation from the Gulbenkian Foundation to become partners in funding AiS. The aim of the scheme was to help three groups of people:

- artists;
- pupils;
- teachers.

It was expected that individual schemes would embrace all three groups and that each residency would:

- place the artist in a new relationship to society, in an economically secure framework, encouraging a new sense of commitment and purpose, and providing new material;
- give pupils an insight into the creative processes at work, and an appreciation of art and artists, thereby demythologizing art;
- encourage teachers to depart from the examination syllabuses and take a broader, humanistic view of education.

A survey of Local Education Authorities in England, Scotland and Wales undertaken for the Arts Council by Macdonald (1980) revealed that many schools already worked with artists, 'that a great deal of activity was taking place . . . probably more than the most optimistic outsider would expect' (1980, p. 2).

The report *The Arts in Schools: Principles, Practice and Provision* (Gulbenkian, 1982) was highly influential in validating and promoting the work of artists in education. It stressed the need to 'clarify what these schemes and visits actually achieved' (p. 125). Following its publication a national curriculum development project was initiated: 'The Arts in Schools Project' (1985–9). This was funded by the Schools Curriculum Development Council, which worked in partnership with 18 LEAs to explore the recommendations of the report, and to develop collaboration between artists, teachers and pupils.

Many of these early programmes included artists, craftspersons and designers, and professional performers from drama, dance and music. Critics of such schemes pointed out that 'the so-called expressive subjects have insufficiently similar aims, objectives, working methods or assessment procedures to enable the integration of these curriculum areas' (Steers, 1993, p. 16).

By the mid-1980s, Drumcroon Education Art Centre was operating the 'Artists in Wigan Schools' scheme. Taylor had already show the value of utilizing the various skills of visual artists via the 'Critical Studies in Art Education' project (1981–4); he was also aware of the potential pitfalls from the AiS project in the United States and early projects in the United Kingdom. He reiterated the importance of partnership:

> I am a great believer in artists-in-schools programmes – but not to by-pass or as an alternative to the classroom teacher; when working together in genuine partnership, it is possible for teacher and artist to offer the young people in their dual charge a quality and range of experiences which neither, working in isolation, can otherwise offer.
>
> (Taylor, 1992, p. 90)

Convinced that artists could make a valuable contribution to curriculum development, Taylor employed various models of engagement. These included using the skills of young local artists and art design teachers from secondary schools to act as artists-in-residence. At Drumcroon Education Art Centre he established a working partnership: school-artist-gallery.

Throughout the second half of the 1980s, schemes to place artists in education were, without a doubt, popular if not 'fashionable'. Numerous Artists-in-Residence (AiR) schemes in schools, museums and galleries were implemented with a view to exploring and exploiting their potential for contributing to the development of a more 'culturally appropriate' curriculum – by providing pupils with direct contact with visual artists of non-European origin. There were notable exceptions, such as those already mentioned, but, too often the aims were not clearly formulated. They claimed to 'demystify art', 'develop creativity', act as a 'role model', 'enrich the curriculum'. Any defensible educational policy must go beyond such vague generalities. It should have clearly articulated educational outcomes in which cognitive aspects are identified.

The year 1988 saw the introduction of the Education Reform Act (ERA). Against this background the National Foundation for Education Research commissioned a two-year study to look into the main benefits and limitations of artists-in-schools' work. The findings were published in *Artists in School* (Sharp and Dust, 1990). This publication has become a seminal text for anyone concerned with residencies. It gives detailed guidance about how to develop each stage of a project, and outlines how a project can be beneficial for all concerned.

EXTENDED DEFINITIONS: PRISONS AND PRIMARY SCHOOLS

There were residency schemes in colleges and universities in the 1950s. The educational institution has, since the 1970s, provided one of many venues; others have included prisons, libraries, shopping centres, football grounds, hospitals, churches, factories and civic centres. It is also a practice which lends itself to an unusually large number of variations on the theme, from 'consultancy surgeries' lasting 15 minutes with designers to three-year placements in independent schools.

Work in education, although diverse, can be divided into the following categories.

Short-term involvement:

- *Workshops* usually involve artists demonstrating techniques and developing ideas related to their own work. They also provide an opportunity for pupils to gain first-hand experience of techniques.
- *Presentations* provide an opportunity for artists to present and discuss their work or the work of an exhibiting artist.
- *Consultancies* use professionals to make expert knowledge available to teachers and pupils.
- *Placements* enable teachers and pupils to work alongside an artist in the artist's place of work (e.g. studio, design company, foundry, etc.).
- *Interpreters* are practising visual artists working in galleries and museums as alternatives to art historians.
- *Outreach* allows practising artists employed by arts organizations or museums and galleries to work in schools with teachers and pupils.

Longer-term involvement:

- *Residencies*. Placements in schools, museums, galleries or arts centres fall into three main categories:

- the artist is engaged in the development of personal work, while teachers and pupils observe at first hand the production of a work of art;
- the artist works directly with pupils on a project which relates to the artist's own approach;
- the artist spends time on the production of a work of art and the congruent instruction of pupils (workshops).

In addition to professional visual artists in education, the contribution made by the work of art and design students should be acknowledged. Some graduate courses include residencies and workshops in schools, art centres, museums and galleries as integral components. Similarly, the role of practising artists in education is seen as a key element of many courses of art and design teacher education. Pioneering work has been undertaken by the Post-Graduate Art Teacher's Certificate course at the South Glamorgan Institute of Higher Education, Cardiff, and by the Post-Graduate Certificate in Education (PGCE) course at the Institute of Education, London.

The artist-in-residence programme in Cardiff, started in 1987, claims to be the first scheme to form part of an initial teacher training course in the United Kingdom. Students spend the first part of the course working in groups in primary schools. It is recognized as a natural way of making the transition from the world of art and design to education – from professional artist to professional educator. The course at the Institute of Education places art and design student teachers in primary school residencies towards the end of their course, when they will have more clearly defined the role of art and design in schools. During these residencies, curriculum development projects in art and design are undertaken for the host schools. Insights into the ways in which residencies can be used as valuable resources for the professional development of serving teachers have resulted from this collaborative work.

SCHOOL ART VERSUS CONTEMPORARY ART: ORTHODOXY OR INNOVATION?

> AiR projects can sweep aside preconceptions about contemporary art and involve pupils in the kind of intensive, concentrated experiences which allow them to re-assess radically their view of art.
>
> (DES, 1991, p. 64)

In addition to the growth of AiR schemes in schools, the introduction of visual artists as educators in museums and galleries has also been witnessed, both as facilitators of practical activities and as interpreters of the work of others. The need for school art to have a relevance to art beyond the confines of the classroom is explicit in these schemes, as it is in the National Curriculum Order. There is widespread recognition of the contribution that can be made to both Attainment Target 1, 'Investigating and Making', and Attainment Target 2, 'Knowledge and Understanding', by pupils working alongside artists, craftspersons and designers in schools, galleries and museums. Underpinning all these schemes is a belief in the importance of contemporary practice. 'The overall and common purpose is to deepen children's understanding of contemporary art in general and of the individual artists' work in particular' (Gulbenkian Foundation, 1982, p. 113).

However, contemporary art can often seem inappropriate in a school environment where an emphasis on the teaching of the basic skills, observational drawing and still-life painting has traditionally dominated the curriculum, and where reference to the 'work of others' has often been restricted to easel painting. Fortunately, there are a growing number of art and design departments that do not fit into this 'school art' category, but far too many still fail to utilize the diverse range of methodologies, materials, issues and concepts that are available through exposure to contemporary practice. It is important to avoid the notion that the 'work of others' is already written and recorded and simply waits to be learned.

These concepts are not new:

> Many art teachers and particularly those trained in a different era, wonder what in the contemporary scene is relevant to their work in schools. Nothing would be less desirable than to attempt merely to keep up with whatever professional artists are producing at the moment, but it is equally dangerous to remain fixed and isolated in one period of time perpetuating its fashion in opposition to the realities of the outside world and the pressures of a changing society.
>
> (DES, 1971, p. 17)

Peake (quoted in Clive and Sellwood, 1992) refers to undemanding and stereotypical 'school art' approaches when she claims:

> there is a false sense of security and a general stodginess about art education . . . there's a need for doubt, risk, experiment . . . somebody pressing forward and stirring up complacency, making more of an attempt to bridge the chasm between what art education and what art – the role of art – is in the outside world. (p. 19)

Does the work of contemporary artists in education offer ways to 'bridge the chasm'? There is a widespread belief that an artist who shares the pupil's life and times is more likely to share the pupil's frame of reference – presenting opportunities for understanding, appreciation and empathy:

> Contemporary art introduces many aspects of popular culture: photography, video, computers. It raises relevant issues, it uses contemporary materials and technologies, it erodes traditional boundaries because it does not always fit neatly into traditional categories of painting, sculpture or print and art, craft or design. If teachers continue to rely exclusively on monographs of well-documented painters, they will be discounting not only many black and female artists, but equally important histories of craft, design and popular culture.
>
> (Burgess and Holman, 1993, p. 9)

TEACHERS: A SHIFT OF EMPHASIS

> There is a growing opinion that teachers are the ones who benefit most from the artist in education projects.
>
> (Dahl, 1990, p. 24)

Traditionally, professional artists in schools, museums and galleries have worked with young people. More recently, the emphasis has shifted and artists are increasingly working in partnership with teachers towards curriculum development. Previously this was seen as a useful but indirect benefit. It is now widely agreed that the element of in-service training (INSET) for teachers, particularly when they are working alongside artists to explore new ideas, issues and technologies, is as important as the benefits for pupils' learning. The National Curriculum requires teachers to extend their knowledge and understanding of professional practice, to establish links with the world of work. Contact with professional artists, craftspersons and designers provides teachers with an opportunity to review, update and extend their own practice, enabling them to fulfil their professional obligations.

Projects involving professional artists are likely to be undervalued unless teachers perceive them as an essential means of extending and enhancing their teaching programmes. If teachers do not regard artists as a significant presence, it is unlikely that they will be valued by pupils. A teacher's attitude and involvement has a marked effect on the whole experience. Ideally the teacher should be involved in the selection of the artist and throughout the planning, implementation and evaluation stages of a project. If proper consideration is not given to the role of the teacher, rather than enhancing provision the presence of an artist can create problems – undermining the teacher's self-confidence and restricting the impact of the residency by the lack of continuity with 'regular' art lessons.

Opportunities for contact between pupils and practitioners are uneven. Taylor (1990) offers an illuminating account of a systematic attempt to place an artist in every school in a Local Education Authority. Although the National Curriculum makes such schemes more relevant, changes in local government policy will make it impossible for this degree of contact to be reproduced elsewhere. Indeed, at the time of writing the continuation of Taylor's work in Wigan is seriously threatened. As the experience in the United States has shown, even with extensive financial support only a small proportion of the school population has any real contact with these professionals. There are many teachers in this country who feel that the possibility of having a residency of even a workshop is so remote as to be barely worth considering. Issues of value for money and entitlement become part of the agenda.

In a recent Arts Council publication, *Live Art in Schools* (Lazell, 1993), the artist Richard Lazell predicted 'it may even be decided that an INSET course where teachers work directly with one or more Live Artist could be more useful than having them work directly with children'. (p. 31)

TRAINING: A PREREQUISITE OR JUST PROBLEMATIC?

The notion of training artists to work in education came about in the mid-1980s, a result of the on-going debate about the ability of artists to communicate their knowledge and expertise to teachers and pupils. It was thought rash to assume that, just because an artist possesses qualities which have the potential for informing the art and design curriculum, they could work successfully in an educated context. Early experiences revealed that artists 'found the experience of working outside the structures for which they had been specifically trained resulted in many difficulties and false starts' (Braden, 1978, p. 7). A lack of understanding about schools can make artists' work with pupils ineffective, even counterproductive. To be able to make any worthwhile contribution to education, a professional artist needs at least a rudimentary knowledge and understanding of how schools function, their goals and the demands of the National Curriculum.

In 1991, Leicester Polytechnic (now De Montfort University) ran a pilot training scheme called 'Artists in Education'. This scheme was specifically designed to train and prepare artists to work in schools. It included a five-day residency in school. Participants agreed that the course had provided 'an ideal opportunity to break the ice and actually be trained instead of stumbling through sessions trying to learn by mistakes' (Artists' Report, 1992, p. 3). Building on the strengths of this project, a number of regional and local initiatives have been set up. Target groups have been identified, such as the Black Artists Training Scheme run by an independent Black Arts organization, and a project run by Charlotte Mason College to train artists to work with pupils with special educational needs.

The response to training programmes has been mixed. Critics claim that training professional artists to work in education is inappropriate, that providing artists with a 'crash course' in teaching can only serve to blur the distinctions between artist and teacher. However, an unpublished survey for the London Arts Board (1993) has shown that artists are keen to participate in such schemes, especially when they result in accreditation. The number of applicants for these courses confirms this. It validates the educational standing of artists' work with pupils and helps them to gain work in schools. Involvement in such programmes puts enormous pressure on the teacher, since the additional organization and preparation needed to make placements work can be considerable. The results of a successful liaison are often sufficient justification. However, if it is to be recognized as professional development for the teachers, training and accreditation for them should also be considered.

FUNDING: A NEW CHALLENGING ENVIRONMENT FOR PARTNERSHIPS

> If schools won't – or more usually can't – pay for them [AiS], they won't survive.
> (Rogers, 1993, p. 1)

Until recently, the most common route into education for professional artists was via Local Education Authority art advisory services, or through intermediary bodies such as Regional Arts Boards and local arts organizations.

An Arts Council strategy document declares that:

> Many arts organisations have pioneered inspiring education programmes, which have helped thousands of people to understand and share the arts. These programmes must be maintained and enhanced. Many of those in both the education and the arts sectors fear the insufficient funding and recent reforms [in the education system – including LMS and opting out], whatever their other benefits, may put this work at risk.
> (Arts Council, 1992, Introduction)

A survey by the Arts Council (Rogers, 1993) reveals a significant reduction in support for the arts in education. It claims that only a quarter of LEAs still have full-time advisers or inspectors for the arts, and only 50 per cent of education authorities continue to fund schemes to place artists into schools. 'The decline is due to the impact of local management, the "privatisation" of many council services, the growth of the grant maintained (GM) sector and the reduction of LEA powers in the 1993 Education Act!' (Spencer, 1994, p. 3). Arts organizations are aware that the long-term future of collaborative work with schools will no longer be dependent on mediation or support from LEAs. They are also aware of the 'ethical and professional consideration of stepping in to fill the gaps left by diminishing LEA services' (London Arts Board, 1992).

As a result of local management, school art and design departments are receiving direct approaches from visual artists with proposals for workshops and residencies. However, very few schools are in a position to respond independently. Schools can rarely meet the full cost of work with professional artists and some kind of subsidy has to be found. Traditionally, schools have relied on external agencies – LEAs, galleries and museums, Regional Arts Boards – to initiate ideas, organize funding and help co-ordinate and evaluate projects and placements. Schemes involving artists, craftspersons and designers have almost always been 'plurally funded'. Subsidies from charitable foundations, business and industry have supported national, regional and local projects. Finding a way through devolved art budgets is more than just a challenge for teachers; it can be a deterrent, especially when coupled with the fact that acc·ss to the information and 'quality control' previously supplied by LEAs is disappearing.

Perhaps the way forward is suggested by new developments which have overcome the hurdles presented by the recent changes. There is a need for a proactive approach rather than the present reactive one – to recognize that recent changes in funding can be seen as creating new and challenging environments for partnership.

A DIFFERENT APPROACH: PARTNERS BY DESIGN

> Very few schools include a study of the work of designers despite the importance of design in the world of work.
>
> (DES, 1991, p. 7)

Over the last decade a number of schemes involving practising artists and craftspersons in education have been subject to monitoring and evaluation in order to provide an understanding of their contributions to the curriculum. However, little research has been undertaken to explore the role of the professional designer in an educational context.

Birmingham LEA hosted a highly acclaimed 'Designers in Schools' project in the 1980s. However, nationally the picture is uneven. The Design Council has remained detached from residency schemes. It claims that models adopted to utilize the skills of professional designers in education do not readily fit those commonly used by other visual artists. The very nature of their professional practice means that designers do not have time for long-term commitments. Contact with a designer is often intermittent or restricted to short 'one-off' sessions. Therefore, teachers are encouraged to identify clearly the areas in which 'expert' help is required and then to contact the relevant design professional. Schemes to involve designers in education fall into two distinct categories:

- *Placements with design consultancies and industry.* Teachers and pupils gain first-hand experience of professional design practice, and insight into how designers work within the constraints of a commercial design environment. This provides professional development for teachers and work experience for pupils, allowing both to gain further skills and understanding which can inform and enrich work back in school.

- *Designers as consultants.* Teachers and pupils receive direct advice from a professional designer via talks, slide shows, design surgeries and INSET.

As early as 1976, a scheme called the National Design Award: The Schools' Design Prize was initiated, its aim being to promote design education in schools. For ten years this scheme continued to provide access to professional practitioners. All entries were judged by practising designers and all participating schools were eligible for design-support visits by a professional.

In England and Wales the scheme was discontinued in 1989. Eileen Taylor, Education Officer at the Design Council, claims: 'It was too much like the "nit nurse" who made an annual visit – the effect was similarly short term. The field [national] was too wide and the funds insufficient' (Taylor, Personal Interview, 1993). In both Northern Ireland and Scotland the picture is different. In 1987 they took over regional control of the Design Award. In Northern Ireland it became 'The Northern Ireland Schools' Design Prize' and in Scotland 'The Scottish Schools' Design Awards'. Economies of scale have meant that these regional developments have succeeded where nationally the scheme proved unwieldly. Over the past five years contact between teachers, young people and professional designers has been sustained and refined and is still in the ascendancy. Models of good practice are now influencing the direction of work nationally.

In Northern Ireland the Schools' Design Prize has stimulated over 100 school visits by professional designers to help pupils with their design development. Such visits focus on all areas of design from animation and engineering to fashion and furniture. An extremely efficient network of designers has been established. They are providing a valuable resource for education. Links between local companies and schools help to foster a real understanding of the design process, introducing pupils to developmental work in design not just the finished product.

All schools entering the competition in Scotland in 1993 were invited to 'Design Support Days' – open surgeries at which professional designers were available to look at pupils' coursework and offer comment and advice on subsequent development. In addition, pupils were also given the opportunity to look at the designers' professional portfolios. The Design Council, Scotland, also uses a touring exhibition of winning designs as a starting point for INSET. Working in association with professional designers, the education staff organize workshops designed to provide teachers with the skills necessary to manage and encourage design projects, promote important links between education and industry, and interpret new curriculum recommendations. The aim of these initiatives is to enable pupils to make connections between classroom practice and the outcomes of designing in the commercial world using professional designers as a resource.

NEW DEVELOPMENTS: RESPONDING TO CHANGE

Developments incorporating the work of professional visual artists exist in every field of art and design education, including photography, media, film and architecture. These are taking place at national, regional and local levels. Many of these projects have evolved over a number of years – the result of building on good practice. They have often predicted and easily assimilated changes in education.

Photographers in education

The Arts Council Photography Officer for Education and Training has co-ordinated the introduction of a three-year scheme, 1994–7, to establish a number of teacher development posts in photography and media education. The posts vary slightly, but essentially the people to be appointed will be photographers with teaching experience. They will work across all phases of education to develop the design, production and delivery of photography and media learning resources (including human resources), distance-learning packages and other work related to INSET needs for the National Curriculum.

The post-holders are expected to make formal connections between the work of the independent photography sector and education; to provide teachers with practical examples and approaches. They are appointed to record, contextualize and disseminate the work of professional photographers to the widest audience via INSET activities, conferences and publications. Through such vehicles innovative work in the field reaches a wider audience and the work of the professional is recorded and translated into curriculum material which can be used both to promote work with practitioners and to enable classroom teachers to develop it independently.

Crafts Council

> We do not consider it helpful in schools to dwell on the divisions between art and craft that seem to exist at the professional level.
>
> (DES, 1991, p. 13)

Since the early 1980s the Crafts Council has participated in a number of programmes to engage craftspersons in education. Although never directly involved in the funding of residencies, the Crafts Council has regularly devolved monies to LEAs, Regional Arts Boards and other arts organizations to facilitate this work, in addition to co-ordinating schemes designed to promote partnership between pupils and craftspersons. The Crafts Council has been keen to ensure that any national initiative involving visual artists in education has had a crafts dimension. As such, the aims of craftspersons in education are not dissimilar to those of artists in education.

The Crafts Council introduced a local outreach project in 1994. This is untypical of the Crafts Council, which usually has a national or regional rather than a local remit. The project comprises three discrete, yet interrelated units:

- *Unit 1 – INSET.* Local teachers were invited to attend INSET sessions at the

Crafts Council. These included an introduction to the project plus some 'hands-on' experience of crafts techniques. Participants were invited to apply for the second unit.

- *Unit 2 – Workshops.* Twelve schools were selected to host two-day placements to provide opportunities for looking into the possibilities of participating in a longer Craftspersons-in-Residence project.
- *Unit 3 – Residencies.* Four schools were selected for ten-day residencies. In their applications they clearly stated the ways they wished to work collaboratively with craftspersons to contribute to curriculum development.

Sustained lines of interest and commitment on behalf of the schools are seen as a prerequisite for a successful residency. Provision is made for teachers and craftspersons working on parallel projects to meet and compare experiences at regular intervals. Schools are expected to contribute 10 per cent towards the cost of the placement. Each school agreed to nominate a 'lead teacher' to carry out practical organization, administration and evaluation of the residency in consultation with the craftsperson. Provision for 'cover' to release the 'lead teacher' and other staff to plan, visit and work with the craftsperson is seen as essential. This type of development demands a substantial commitment from the school as a whole rather than an *ad hoc* arrangement with the art and design department.

Camden Arts Centre (CAC)

There has been a trend in museum and gallery education over the last decade to use professional artists rather than art historians as mediators between the work on display and the gallery audiences of all ages. 'We've found that the best person to talk about art in the gallery is an artist who is interested in the work on show and has some sympathy for it' (Graham-Dixon, 1989, p. 9). This is done at CAC in the belief that an artist who works in a similar way or deals with similar themes is better able to communicate to others the intentions of the artist whose work is on display.

At CAC, residencies in the studio space involving young people forms an important part of the Centre's work in the field of education. Residencies that take place in this contemporary art gallery are about experimenting, risk-taking and understanding the whole process of art *now*. The Centre also runs daily workshops for schools, colleges and PGCE courses. Led by practising visual artists, they provide an opportunity for pupils and their teachers to explore the concepts of the work on exhibition through making. This provides them with a 'way in' to avant-garde art that they might otherwise find inaccessible. The workshops concentrate on exploring concepts and themes that transcend those of a specific artist or art object. As a result, pupils develop a deeper understanding of ideas and methodologies avoiding the questionable practice of merely copying work on display. Establishing 'relationships' with schools is seen as a prerequisite for this work. Pupils who are given the opportunity to visit only one contemporary art exhibition run the risk of developing a limited view of contemporary practice rather than an appreciation of its rich diversity.

Following discussions with an advisory panel of teachers, heads and governors,

CAC has developed a programme of in-house, artist-led workshops for local schools. This requires participating schools to make a long-term commitment to working with the gallery. Schools are encouraged to pay an annual subscription and book a block of six artist-led workshops to coincide with the six contemporary exhibitions held annually. Close collaborations of this kind allow for proper consideration to be given to how the work relates to the school syllabus, and shared INSET sessions with the participating schools will further highlight this aspect. Resource packs for teachers and pupils accompany each exhibition. Every pupil is issued with a 'scrapbook' in which to document each workshop and exhibition, providing an opportunity to record and evaluate their experience.

The CAC scheme should make a strong contribution to curriculum development in the participating schools, and provide exemplary material for wider dissemination.

The Whitechapel Art Gallery

The Whitechapel Art Gallery is the gallery with the longest history of working with professional visual artists in education. Its education programme is just recovering from a two-year period of instability. Loss, during this time, of their LEA support grant has made them look at a pattern of diversity – of mixed funding. Although it has recovered its LEA grant through a Service Level Agreement (SLA), it now recognizes the vulnerability created by dependence on any one body for a considerable part of its capitation.

Situated on the edge of the City of London, it has been able to tap into a number of development funds including Docklands Development and City Challenge. Through these it has become involved in environmental and public arts projects which include schools and gallery artists working as partners on community development projects. New funding arrangements have meant that the form and content of residencies have changed. Previously the content of placements was decided by the gallery, artist and school. Now the interest of the sponsor has become part of the equation. Dialogue and planning between the various interested parties has been fruitful; it has resulted in innovative work using a diversity of materials on a range of sites.

As a consequence, a new direction in the educational work has been developed which is concerned more with exploring *outreach* (off-site work) and less with gallery-based initiatives which are well established. Outreach involves artists visiting schools, asking questions of teachers, and identifying their needs and concerns in an attempt to make sure that their educational work is fulfilling a perceived need. Outreach work in schools has also encouraged young people to attend Saturday morning sessions at the gallery where, working with professional artists, GCSE candidates are encouraged to extend and develop their coursework portfolios. Response from the participants and feed-back from teachers continues to contribute to the changing content and methodology adopted during the sessions.

Galleries, museums and art organizations with a record of work with professional visual artists are in the strongest position to negotiate projects with sponsors. Numerous organizations have tried-and-tested codes of practice, contracts and evaluation procedures which have been developed, reviewed and updated over a number of years to ensure that collaboration is effective.

Partnership has become a 'buzz-word' in education during the last few years. The need for mutual support and collaboration between artists, craftspersons, designers, schools and arts organizations has been reiterated. The purpose of such collaboration is to identify common aims and understand different ways of working with a view to producing long-term changes in the nature of the experience on offer to pupils. At the same time there is a need to acknowledge that organizations are at different stages of development, responding to different audiences. It also needs to be recognized that the diversity of current educational work in the field of art and design is one of its strengths.

Experience gained to date provides a sound basis for alternative models and extended activities to be considered for artists working in educational contexts; ways in which pupils and teachers are able to benefit through direct and indirect participation with practitioners. It could be argued forcefully that there is no substitute for direct involvement, for the artist working with pupils. Strategies to maximize pupils' access to contemporary practice, such as artists working across 'federations' or 'cluster groups' of schools, are still possible. But given the rapid rate of educational change and the constraints on funding, these models are still available only to a few schools. Schemes currently being developed ensure that the benefits of working with professional artists are open to greater numbers of pupils. New schemes utilizing the facilities of arts centres, museums and galleries offer the possibility of the widest dissemination of ideas through direct contact, in-service courses and the production of distance-learning materials. As Mary Kelly claimed: 'You should have a practice in art that actually looks forward to a moment that will be different' (1984, p. 91).

REFERENCES

Arts Council (1992) *A Creative Strategy for Arts, Crafts and Media in Great Britain.* London: Arts Council of Great Britain.

Braden, S. (1978) *Artists and People.* London: Routledge and Kegan Paul.

Burgess, L., and Holman, V. (1993) Live art. *Times Educational Supplement,* 2 June.

Clive, S., and Sellwood, S. (1992) *Substance and Shadow.* London: London Arts Board.

Dahl, D. (1990) *Residencies in Education.* Sunderland: AN Publications.

Department of Education and Science (DES) (1971) *Arts in Schools Educational Survey.* London: HMSO.

Department of Education and Science (DES) (1991) *National Curriculum: Art for ages 5–14.* London: HMSO.

Eisner, E. (1974) Is the artist in the school program really effective? *Art Education* **27**, 12–19.

Graham-Dixon, A. (1989) *Artists and Schools.* London: Whitechapel Art Gallery.

Gulbenkian Foundation (1982) *The Arts in Schools: Principles, Practice and Provisions.* London: Gulbenkian Foundation.

Hanks, N. (1971) Education through art: a gateway. *Art Education* **24**(7), 11–15.

Kelly, M. (1984) Reviewing modernist criticism. In Wallis, B. (ed.), *Art After Modernism.* Boston, Mass.: New Museum of Contemporary Art, NY, in association with Godine.

Lazell, R. (1993) *Live Art in Schools.* London: Arts Council of Great Britain.

Macdonald, I (1980) *Professional Arts and Schools: A Discussion Document.* London: Arts Council of Great Britain.

Rogers, R. (1993) *Looking Over the Edge.* London: Arts Council of Great Britain.

Sharp, C., and Dust, K. (1990) *Artists in Schools*. London: Bedford Square Press.
Smith, R. A. (1977) A policy analysis and criticism of the Artist-in-Schools program of the National Endowment for the Arts. *Art Education*, September.
Spencer, D. (1994) Budgeting brush-off for Arts. *Times Educational Supplement*, 4 February.
Steers, J. (1993) New realities for Art & Design. *Journal of Art & Design Education* **12**(1), 9–24.
Taylor, R. (1990) *The Artists in Wigan Schools*. London: Calouste Gulbenkian Foundation.
Taylor, R. (1992) *Visual Artists in Education*. Lewes: Falmer Press.

Chapter 9

The National Curriculum for Art: Translating it into Practice

Colin Robinson

Prior to the publication of the Order for Art in the National Curriculum (NC) in 1992, primary school teachers and art and design teachers in secondary schools were responsible for deciding what to teach in art lessons and why to teach it. They were subject only to the obligation which applies to any teacher, that their teaching programme has the support of their pupils' parents, the schools governors and the headteacher. The freedom inherent in such a responsibility no longer exists. Teachers now have to exercise a different kind of responsibility, that of translating the statutory requirements of the NC into practice. They have the demanding task, and valuable opportunity, of designing and teaching courses of study to meet given objectives in such a way as to be able to teach with personal commitment.

In this chapter a selection has been made of what are considered to be those features of the Order for Art which are of central importance for teachers as they translate the Order into practice. These are discussed, sometimes considering their sources in the recent development of art and design education, sometimes accompanied by digressions which seek to clarify the concepts concerned, but always with the intention of enabling teachers to improve the quality of their pupils' work in art and design.

For readers who may be unfamiliar with recent developments in education in England, it might be helpful at the outset to describe in very broad terms the development of art and design in the curricula of primary and secondary schools. The inclusion of art as one of the ten subjects in the NC, which became statutory through the Education Reform Act of 1988, was a tribute to those teachers and teacher educators who worked to establish and develop the subject in schools over the past seventy or eighty years.

Simple copying and drawing skills began to be taught in schools towards the end of the last century and, as the primary school curriculum developed during the early years of this century, particularly after the First World War, the range of practical activities constituting art in schools started to extend beyond drawing. Painting and simple printmaking techniques were introduced, eventually being complemented by work in three-dimensional materials and fabrics, but more importantly, the educational value for children of engaging in practical art activities became widely recognized.

The range of such activities became broad. Some of them were valued because they helped children to develop fine manual control. Some of them enabled children to experience achievement in the mastery of simple craft skills. Some activities were more demanding and required pupils to think and act like artists, craftspersons or designers, or learn to appreciate works of art and artefacts and see art in historical and social contexts. The current status of the subject is reflected in the fact that now about a third of pupils aged 16 opt to be examined in art and design, as the subject has come to be called. At that age most pupils take the General Certificate of Secondary Education (GCSE) in English language. In 1994, 630,000 did so, and 212,000 were examined in art and design.

ART AND DESIGN

Over the years the titles used to describe this area of the curriculum have included art, craft, handwork, art and craft, light crafts, handicrafts and, more recently, art and design. It is worth exploring the use of the term 'art and design' because of its significance in the subsequent analysis of the Order for Art. Names, titles and labels can exert powerful influences. The activities of artists are different from those of designers. The intentions of artists are different from those of designers, and the thinking and feeling processes in which each of them engages are not the same. Artists make imagery in response to, and to comment on, human experience. Designers make or improve artefacts, environments and systems. The differences between them are significant enough to have required the continuing use of the two terms 'artist' and 'designer' in order to distinguish between them. Practitioners in the field are usually very clear about whether they perceive themselves as artists or designers.

It is also true to say that the activities of making art and designing have common features. Artists and designers share an interest in creativity and imagination, and in the making of two- and three-dimensional objects. Sometimes both are involved in making their objects, more so in the case of artists than in that of designers, and they have a concern for the sensitive and appropriate use of materials; a concern which is well described as 'craftsmanship'. Their professional training is usually undertaken in departments or faculties of art *and* design. They share a common currency of visual and aesthetic ideas, and to a large extent they share a technical vocabulary. There is, therefore, a considerable degree of overlap of interest and conceptual interdependence between artists and designers, *but they do not share a common purpose*. Their contributions to society are different, and as a consequence the contributions of art- and design-related activities to the curriculum in schools are different. One of the first decisions which teachers have to make in the process of translating the Order for Art into practice is whether they should teach art, or art and design. The Order itself is not as helpful as it ought to be in assisting them with this decision, as will be seen later.

TWO ATTAINMENT TARGETS

All the subjects in the NC were required to be published within a common frame-work, part of which specified the skills, knowledge and understanding which pupils should be expected to attain in that subject by the end of four Key Stages of their compulsory schooling. These objectives are called 'Attainment Targets' (ATs). It might reasonably be assumed that the number of Attainment Targets for a given subject should be related to the nature and structure of that subject in an educational context. That number should have conceptual integrity and be capable of being underpinned by a rationale. Art in the NC has two Attainment Targets, and yet for the past twenty years no major contributor to curriculum development in art and design education has developed a curriculum model with fewer than three compo-nents. Barrett (1979) used the three terms conception, operation and synthesis. Clement (1986) identified three elements: the personal or conceptual; the technical; and the visual. From 1986 the GCSE for Art and Design used three 'domains' in its assessment arrangements: the Conceptual; the Productive; and the Contextual and Critical. There was no general consensus about the nature of the organizing categories, but it was clear that the complexities of the subject did not allow for the use of fewer than three.

The process of formulating statutory requirements for each subject in the NC, which became known as a subject's 'Order', started with the setting up of Working Groups for each subject. These consisted of groups of a dozen or more members, appointed by the Secretary of State for Education, and drawn from each subject's professional and educational communities. The Art Working Group recommended to the Secretary of State in 1991 that there should be three ATs: Understanding; Making; and Investigating (DES, 1991). When published in 1992, the Order for Art revealed that, contrary to that advice, the Secretary of State had decided that Art should have two ATs: Investigating and Making; and Knowledge and Under-standing. It is significant that there are two concepts in each AT. No educational rationale is offered for having two ATs, either in the Order or in the Non-Statutory Guidelines (NSG); probably because one does not exist.

The National Curriculum Council (NCC) had been set up to advise the Secretary of State, and by the time each of the Orders for Art, Music and Physical Education were being formulated by the NCC in 1991, there was growing concern about the increasing size and complexity of the NC. Not surprisingly, in view of the sequential rather than holistic development of the NC in its entirety, the writers of the Orders of the subjects published earlier had made sure that the status of their subjects was demonstrated by the amount of content and large number of ATs required as a consequence. Mathematics (1989) had 14, Science (1989) had 17, English and Tech-nology (1990) had 5. By the time the Orders for Modern Foreign Languages, Geography and History were being formulated in 1991, the reduction of the number of a subject's ATs was seen by the government as a means of meeting the concerns over the size and complexity of the NC, and of reducing the growing pressure on school timetables. Consequently, by the time the last three of the ten subjects came to be considered in 1991–2, the NCC was required to ensure that each of them, Music, Physical Education and Art, had only two ATs. That is why Art in the National Curriculum has two ATs. Conceptual integrity never entered into it. This detailed explanation of the process has been given in order to warn teachers against assuming that there is any educational significance in the number of ATs in art. It is for them to decide how many main organizing categories they use to structure their schemes of work for art and design.

It might reasonably be assumed that because there are two, and because the space in the Order devoted to each is more or less equal, teachers should give equal weight to each when planning programmes and expenditure on resources. This, however, is not the intention. The NSG in Note B1.2 states that 'The expectation is that more attention will be given to the practical elements . . . it is intended that the assessment Order will weight the ATs two in one in favour of the first.' This reflects the current practice of those teachers who are at the forefront of developing work in critical and historical studies. It has never been their intention to threaten the predominance of the practical dimension of art and design education. Their argument is that such practice is complemented by critical awareness and appreciation, and vice versa. Indeed, the third 'strand' of AT2 is called 'Applying knowledge of the work of other artists to their own work' and seeks to ensure that complementarity by requiring practical work to emanate from AT2. The intention of the Order is therefore that 'more attention will be given to the practical elements'. How *much* more is for teachers to decide, and this gives them valuable scope for exercising judgement.

The origins of AT1: Investigating and Making

The term 'practical work' describes the activity of making things – products, objects or artefacts – in two and three dimensions and for a variety of purposes. Practical work conveys the sense of physical involvement in the manipulation of matter to make an object. Making a painting would be described as 'practical work', but making a poem would not. Strictly speaking, writing a poem also involves manipulating matter, a pen and paper, to make an object, a poem written on a piece of paper, but writing a poem is not thought of as practical work. The manipulative process of using hands, tools, equipment and materials to make something is the distinctive attribute of practical work. In art and design lessons, pupils usually paint, draw, print, weave, embroider, carve, model, construct and make collages, pots and sculptures, all of which constitute work related to AT1. AT1 is about practical work in art and design, and AT1 maintains the practical dimension of the subject which has been central to the subject's development since its origin.

It is in relation to AT1 that teachers have the most scope for planning the aims and content of their programmes. Although the Order sets out statutory requirements about what pupils should be able to do at the end of each Key Stage and how they should go about that work, the End of Key State Statements and Programmes of Study are couched in very broad terms which allow for wide interpretation. For example, the Order does not make statutory requirements about subject matter. Teachers are free to choose aspects of human experience on which to focus pupils' attention. Pupils may or may not make images of landscapes, or interiors, or objects, or themselves, or their friends and families, or animals, or their sporting heroes or their pop idols. Similarly, teachers are free to choose the kinds of object for pupils to design and make, from any point on the continuum between functional and decorative; a system of directional signs for the school, a poster for the school play, a screen-printed T-shirt, or a piece of jewellery.

These choices are crucial. They affect what pupils learn and should therefore relate to the aims underpinning a particular course of study. Interestingly, and valuably for teachers seeking to teach from the basis of personal commitment, there are no explicitly stated aims in either the statutory section of the Order or the NSG. The ATs and Programmes of Study are presented as if their implicit aims are self-evidently valuable. There are no rationales for the inclusion of this or that require-ment. For example, there is a statutory General Requirement that pupils should 'work individually, in groups, and as a whole class', but we are not told why this is educationally valuable or why it is important that pupils should 'make appropriate use of information technology'. Answers to those questions and rationales to explain choices of the content of programmes are left for individual teachers to provide in their schemes of work, thereby providing the opportunity to translate the Order into personally convincing courses of study to teach.

One of the Order's statutory General Requirements is that pupils should be given opportunities to 'evaluate their own and others' work'. This requirement is another of the Order's strengths in the recognition it gives to the role of communication in the learning process. While artists can afford to remain inarticulate about their work, art and design teachers cannot. Unless teachers are able to explain clearly the criteria by which they are judging progress and on which they are basing their advice, their teaching can be little more than a form of tyranny in which pupils learn merely to obey instructions without understanding. The requirement for pupils to learn to evaluate their own work and that of others not only has a vital role to play in teaching related to AT1, but also enables pupils to strengthen conceptual links between AT1 and AT2 by articulating them in discussion.

The origins of AT2: Knowledge and Understanding

AT2 is about the history and appreciation of art and design. It is certainly not intended to be the theoretical complement to the practical dimension of AT1. If the NC for Art had been created twenty years ago, it is doubtful whether work involving the study and critical appreciation of the artefacts of artists and designers would have been a major feature, though the desirability of this has long been recognized. Many of the contributors to Thistlewood's (1989) *Critical Studies in Art and Design Education* start their essays by drawing support from seminal writers from as far back as Read (1937) through to more recent ones, notably Taylor (1986). However, reports by Her Majesty's Inspectors of Schools show that the impact of these writings on the practice of most primary teachers and a considerable number of secondary art and design teachers has been small.

The National Criteria for Art and Design (GCSE, 1985) stated that 'critical and historical studies *could* form part of the content of a syllabus in art and design', but it was significant that only one of the five examination groups made such work compulsory. The NC Working Group included as one of the aims of art that 'art education . . . should develop pupils' ability to value the contribution made by artists, craftworkers and designers and to respond thoughtfully, critically and imaginatively to ideas, images and objects of many kinds and from many cultures' (Section 4.1). Its first AT required pupils to 'respond practically and imaginatively to the work of artists, craftworkers and designers' (DES, 1991). AT2 has at last made the critical study of artefacts a statutory requirement, but again teachers have scope for selecting the detailed content of such studies within the given framework.

ART, CRAFT AND DESIGN

The way in which the name of the subject has evolved has already been commented on, but it merits further discussion because there is power in a name. The NC Working Group for Art did not attempt to define art, craft and design; probably wisely in view of the complex and contentious nature of the debate. Their solution to the terminological problem was to use all three terms throughout their report: 'the teaching of art, craft and design'; 'craft, for example, in pottery, textiles and jewellery'; and 'the division between art and craft'. The tenor of their report suggests that they would have liked to call the subject 'art and design', but existing legislation, the Education Reform Act of 1988, had already labelled the subject 'art', and 'art' it had to remain. The problem was recognized in the Order for Art in the General Requirement, which states: ' "Art" should be interpreted to mean "art, craft and design" throughout and "artists" should be interpreted to mean "artists, craftworkers and designers".' The same requirement to see art, craft and design as a 'subject field' is echoed in the summary statements accompanying the ATs, both of which make use of the phrase 'art, craft and design'. Unfortunately, slippage starts to occur in relation to AT2, which refers to 'history of art' (not design), 'our artistic heritage' (not design), and 'other artistic (not design) traditions'. This slippage is indicative of a flaw which runs through the Order and further erodes its conceptual integrity. The claim is made that the Order is about art, craft and design, but apart from a minority of design activities in the NSG such as 'design and print a poster', 'in preparation for design-based work, e.g. a printed textile', and 'compare the way in which the design of clothes has changed over the centuries', the Order is over-whelmingly about art.

The spirit of the Order, however, and one which is supported by the majority of the subject community, is that both art- and design-related activities have educational value, and pupils should engage in both of them. The statutory parts of the Order speak only of art, whereas the non-statutory examples and the Non-Statutory Guide-lines speak of art *and* design. Future revisions of the Order should address this inconsistency so that teachers are given clearer guidance in planning their teaching programmes. In the meantime they should take advantage of the scope they have to set their own balance between art- and design-related activities to which they can feel personally committed.

OBSERVE, REMEMBER AND IMAGINE

A painting is different from a print because the materials and technical processes used in making each of them are different. By just as fundamental an influence on the outcome is the nature of the source, or sources, of imagery from which the final visual image is derived. Making an image from a directly observed object or copying someone else's ready-made image, both of which constitute working from observation, are different from making imagery based on remembered experiences, or imagining something which does not exist in the real world. The decision-making processes of working from each of the three sources are quite distinct because of the differences between the kinds of decision involved; deliberate or spontaneous, conscious or unconscious, rational or intuitive. It is these decision-making processes in which the teacher is interested and which are central to any rationale for justifying the educational value of a particular activity. Whether the result of such an activity is a painting or a print is relatively unimportant as far as educational value is concerned. What matters is the kind and quality of thinking and feeling in which pupils engage during the process of making that imagery. The ways in which these might contribute to that pupil's education are explored below.

When working from observation, for example, in life drawing or painting a landscape on location, the distinctive feature of the activity is that the response to the subject matter can be maintained throughout the making process. The discipline of writing clarifies one's understanding of motivations and intentions as a result of the conscious selection and prioritization of ideas which occur in the process of writing. There is a similarity in making imagery from observation. Awareness is gained about the nature of the subject matter, but also why it has been responded to, and why it is seen as important and worth commenting on. This means of gaining access to self-awareness has educational value. A similar self-questioning occurs when records of observation in th form of drawings or photographs are used as intermediary stages in the process of working towards the final version of an artefact. The act of recording requires questions to be answered such as: What aspects of the subject matter need to be recorded? What medium is best to use in the time available? What can be remembered and what is too significant to risk losing by trusting to fallible memory? Such self-questioning is educationally valuable.

Working from memories of a personal experience gives freedom to move away from a primary concern with the visual appearance of phenomena in order to explore other dimensions of personal experience, particularly the inner world of feelings and attitudes about the events on which the memories are based. Scale, colour and juxtapositions can be symbolic and metaphoric. Vagueness and suggestion can coexist with clarity and unambiguous statement. Working from memory can provide another means of access to self-awareness which has educational value.

Strictly speaking, the creation of imagery from imagination is not a distinct mode of working because the imagination is involved in all art-making processes. Imagination is the capacity of the mind to recombine stored and recalled mental images to form new ones. Even when drawing from direct observation one imagines the result of the next mark before it is made, and using materials inventively necessarily involves the imagination. All art and design activities, therefore, have an imaginative dimension, but in the context of art education, working from imagination has come to mean 'making things up' rather than working from direct observation. It has a long history, from the teaching of Marion Richardson onwards, and is legitimated by the practice of many artists from different cultures working from imagination. In terms of time, working from observation takes place in the present. Working from memory gives the opportunity to explore past experience. To work from imagination completes the range of sources of imagery by creating freedom to explore anything, anywhere, and not necessarily in relation to time. Responding to such freedom has educational value.

There is a key phrase, repeated in the End of Key Stage Statements for each Key Stage, which requires pupils to use three sources for the imagery of their work relating AT1: Investigating and Making. Pupils are required to 'communicate ideas and feelings in visual form based on what they *observe, remember and imagine*'. The breadth of this range of three sources of imagery is one of the Order's strengths, and presents yet another set of decisions about balance which need to be made by teachers in the planning of courses.

INVESTIGATING AND MAKING

The title of AT1 is 'Investigating and Making'. Some years ago it might have been acceptable to teachers to convey the practical dimension of the art curriculum by simply calling the AT 'Making'. That would be unacceptable today because of the growing realization by teachers that the quality of pupils' art and design work is greatly affected by the quality of preparation and research which precedes and continues throughout the making stage of the process. The emphasis given to the importance of this through the name of AT1 is one of the Order's strengths.

The second strand of the End of Key Stage Statements and Programmes of Study which run through the Key Stages of AT1 are usefully set out in the NSG (Section C3), and convey well the importance of establishing a rich range of stimulus material to feed the image-making process which is central to AT1. This emphasis is another of the Order's strengths and is valuably reinforced by the statutory requirement for pupils to keep sketchbooks in Key Stage 3.

The third strand focuses on 'making', and the examples in the Order and the comments on 'making' in the NSG rightly describe a wide range of two- and three-dimensional materials and processes which can be made available. There is, however, no mention of quality of craftsmanship. Quality of expression depends on mastery of the medium being used. Quality of design-related work depends on mastery of tools and materials. Because there can never be sufficient time allocated to the subject to enable pupils to gain mastery of many media and materials, some degree of specialization should be made by pupils in later Key Stages in order to enable them to produce work of high quality. The absence of such a recommendation is one of the Order's weaknesses.

Within the third strand, the term 'elements of art' is introduced. This term replaces the more widely used one in the subject community of 'formal elements', which harks back to the days of Basic Design. 'Elements of art' loses nothing by dropping the term 'formal'. The 'elements of art' are defined in Section C5 of the NSG as 'line, tone, pattern and texture, colour, shape, form and space'. Before the introduction of the Order for Art, teachers' schemes of work were often categorized in terms of materials and processes, or the formal elements. Headings for the work of each year group might be, for example, 'Year 7: introduction to painting, printmaking and sculpture'; or, 'Year 8: projects related to tone, line and colour'. The way in which concepts are organized into categories inevitably reflects underpinning priorities. The importance given to 'materials and processes' and 'formal elements' reflected a widely held view, often implicitly held rather than explicitly stated, that learning the 'language' of art and design constituted the preliminary learning necessary for subsequent art- and design-related activities.

There is some truth in that view, but there is also a danger. It is true that developing competence in the skills of controlling processes and materials, and developing an awareness of the elements of art, are necessary for transforming a material into a medium of expression. But the means of making messages is no substitute for having messages to convey. Art in schools too often and too easily slides into mere picture-making rather than the expression of ideas and feelings about highly significant personal experience, which is what art should be about. Similarly, pupils can sometimes be observed in schools engaged in a form of pseudo-designing in which they are asked to design such things as compact disc covers when they know that their products will never cover a compact disc. The scale and complexity of such design problems far exceed the knowledge they have in order to make well-informed decisions, which is central to what designing should be about.

The choice of headings by which to categorize a scheme of work is vital. Headings reveal clearly the priorities of the course designer because they distinguish between those parts of the curriculum which it is important for all pupils to cover, and those parts about which choices can be left to the discretion of the individual teacher operating within guidelines provided by the scheme of work. The parts to be covered by all pupils will be those that have been organized to ensure progression and continuity, which are valuably encouraged in the Order and NSG. However, critical decisions still rest with the course planner. Is it more important to ensure that all pupils work from observation, memory and imagination, which could be headings in a scheme of work, or in two- and three-dimensional materials? Should ATs constitute one axis of a matrix with materials and processes the other? Would different kinds of subject matter, such as landscape, interiors and people, merit elevation to headings? It all depends on how the course planner's priorities can be related to statutory requirements, but to fail to achieve integration in the planning of a scheme of work is to risk loss of commitment in the transaction stage in the classroom.

ACHIEVING PROFESSIONAL INTEGRITY

The point has been made that adequate motivation to teach a course of study is best achieved through a personal commitment to the values of that course of study on the part of the teacher teaching it. The attempt has been made in this chapter to reveal the scope which teachers have to translate a National Curriculum for Art into teaching programmes to which they can commit themselves with professional integrity. There are two other forms of integrity which can contribute significantly towards achieving the same goal.

Some years ago a study was made of the progress of young art and design teachers in their first two years of teaching (Robinson, 1978). It was found that those who were making the most progress shared two attributes. In general, they had gained better than average degree classifications, and this confidence in their subject expertise carried over into their teaching. They had also maintained their practice as artists and designers, and had found ways of informing their pupils of this, thereby greatly enhancing their credibility in the pupils' eyes. The pupils could see that art and design activity was important to them at a personal level, and meant more to them than just a subject on the timetable. The concepts central to their thinking about art and design education were enriched by their practice as artists or designers. It was typical that in discussions with pupils they often referred to their own work when, for example, exemplifying specialist technical terms. Operating in the field of art, craft or design *and* as teachers gave their teaching professional integrity. Following on from this study, observation of several mid-career art and design teachers revealed that their teaching was at its best when there were strong connections between what they were teaching in the classroom and their wider belief systems. In those situations their motivation was springing from deep personal conviction. They cared about what they were teaching, and taught it well because they believed in it.

A teacher of art and design is required to teach within the statutory curricular framework provided by the Order for Art in the NC, and has the responsibility for creating a scheme of work and teaching courses which will enable pupils to achieve the subject's Attainment Targets. A major strength of the Order is the provision of a framework that gives a clear sense of direction and yet leaves a significant amount of scope for teachers to construct programmes to match their schools' and departments' resources of materials and equipment, and the expertise, enthusiasms and beliefs of the teachers involved. This opportunity is the key to enabling pupils to achieve work of high quality – pupils taught by teachers who have achieved an integration between externally imposed statutory requirements and personal commitment rooted in their own belief systems.

REFERENCES

Barrett, M. (1979) *Art Education*. London: Heinemann.
Clement, R. (1986) *The Art Teacher's Handbook*. London: Hutchinson.
Department of Education and Science (DES) (1991) *National Curriculum: Art for Ages 5 to 14*. London: HMSO.
GCSE (1985) *Art and Design: The National Criteria*. London: Department of Education and Science and the Welsh Office.
Read, H. (1937) *Education Through Art*. London: Faber.
Robinson, C. (1978) Young art teachers. Unpublished M. Phil. thesis, CNAA, University of Brighton.
Taylor, R. (1986) *Educating for Art*. Harlow: Longman.
Thistlewood, D. (ed.) (1989) *Critical Studies in Art and Design Education*. Harlow: Longman.

Chapter 10

Approaching Curriculum Planning: A Strategy in the Face of an Impossible Task

James Hall

> Teachers must be educated to develop their art, not master it, for the claim to mastery merely signals the abandonment of aspiration. Teaching is not be regarded as a static accomplishment like riding a bicycle or keeping a ledger; it is, like all arts of high ambition, a strategy in the face of an impossible task.
>
> (Stenhouse, 1983, p. 189)

> There can be no school without a program; that program is the curriculum … Just as the curriculum lies at the heart of the school, the learning activity lies at the heart of the curriculum. The learning activity, whether planned by student, teacher, or curriculum committee, is the imaginative invention of a vehicle designed to help children learn or experience something having educational value.
>
> (Eisner, 1972, p. 162)

Part of the art of teaching is the thinking and decision-making that teachers engage in to guide what and how they should teach. This thinking or planning occurs at various levels, from the objective and explicit level on which curriculum documents and plans are written, to the more intuitive and spontaneous level of the curriculum in operation – the lesson itself. Curriculum can be conceived as all that is taught to pupils; and as all that is learned by pupils. Clearly, there can be a gap between intention and outcome. Eisner (1984) distinguishes between the intended curriculum, the plans and materials intended to support children's learning, and the operational curriculum, the learning that actually transpires in classrooms.

> In the end, questions of which approach to development and how much prescriptiveness materials ought to have must be determined not by examining the intended curriculum,

but by getting into classrooms and assessing the curriculum in use – what I have called the operational curriculum. It is this curriculum, not simply the materials, that make the difference in the lives of children being taught. Significant curriculum reform and better curriculum theory and development ultimately rest upon what we have yet to learn about how classrooms work. (p. 264)

Curriculum is conceptualized by Eisner (1984) and Stenhouse (1983) as a means of helping teachers to teach and pupils to learn. The curriculum is seen as both the means of learning for pupils and the means of professional development for teachers. Teachers are extended by access to new ideas and are challenged to skilfully adapt and adjust those ideas to fit their established patterns of teaching and learning within their own framework of values. Equally, given the introduction of a National Curriculum for Art (DES, 1992), teachers are challenged to adapt and adjust their patterns of learning and teaching, and to question their framework of values.

The ideas of both Stenhouse and Eisner make clear the notion of curriculum planning as a creative and imaginative process, in which curriculum, as a set of plans or intentions, is seen as problematic and hypothetical. For Stenhouse, there is no good or right curriculum, only interesting and engaging ideas or theories that are worth testing and exploring in classrooms. This propositional view of curriculum requires teachers and pupils to critically review and evaluate the ideas and plans that are put into practice, modifying and adapting those ideas according to their changing needs and contexts. Such an interpretation of curriculum recognizes the autonomous decision-making function of teachers in shaping curriculum materials to their own requirements, and recognizes the role of pupils in identifying aims and plans of their own. How does this view of curriculum planning sit along-side the statutory obligation teachers have to teach the National Curriculum for Art? How can student teachers of art and design learn to plan lessons and projects effectively?

Courses of initial teacher education should foster the growth of reflective prac-titioners who are capable of evaluating and developing their practice. It is not enough that they produce competent practitioners who are able to 'produce coherent lesson plans which take account of National Curriculum Attainment Targets and of the school's curriculum policies' (DFE, 1992, Annex A, 2.3.1). Teachers need to be critically reflective as 'user-developers' (Connelly, 1972) of the curriculum, skilfully adopting, adapting and adjusting materials appropriate to their situations. Teachers of art and design need to respond both to external requirements, in the form of the National Curriculum framework or an examination syllabus, and to the local requirements, opportunities and constraints experienced in their own schools. Stu-dent teachers must gain access to the broader, generalized and explicit criteria that teachers need to respond to when making planning decisions; and to the contextual-ized knowledge and understanding that experienced teachers possess and respond to in their teaching. The local circumstances influencing teachers' decision-making will include the pupils' needs and interests, the teachers' abilities and interests, the resources available, including time and materials, the whole-school curriculum and the relationship between art and design and other subjects. Teachers' thinking will also be guided by their personal orientations as artists or designers and as educators, by their own values and beliefs, and these need to be articulated in the form of statements of aims and rationales for art and design education.

At the level of classroom practice and the individual lesson, an infinite range of additional considerations come into play. These include the immediate circumstances of the lesson, the unforeseen events and situations, and pupils' reactions, which teachers have to respond to in the context of the lesson. Teachers' spontaneous 'planning' and decision-making at this level is largely intuitive; aims and strategies for a single lesson or part of it are rarely explicitly stated, but are embedded in the skills and knowledge that teachers have built up from experience. Most situations or similar ones have been met before, and teachers develop repertoires of strategies, which they can call upon and adapt to particular situations (Schon, 1983).

It is possible to identify three challenges that teachers of art and design face in the context of curriculum planning. The first challenge concerns how to respond to what Eisner (1984) refers to as a 'mixed mode' of curriculum development:

> In the mixed mode, teachers respond to the external structures that are provided by others, in the form of frameworks or guidelines, by working within and being stimulated by those structures to develop specific aims, strategies and outcomes appropriate to the local contexts of their schools. (p. 263)

Teachers need to respond to the statutory framework of the National Curriculum for Art in their curriculum planning. This is not an entirely new situation as teachers have worked within the framework of the General Certificate of Secondary Education (GCSE) since 1986.

The second challenge is for student and newly qualified teachers (NQTs) of art and design, their mentors in the school-based models of initial teacher education and their tutors in higher education institutions. During student teachers' school experience or newly qualified teachers' experience in their first post, they lack the deep contextualized knowledge of schools, pupils, colleagues and resources that is so crucial to curriculum planning. Student teachers and NQTs need access to this knowledge so that they can develop a full understanding of curriculum planning and the thinking behind it, including the reasons for teachers' decisions. Obviously, student and recently qualified teachers will not have the tacit, practical knowledge possessed by experienced teachers as this can only be gained over time. However, novice teachers also need access to the 'knowledge-in-action' (Schon, 1983) that experienced teachers use so fluently in order to gain insights into expert practice.

The third challenge underlines the need for a curriculum that is flexible and open to negotiation. Teachers need to make curriculum statements in order to be clear about their intentions and to help them plan and structure learning experiences for their pupils. Teachers also need to communicate their intentions clearly to their pupils in order to encourage pupils to go on and formulate some aims of their own in relation to the project or task. The pupils' involvement in their own learning is less likely to take place where too little structure exists, aims and directions are unclear, and hence pupils lack the confidence to work with independence. Conversely, where the structure is too tight, with little or no room for manoeuvre, pupils will be unable to develop their own differentiated responses and forge some directions of their own. Pupils need to be provided with opportunities to develop their creative imaginations and to develop the practical skills necessary to realize their ideas.

It is the teachers' task to respond to these two essential requirements. The balance between freedom and control is the greatest of our professional responsibilities. Total freedom can lead to anarchy; total control to dictatorship. Neither of these strategies, in isolation, can provide a useful guide to the process of learning.

(Hampshire County Council, 1992, p. 101)

This chapter explores the range of factors that teachers need to consider when planning an art and design curriculum. Different considerations need to be addressed at different tiers of thinking and planning. Seven tiers of planning are identified from the explicit level of broad aims and rationales to the implicit level of classroom activity and the learning of individual pupils. Where appropriate, reference is made to examples from schools within the University of Reading and Schools Partnership Scheme, which is responsible for the Postgraduate Certificate in Education course. The implications of this broad conceptualization of curriculum planning for student teachers and their mentors are discussed. Of particular concern is the way in which student teachers of art and design can be supported in their learning, and the manner in which they are introduced to classroom decision-making as a form of creative research and continuing professional development. A simple theory-into-practice model of curriculum planning in art and design is inadequate as no theory could encompass or predict the range of things a teacher needs to consider when planning at either the departmental or individual level. A critically reflective approach is suggested, whereby the range of considerations facing teachers is kept under continuous critical review and is evaluated through documented practice and discussion with colleagues.

TERMINOLOGIES, ISSUES AND QUESTIONS

Before looking at possible strategies for designing a curriculum, it is necessary to pay some attention to terminology. Rowntree (1974) suggests 'The literature of educational intention is a minefield of terminological confusion. Statements of purpose operate at several different levels and there are many different words used to denote the levels, eg. aim, goal, objective, standard, learning outcome, criterion, etc.' (p. 19). Any teminological confusion that art and design teachers may have suffered from has been compounded by the fact that many teachers have been unused to explicating or even debating their practice. Reid and Walker (1975, p. 249) point to 'the existence among teachers of stable bodies of ideas about how and what to teach'. Until more recently, in art and design education, these ideas have often remained implicit in teachers' practice and were rarely brought out into the open, shared and explored. Curriculum development initiatives in the 1960s and 1970s seemed to pass art and design education by: Barrett (1979, p. 1) refers to art teachers' 'unwillingness or inability' to formulate a case to justify and clarify the subject's place in the curriculum. Barrett (1983) also draws attention to the apparent 'uneven partnership' between those he termed the theoreticians, who 'lack the detailed knowledge of the classroom' and the practitioners who lack the ability 'to articulate their ideas and develop their expertise through their colleagues' (p. 286).

It is considered that developments within the last ten to fifteen years signal a much closer and healthier articulation between theory and practice in the field of art and design education. Curriculum developers and analysts in the field have drawn on theoretical perspectives and existing practice to identify the general principles that underpin effective practice in a variety of contexts. Taylor's (1986) and Clement's (1993) methodologies, though supporting different aims, are exemplars of this approach.

Curriculum

A subject is not a curriculum. Subject matters have to be converted into educational events to have the status of curriculum. Eisner (1984, p. 259) defines curriculum as 'a series of events designed to have educational consequences, often conceived as a set of plans or materials'. The curriculum is a broad statement providing a long-term view of a varied and balanced programme of learning.

Syllabus

While some educators would see a syllabus as an example of a curriculum, others conceive a syllabus as a more concise statement of course aims, content and suggested activities. Barrett (19798, p. vi), sees a syllabus as 'a set of decisions made about the strategies employed to achieve a general or specific outcome'. Barrett points out that, although a syllabus is a formal document of outcomes, this does not mean it will be formal in operation. A syllabus would normally define a course of study for a specific age group.

Aims and objectives

Aims and objectives operate at a number of difference levels of increasing specificity. An aim is a broad statement of educational intent. Aims can relate to the curriculum at the whole-school level (e.g. to foster children's creativity and imagination, and at the subject level (e.g. to encourage creative and imaginative responses to ideas, themes or subjects).

Objectives are more precise statements of intended outcomes and are formulated to achieve the more general aims. Objectives 'switch the emphasis from the teacher's teaching to the learner's learning' (Rowntree, 1974, p. 20).

Important issues in curriculum development and planning remain: Barrett (1979) discusses the alternative merits of a syllabus based upon objectives and a process model for the syllabus. In an objectives model, derived from the work of Tyler (1950), specific learning outcomes, or objectives, are defined and these determine the content, methods and evaluation procedures to be used. The limitations of prescribing intended outcomes in art and design and allowing these objectives to determine the syllabus are recognized by Eisner (1972), Stenhouse (1970) and Barrett (1979). A syllabus based upon defined outcomes can fail to take account of the nature of learning in art and design, local circumstances, the varied and changing contexts for learning, the teacher's role and the pupil's role, and their impact upon what is taught and learned.

Eisner (1972) sought to get around this difficulty by distinguishing between instructional or behavioural objectives and expressive objectives. An expressive objective defines an educational encounter or task, but does not specify the outcome, or what pupils are to learn from their encounter with that situation or problem. Thus more open-ended activities are described, in which outcomes are varied and negotiable, and the processes of investigating and learning are emphasized. Barrett (1979) argues that the process model is a more suitable structure for an art and design syllabus. Here content is specified rather than the objectives. Specific activities are seen as worthwhile in themselves rather than as a means towards outcomes. Education is the process of being involved in those worthwhile activities, which have their own built-in standards of excellence, or inherent criteria. 'Disciplines allow us to specify input rather than output in the educational process. This is fairer to the needs of individual students because relative to objectives, disciplined content is liberating to the individual' (Stenhouse, 1970, p. 86).

Stenhouse's view has echoes with art and design curriculum development in North America, where Eisner has been a prime mover in the Discipline Based Art Education movement (Getty, 1985). In this rationale, the curriculum is based upon the four disciplines of Art Criticism, Art History, Aesthetics and Studio Practice. Questions of balance and integration face teachers as they seek to use this structure, a situation which has obvious parallels with teachers in England and Wales as they interpret and use the National Curriculum for Art.

While a traditional objectives model of curriculum planning has been found to be inadequate for the needs of art and design in education, the National Curriculum for Art is defined in terms of outcomes or skills, knowledge and understanding that pupils should attain by the age of 14. However, a curriculum based on objectives tends not to specify how these objectives should be attained; a curriculum based on the process model specifies worthwhile activities and offers criteria for structuring these activities. Perhaps within the framework of the National Curriculum, the two approaches to curriculum planning are not incompatible. It is felt to be sufficiently broad and general (Clement, 1993) to allow teachers to develop different strategies and approaches to their planning and teaching.

THE TIERS OF CURRICULUM PLANNING

There are various tiers of curriculum planning which guide teachers' thinking and decision-making about their pupils' learning, from the level of the National Curriculum and the school curriculum to the learning experiences of individual pupils. For the purposes of discussion, seven tiers of planning are identified, as they apply to pupils aged 11 to 12 years (see Figure 10.1).

This process takes planning from broad to specific considerations, from defined to open and negotiable criteria, from the explicit to the implicit level of planning teaching and learning in art and design. The process could be stratified more finely if, for example, the complex layers of thinking and decision-making at the classroom level were considered. Also, at the broader level of planning, guidelines or frameworks for curriculum planning are produced by Local Education Authorities (LEAs), often through teams of teachers and advisers working collaboratively, and these documents provide useful support for teachers (Hampshire County Council, 1992).

However, the question of the number of tiers or the distinction between them is not as important as the recognition that teachers' thinking and decision-making permeate various layers of planning considerations. This is not intended to be read as a hierarchical structure, whereby the National Curriculum framework is seen as dominant and more valuable than the colouring the individual teacher and pupil lends the curriculum at its operational level. At all levels of planning, local circumstances will influence teachers' thinking and decision-making. It is assumed that teachers will have an intimate knowledge of the local criteria and will consider them at each level of planning. Local circumstances include the following.

Pupils

What is taught and how it is taught will, in part, be determined by the age of pupils, their stage of development and prior learning, their skills and interests, and the number of pupils in the group. At the operational level of the classroom, knowledge of group dynamics and the personalities and behaviour of individual pupils becomes important as continuous adjustments and modifications are made.

Teachers

Curriculum planning is informed by teachers' personal values and beliefs, as individuals, artists, designers and teachers; these ideas help to shape their rationales for the subject. The curriculum is also determined, in part, by the skills, interests, strengths and expertise of teachers. Any curriculum should be kept under review so that it can be developed and modified to meet changing needs and circumstances. Such changes generate teacher development needs and these should be met through appropriate in-service training (INSET) provision.

Resources

What is taught and how it is taught will also be influenced by the resources that are available to teachers and pupils, and the opportunities and constraints that they are faced with. The size and quality of accommodation and how teachers make use of the available space; the facilities, equipment and materials available for learning; and the length and frequency of lessons are all important considerations for teachers' planning.

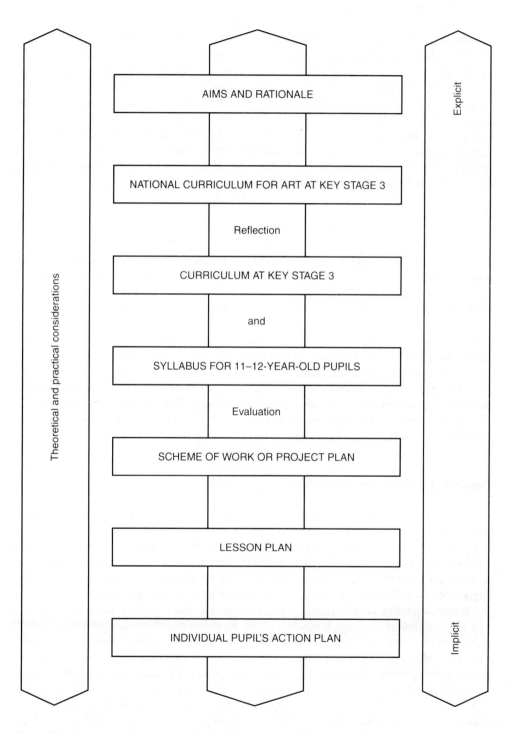

AIMS AND RATIONALE

NATIONAL CURRICULUM FOR ART AT KEY STAGE 3

Reflection

CURRICULUM AT KEY STAGE 3

and

SYLLABUS FOR 11–12-YEAR-OLD PUPILS

Evaluation

SCHEME OF WORK OR PROJECT PLAN

LESSON PLAN

INDIVIDUAL PUPIL'S ACTION PLAN

Explicit

Implicit

Theoretical and practical considerations

Figure 10.1 *Seven tiers of curriculum planning for a secondary school department of art and design*

Curriculum organization

Curriculum organization in the school as a whole will determine how subjects or areas of the curriculum are structured and organized. Art and design may be organized as a discrete subject area or as part of a faculty structure, allied to other areas of the curriculum. Art and design may be in a faculty with technology or in an expressive arts consortium with, for example, music, drama and dance. Projects or schemes of work may be jointly planned and taught by teachers from these different areas of the curriculum. Alternatively, planning can continue separately but with broad, thematic links between learning in different subject areas. Clearly, national criteria have to allow for differences of approach and provision; different established methods of working within different frameworks of values.

EXEMPLARS

The seven tiers of planning identified above will now be discussed in turn. Reference will be made to the curriculum plans for art and design of two schools. Frogmore Community School in Yateley, and Fernhill Community School in Farnborough. Both schools are Hampshire LEA supported and make use of, and have contributed to, Hampshire LEA's *Further Guidelines for Art Education* (Hampshire County Council, 1992). Maurice Barrett contributed the discussion papers for this document, providing a link to the rationales for curriculum development discussed earlier.

Both Frogmore and Fernhill Schools are members of the Reading University and Schools Partnership Scheme and contribute to the PGCE course, by offering placements to pairs of student teachers of art and design. The students are supported by a mentor, known as a 'supervising teacher' in the Reading scheme; at Frogmore and Fernhill, this role is adopted by the head of department.

Departmental aims and rationale

Before teachers of art and design decide what and how they are going to teach, they need to consider why art and design should be taught at all. In other words, teachers need to identify a rationale for the subject and some worthwhile aims for art and design education. These statements are at a broad, philosophical level in which a framework of values is established; the statements describe the ethos of the department rather than the content of teaching or the strategies adopted.

Clearly, with the introduction of the National Curriculum for Art, with its own, implicit framework of values, teachers will need to review the documents outlining their particular orientation to the subject. Often, these broad statements of aims and rationales will be framed within the context of a departmental policy document, sometimes supported by a development plan, in which the current and future needs of the department are identified. Heads of department may be expected to publish a policy document for the department for the purposes of internal monitoring and review of the curriculum and for the external inspection of the school.

Frogmore has a curriculum framework document for art. The introduction reads:

The concept of Art is one which encompasses both practical and theoretical activities of the creative, visual and tactile aspects of the subject.

It is intended that through first-hand practical experience, an increased understanding of the work of artists, designers, architects and craftsworkers is built up. This will lead to a more lively appreciation and a greater awareness of the natural and human environment and mankind's cultural achievements, so enriching the pupil's experience of life.

Learning in art provides pupils with a way of perceiving themselves and the world which is not taught in other areas of the school curriculum and which is essential to basic education. This visual understanding deepens their creative awareness by enhancing the imagination and intensifying feelings, ideas and sensitivities.

It is the intention of the curriculum framework to provide for the needs and preferences of pupils of differing abilities, background and interests, in an exciting, innovative and balanced programme in line with the requirements of Art in the National Curriculum.

(Frogmore Community School, 1992)

This introductory statement is followed by a list of broad aims and objectives for the department, which draws upon national criteria for GCSE Art and Design.

Fernhill's document is the result of a collaboration with staff at a nearby school in Farnborough, The Cove School. The two heads of department have worked closely in their respective schools for over twenty years, 'arguing and debating Art Education ... [and] now seemed an appropriate time to draw some conclusions' (Fernhill Community School, 1993). The introduction to this document reads:

Art is both mysterious and elusive, it can give insights into a person's thoughts, it can confound.

It may lead you straight back to the front door or lead you a tenuous route through back lanes and diversions before, if then, arriving at your destination.

It can be concrete, arrived at through precise, laid-down processes.

It can be the result of long-term study or a split-second insight.

At its broadest it has no boundaries, at its narrowest it can be quite specific.

The idea may lead to the selection of a specific medium for its realisation but equally, the medium itself might be the catalyst for expressive activity.

Outcomes are not predictable, an idea expressed through one medium may well lead to a totally different outcome when explored through another.

It is this variety of response that must be cherished, even if it does not allow the subject to fit neatly into tight little boxes.

If it seems out of step then maybe it shouldn't have been in the march in the first place, for I believe that it is these idiosyncratic responses that allow man to make his own, individual mark on the world and, in so doing, enrich the lives of others.

(Fernhill Community School, 1993)

National Curriculum for Art at Key Stage 3

The National Curriculum for Art (DES, 1992) established a statutory framework of learning in art for all pupils aged from 5 to 14 in maintained schools in England and Wales. The main aspects of the subject are defined in Attainment Targets (ATs), which contain End of Key Stage Statements against which pupils are assessed. Programmes of Study set out the range of knowledge, skills and understanding that pupils should be taught during their time at school.

Both the Frogmore and Fernhill documents include the National Curriculum for Art End of Key Stage Statements and Programmes of Study for Key Stage 3.

Curriculum at Key Stage 3

How is the National Curriculum for Art at Key Stage 3 interpreted and implemented given all the local considerations discussed earlier? At this level of planning, the department devises a curriculum for all pupils at Key Stage 3, aged 11 to 14, basing their plans on, or checking them against, the requirements of the National Curriculum. At Frogmore School, the art and design curriculum for Key Stage 3 is described in three phases: 'Introduction' in Year 7; 'Exploration' in Year 8; and 'Sowing a Seed of Interest' in Year 9. The art and design curriculum time for each pupil at Frogmore School is 90 minutes a week. In Year 7, art and design is taught as part of a creative arts course, including music, drama and dance.

> *Introduction*
> Art is an essential part of the Key Stage 2 experience which, as a mode of non-verbal communication and expression, should be maintained and increased in order to direct the pupils to a more versatile and re-active form of expression. The creative arts course at Key Stage 3 should be a continuation of the pupils' creative and expressive development, increasing the aesthetic vocabulary through resource-based and active learning across the creative arts areas.
>
> *Exploration*
> The continued introduction and deeper exploration of technical skills at Key Stage 3, acquired through understanding, making and investigating in thematic and creative responses to a variety of media and stimuli.
>
> *Sowing a Seed of Interest*
> At this point pupils can develop further skills in art involving new and diverse practical experience. The process of research–development–execution–evaluation is strengthened. Pupils are encouraged to develop and pursue a personal response to stimuli and to foster a keen interest and involvement with the subject, leading to pupils wanting to continue art as a GCSE option.
>
> (Frogmore Community School, 1992)

Syllabus for 11- to 12-year-old pupils

This level of planning is concerned with a syllabus over one year of a pupil's experience, in this case an 11- or 12-year-old pupil in Year 7. The plans should represent an overview of the content and activities each pupil will cover during the year. The key issues of progression and continuity are vital, but somewhat problematic. To relate a pupil's knowledge, skills and understanding to what has been learned in the primary school assumes a close relationship with the primary schools transferring pupils to a secondary school. The open-enrolment policy resulting from the Education Reform Act (DES, 1988) implies that pupils can be recruited from any primary school, making liaison very difficult. However, in practice, the majority of pupils transfer to secondary schools designated by the LEA. The National Curriculum has been introduced, in part, to address this problem. Wherever pupils transfer to, teachers will have a knowledge of the framework of learning that pupils should have engaged in.

Frogmore's curriculum framework specifies the content and media that 11- to 12-year-old pupils will be expected to engage in over the year. The following examples list pupils' experiences in printing, graphics and information technology.

Printing
Mono printing; relief printing; ink preparation and use of rollers; print assemblages; surface textures; colour mixing; pattern-making and repetition; understanding purpose and history of printing.

Graphics
Colour; image; balance; layout; basic letter construction and manipulation; communication and message; role and history of graphics.

Information technology
Using the Archimedes computer as a tool within art and design; use of artisan software; basic shape construction, manipulation; colour experimentation; lettering; free drawing; saving work; use of computer in a wider context.

(Frogmore Community School, 1992)

Fernhill identifies five priorities as selected points of focus for Year 7:

Selected focus for year seven
The following priorities will form the core of experiences for Year 7 and at least 80% of all lesson plans will be distilled from the following:
1) Visual investigation.
2) Engender a sense of the new.
3) Imaginative responses.
4) Making in 3D.
5) Critical/aesthetic appreciation.

(Fernhill Community School, 1993)

Scheme of work or project plan

The scheme of work involves a detailed breakdown of content and activities for a particular unit of learning or project. A project could be expected to extend over several lessons and weeks, and may, in some cases, extend to half a term, or even a whole term's work. A cross-curricular dimension may be included, such as one of the National Curriculum themes (e.g. Environmental Education, Economic and Industrial Understanding) or a link to another subject, such as English or drama.

Considerations for teachers will include continuity with prior and subsequent learning; the sequence of learning and activities within the unit of work; and the complexity of the tasks related to the ability levels of the pupils. Further questions for teachers are: How flexible is the approach to the theme or topic and how much scope is there for pupils to make a personal response? Are there different options and choices within the unit? It is also expected that the unit of work will be fine-tuned in relation to a particular class of pupils, drawings on the teacher's knowledge of the group and of individual pupils. Will the unit's content be negotiable with the pupils? Are the ideas and plans shaped by and with the pupils?

Fernhill's rationale for planning the unit of work is as follows:

This is a means of structuring the unit of work.

It should enable the teacher to clarify thoughts, prepare materials and other resources and show the initial purpose of intent.

It will be distilled from the Priorities and Foci.

It will show the research/homework expectations.

It will highlight essential elements within the unit.

It will indicate the duration of the unit (50 minutes to several weeks).

It will help to develop language by identifying words and terms that could cause confusion.

It will indicate the National Curriculum Attainment Targets and Programmes of Study.

(Fernhill Community School, 1993)

An example of a scheme of work from Fernhill School is shown in Figure 10.2.

Lesson plan

The educational thinking and planning that teachers engage in continuously at the operational level of the curriculum, in the classroom, is the most difficult level of strategic decision-making to access for student teachers.

The lesson plan is a detailed breakdown of a lesson into its objectives, sequence of activities, including introduction and conclusion, key concepts and vocabulary to be used, and resources required. This involves implementation of the curriculum at its most flexible and negotiated level, when teachers need to consider an ever-expanding range of factors in their decision-making. Experienced teachers would not normally plan at an explicit level, but would rely intuitively on their former experience of similar situations and on their repertoire of knowledge and skills (Schon, 1983).

The thinking and decision-making that informs and guides these actions is deeply embedded in teachers' practical knowledge (Elbaz, 1983). Increasingly complex skills, actions and decision-making have become routinized and almost invisible, lending the expert teacher's practice a fluency and flexibility that looks tantalizingly easy to the student or novice teacher. Flexibility comes from expert teachers holding many different strategies for realizing an objective: they have met so many similar situations before that they can draw on 'the wealth of ideas about what and how to teach' (Reid and Walker, 1975, p. 249) and adjust their actions to 'fit' the new situation.

The planning and decision-making of experienced teachers occurring at the operational level of the curriculum are implicit and difficult to access and discuss both for student teachers and for teacher mentors. However, student teachers need to plan their first lessons and projects on an explicit, objective basis and be prepared to discuss the content and strategies, justifying their decisions, with their teacher mentors and tutors. With no 'back-catalogue' of ideas and experiences to guide their decisions at the operational level, student teachers are challenged to hold to their objective planning while responding to the unfolding event of the lesson in all its complexity. One way around this is for student teachers to be introduced to planning by working collaboratively with teacher mentors for their initial experiences

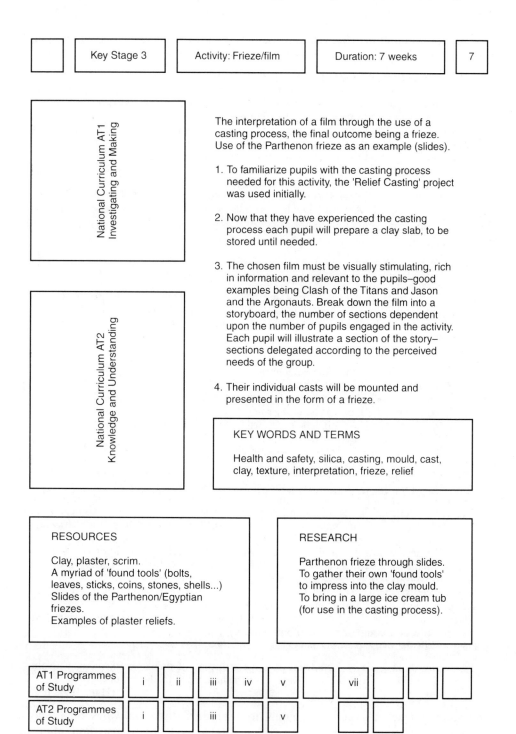

| | Key Stage 3 | Activity: Frieze/film | Duration: 7 weeks | 7 |

National Curriculum AT1 Investigating and Making

National Curriculum AT2 Knowledge and Understanding

The interpretation of a film through the use of a casting process, the final outcome being a frieze. Use of the Parthenon frieze as an example (slides).

1. To familiarize pupils with the casting process needed for this activity, the 'Relief Casting' project was used initially.

2. Now that they have experienced the casting process each pupil will prepare a clay slab, to be stored until needed.

3. The chosen film must be visually stimulating, rich in information and relevant to the pupils–good examples being Clash of the Titans and Jason and the Argonauts. Break down the film into a storyboard, the number of sections dependent upon the number of pupils engaged in the activity. Each pupil will illustrate a section of the story–sections delegated according to the perceived needs of the group.

4. Their individual casts will be mounted and presented in the form of a frieze.

KEY WORDS AND TERMS

Health and safety, silica, casting, mould, cast, clay, texture, interpretation, frieze, relief

RESOURCES

Clay, plaster, scrim.
A myriad of 'found tools' (bolts, leaves, sticks, coins, stones, shells...)
Slides of the Parthenon/Egyptian friezes.
Examples of plaster reliefs.

RESEARCH

Parthenon frieze through slides.
To gather their own 'found tools' to impress into the clay mould.
To bring in a large ice cream tub (for use in the casting process).

| AT1 Programmes of Study | i | ii | iii | iv | v | | vii | | |
| AT2 Programmes of Study | i | | iii | | v | | | |

Figure 10.2 *An example of a scheme of work*

of teaching. Student teachers can work closely with experienced teachers, jointly planning and teaching lessons in order to develop new skills and understandings.

> Collaborative teaching makes two kinds of learning possible:
> Planning – learning to plan lessons carefully through being involved in joint planning with [experienced teachers], finding out what [experienced teachers] take account of, and identifying with the planning and its consequences.
> Classroom teaching skills – learning certain skills through having responsibility for a specified component of the lesson while at the same time identifying with the whole lesson and recognizing the relationship of the part to the whole.
> (Hagger *et al.*, 1993, p. 61)

The following example of collaborative teaching took place as part of the University of Reading PGCE Art and Design course. Student teachers worked in teams of three with an experienced teacher, one of whom provided the following briefing notes in advance of their first visit and planning meeting.

Project: African Outcomes

Introduction
These notes are to prepare you in some way for next Thursday. We are all looking forward to your visits. I thought it might help you if I gave you some information but please feel free to bring to the teaching experience your own ideas. The following is only a starter.

Aims
- further awareness of cultural influences
- appreciation of ethnic crafts, etc.
- acquire knowledge through drawing, exploration of texture, form, etc.
- gain confidence by looking, handling and recording information
- explore the potential of objects as a starting point for more personal study and expressive, imaginative work
- enjoy exploring new methods of working and assessing outcomes

I have borrowed African objects from the Reading Museum Education Loan Service – costumes, belts, sculptures, cooking implements, snake skins, etc. So far the pupils have chosen an object and made careful analytical drawings. I will split the group so that you have a group of five or six pupils to work with over the four weeks. You can have them working individually or as a group. They can work directly from their drawings or refer back to the objects.

You can decide how the pupils work and with what materials. It is important that you make some decisions for them and with them. The following list provides suggestions – I am sure you have lots more to offer.
Textiles: tie dye, batik, screen-print, block-print, weave, paper, wool.
Sculpture: card, paper, found materials, papier mâché, etc. (not clay).
Graphics: illustration with introduced poetry, layout, product or packaging design. (We have the use of a computer and colour printer.)
Painting: all the usual painting materials.

By the fourth Thursday I would like to have a display of pupils' work along with the objects. I would also like the groups to explain their work to the others.
(Hall, 1992, p. 7)

One student teacher asked her pupils to reproduce their drawings on tissue as preparation for a fabric print or weaving. In an evaluative discussion after the placement, the student said:

> I spent a lot of time with four of them because they needed continuous input into what

they were doing along with help on how to think the process through. They were quite prepared to work ... one pupil was doing a block-print, one a screen-print, another a weaving ... you're giving lots of information to different people all the time. It's very demanding but it's close to the way I work.

(Hall, 1992, p. 8)

In this reflection on her first experience of teaching, the student teacher's own practice and creative methodology as a textile designer is clearly an important reference point.

Another student teacher, having read the teacher's briefing notes, decided to focus on graphic design, asking the pupils to design either a poster for an exhibition of African art or a design for the door surround as part of the exhibition design.

As soon as we started I realised first that it was quite complicated; secondly, that you had to give them a lot of information and incentive, which I hadn't worked on and I was just floundering ... so we started off and discussed the brief, jotted down some of the main points ... and I quickly realised I was going to have to change direction. So I asked [the teacher] if we could do some printmaking – making a printed background based on African symbols to be used either for the poster or the door surround which gave us something to work with because they were sitting there trying to work out ideas, which is something I find difficult to do.

(Hall, 1992, p. 9)

This student teacher clearly reflected on how to approach the planning of a lesson, the sequence of activities and learning, and the timing and relationship of practical investigation to discussion.

Other key aspects of planning were discussed in the evaluations of these placements, including the importance of language, concepts, aims and objectives, the organization of resources, and lesson management issues. Through this initial experience of planning and teaching, student teachers are introduced to the complexities of the curriculum in action, and how teachers skilfully tailor their intentions to meet each pupil's needs and interests.

Later in the PGCE course, as student teachers assume greater and eventually full responsibility for lessons, the leading responsibility for planning shifts from the teacher mentor to the student teacher.

At Reading, students are offered the following format for their lesson planning:

Date, time and length of lesson

Name of class or form and number of pupils

Aims (usually only necessary for a series of lessons)

Objectives (refer to NC strands and Programmes of Study)

Resources (materials, tools and equipment needed, including slides, books, etc.)

Plan (a clear sequence of instructions to be given, ideas and materials to be presented and activities to be undertaken. Each lesson should have an introduction and a conclusion. There should be a note of such points as questions to be asked, the timing and pace of the lesson, organisation of groups, etc.)

Evaluation (The most effective way to improve your performance as a teacher is to analyse your teaching and the resulting pupil activity and achievement after each lesson or session. It is equally important to examine your successes and build on those as to examine any performances which you feel were less good than you intended.)

Homework (If homework is an integral part of your responsibility for a group during your practice, then a separate note will be required for this.)

Visual material (It may be useful to illustrate your lesson notes, or use diagrams if appropriate.)

The role of reflection and evaluation in the cycle of planning, teaching, evaluating and further planning is stressed, and student teachers are offered a pro forma for their self-evaluation, derived from the work of Kyriacou (1986).

> Reflection and evaluation regarding one's teaching is crucial for the continuing develop-
> ment of teaching skills in general, and for specific knowledge about how a particular
> lesson could have been improved (with implications for similar lessons). Each teacher
> has intentions about his or her own teaching; teachers may differ both in terms of the
> educational outcomes they wish to emphasise and the types of learning experiences
> they wish to use. In this respect, one teacher may feel a lesson has gone well, whilst
> an observer may well feel that other educational outcomes or learning experiences
> could more usefully have been involved. Periodically, teachers need to reflect on the
> general character of their teaching and relate this to curriculum developments aimed
> at improving the quality of education. (p. 126)

Individual pupils' action plan

The broad conception of curriculum planning – all the thinking and decision-making that supports pupils' learning and teachers' teaching – cannot stop at the lesson plan, but must continue to the heart of the learning activity: the pupil's role. Pupils make decisions about what they are going to learn and how they are going to learn it. There may be occasions when pupils' decision-making is not high on the agenda – the lesson content may demand a more prescribed response on occasions. However, most teaching and learning in art and design occurs in a context of negotiated enquiry. The National Curriculum framework and GCSE criteria stress pupil owner-ship of their learning, with pupils learning to make their own decisions, and planning goals and aims for themselves.

In responding to the experience of the lesson, pupils interpret the teacher's intentions, which are either implicit in the task or explicitly stated. In so doing, pupils are establishing criteria or aims of their own to which the teacher must be sensitive. Pupils' individual criteria, together with the general criteria of the lesson or project, inform the dialogue between teachers and their pupils, through which their learning is guided and negotiated. This is the learning activity which is at the heart of the curriculum, and it is a learning experience for teachers as well as for pupils. It is the richness and quality of this experience for pupils, and for teachers, that the preceding six levels of curriculum planning have been facilitating.

CONCLUSION

Curriculum planning in art and design is a complex process of decision-making on a number of different levels, ranging from the explicit, objective level of curriculum statements and frameworks, to the implicit, more intuitive level of the teaching and learning activity in the classroom. At the operational level, when teachers' planning is influenced by an infinite range of factors, many of which teachers respond to spontaneously, student teachers and their teacher mentors and university tutors are challenged to access and analyse the 'invisible' skills of the expert teacher (Hagger *et al.*, 1993).

Student teachers of art and design need to be guided and supported in their efforts to make connections between these different levels of curriculum planning. They need to reflect on the broad aims and intentions of their teaching as a result of their pupils' responses to the lesson or series of lessons. Student teachers should aspire to become reflective practitioners rather than merely competent teachers. The attainment of the competences against which PGCE student teachers are now assessed (DFE, 1992) should be seen not as the summation of achievement, but rather as the minimum level of ability required to qualify as a teacher. The assessment criteria that the competences embody seek to define those aspects of teaching that are capable of objective definition. A much broader range of criteria, which include the contextualized, personal and qualitative aspects of teaching, must be brought into play, once student teachers cross the competence threshold. Student teachers should be encouraged to set goals of their own to work towards, and to evaluate their own steps towards achieving those goals.

There are parallels between the reform of courses of initial teacher education and the introduction of a National Curriculum for Art. Both reforms are assessment led and specify the outcomes of learning, in the form of skills, knowledge and understanding to be demonstrated by the learner, rather than specifying input or content. With the emphasis on outcomes, the tendency is for assessment to concentrate on the acquisition of these skills rather than on the qualitative aspects of learning and the development of the individual. As is the case with the competences of teaching for courses of initial teacher education, the Attainment Targets for Art in the National Curriculum are not the sole criteria for learning in art. Further criteria are implicit in the response of the individual pupil, and it is part of the task of the teacher to use these criteria in their dialogue with the pupil and to inform their professional judgements. 'The character of the pupil's effort is judged on a wide range of criteria after it emerges' (Eisner, 1972, p. 155).

Student teachers of art and design need to be encouraged to use this full range of criteria, at the explicit and implicit levels, to guide the planning and evaluation of their teaching. Through this open-minded and enquiring approach, student teachers will be researching their own practice, attempting to understand how and why people acted as they did. The understanding gained – the reasons, principles and explanations – can be called theory.

If a curriculum is a set of ideas grounded in practice, curriculum evaluation involves judgements about the ideas and the practice. The ideas are usually expressed as explicit statements of intent; practice is complex and difficult to explain and evaluate. Ways need to be found of helping student teachers to review critically the curriculum in action as the means of developing their pupils and themselves.

REFERENCES

Barrett, M. (1979) *Art Education: A Strategy for Course Design.* London: Heinemann.
Barrett, M. (1983) A Framework for the Consideration of Art Education. *Journal of Art and Design Education* **2**(3), 279–87.
Clement, R. (1993) *The Art Teacher's Handbook*, 2nd edn. Cheltenham: Stanley Thomas.
Connelly, F. Michael (1972) The function of curriculum development. *Interchange* **3**(2–3), 161–77.
Department for Education (DFE) (1992) *Initial Teacher Training (Secondary Phase).* Circular 9/92. London: HMSO.
Department of Education and Science (DES) (1988) *Education Reform Act.* London: HMSO.
Department of Education and Science (DES) (1992) *Art in the National Curriculum (England).* London: HMSO.
Eisner, Elliott W. (1972) *Educating Artistic Vision.* London: Collier-Macmillan.
Eisner, Elliott W. (1984) Alternative approaches to curriculum development in art education. *Studies in Art Education* **25**(4), 259–64.
Elbaz, Freema (1983) *Teacher Thinking: A Study of Practical Knowledge.* London: Croom Helm.
Fernhill Community School (1993) *Art and Design Departmental Handbook.*
Frogmore Community School (1992) *Art: Curriculum Framework.*
Getty Center for Education in the Arts (1985) *Beyond Creating: The Place for Art in America's Schools.* Los Angeles: The Getty Center for Education in the Arts.
Hagger, H., Burn, K., and McIntyre, D. (1993) *The School Mentor Handbook.* London: Kogan Page.
Hall, James (1992) Teaching and learning in art and design. Unpublished evaluation of IT-INSET project at the University of Reading.
Hampshire County Council (1992) *Further Guidelines for Art Education Key Stages 1–5.* Winchester: Hampshire County Council.
Kyriacou, C. (1986) *Effective Teaching in Schools.* Oxford: Blackwell.
Reid, William A., and Walker, Decker F. (1975) *Case Studies in Curriculum Change.* London: Routledge and Kegan Paul.
Rowntree, Derek (1974) *Educational Technology in Curriculum Development.* London: Harper and Row.
Schon, D. (1983) *The Reflective Practitioner.* London: Temple Smith.
Stenhouse, L. (1970) Some limitations of the use of objectives in curriculum research and planning. *Paedagogica Europaea* **6**, 73–86.
Stenhouse, L. (183) Research as a basis for teaching. Inaugural lecture given at the University of East Anglia, 1979. In Stenhouse, L., *Authority, Education and Emancipation.* London: Heinemann.
Taylor, R. (1986) *Educating for Art*, London: Longman.
Tyler, Ralph (1950) *Basic Principles of Curriculum and Instruction.* Chicago: University of Chicago Press.

Chapter 11

Creating Cross-Curricular Connections

Arthur Hughes

This publication comes at a time of national longing for things past: a hankering daily visible in suburban mock Jacobian 'executive dwellings', estates of newly constructed 'barn conversions' and hypermarkets that bear a crude and passing resemblance to the Newmarket stables of George Stubbs (replete with dovecots and bell towers). It is also apparent in no less tangible form in schools, where this flight from present imperatives has been marked by the tortuous development of the National Curriculum for England and Wales, a well-documented and sometimes unedifying spectacle of vested interests, political imperatives, prejudice and malad-ministration (see Graham and Tytler, 1993).

What was promised as a radical initiative for the education of children in the state sector culminated in a reaffirmation of traditional curriculum structures and a subject-orientated curriculum endorsed by Her Majesty's Inspectorate for Schools (DES, 1988), but marked by squabbles over content, time and resource allocation. The result has been called 'a sort of romantic Matthew Arnold curriculum' (Graham and Tytler, 1993, p. 3).

Art in the National Curriculum (what teachers still rightly insist on calling *art and design*) has been separated from both craft and design, which continue to exist in the art curriculum largely courtesy of those schools who still see fit to employ trained ceramicists, textile designers, jewellers, product designers or graphic designers.

The innovation of making Technology a compulsory curriculum *area* briefly prom-ised a new and interesting extension to the art curriculum, since art was offered a seat round the technology table because of the contribution it could make to the teaching of design. Art could still be taught in traditional ways (the National Curricu-lum for Art is extremely orthodox and challenges few of the conventions of the last twenty years), while also contributing its more technological and design-related aspects to the technology curriculum. Subsequent revisions notionally retained this role, although as Steers (commenting for the National Society for Education in Art and Design, NSEAD) said in his response to the 1993 recommendations for revised

Technology Programmes of Study and Attainment Targets, 'there is a danger that this is becoming little more than an oft-repeated pious hope' (NSEAD, 1993, p. 5).

The faltering of technology as a worthwhile alternative to its generously resourced but largely discredited predecessor, Craft, Design and Technology (CDT), can be linked to the decision by many schools (and accepted by the Department for Education) to turn it back into a discrete subject. In so doing, the original intentions for Technology were thwarted as this new cross-subject area of knowledge and experience became entrusted to the stewardship of one of the more educationally conservative subjects, CDT. Many of the difficulties can undoubtedly be attributed to the relatively short history of technological education for 5- to 18-year-olds in Britain, and the lack of an adequate intellectual or pedagogical foundation. As recently as 1980 Her Majesty's Inspectorate could find no independent place for Technology in the school curriculum, but a location for its close relation, CDT, under the generic heading of 'the arts and applied crafts' (DES, 1980). Eight years later there was a shift and it was the 'technological' that was being talked about by HMI, who at that time recommended that it should become an *'area* of learning and experience' (my italics) that has 'a special contribution to make to the education of every individual' (DES, p. 9).

As the National Curriculum came on stream, subject by subject, a complex picture emerged and discussion developed into the ways that the many Statements of Attainment could be made more manageable for teachers. Proposals were put forward for a cross-curriculum or cross-subject approach to delivery and assessment, especially in the primary school. This process of rationalization culminated in the Dearing Report (1993), and subsequent reductions to subject content proposed by this same body. Art and design teachers, confronted with pressures to adopt a more 'whole-school' approach, were led to espouse a more instrumental view of their subject than many would have liked – a position from which they had moved firmly away in the early 1970s, and which had been endorsed as recently as 1983 by HMI.

In their last major publication on art and design, HMI promulgated a predominantly essentialist approach in which values, practices and procedures regarded as intrinsic to the subject form the adequate justification for its place in the curriculum (DES, 1983). Art and design was considered sufficient unto itself, and apparently had no need of forced or even recommended links with other subjects. Any 'useful' spin-offs in terms of cross-curriculum links were of course to be welcomed, but in the main, art and design education was marked out by 'the skills and understandings rooted in the senses of sight and touch, as well as feeling and intellect' (p. 64). In this publication, *Art in Secondary Education 11–16*, HMI presented what now seems a very simple, uncomplicated, even naive attitude to the subject. 'Distinctive and convincing personal expression' was, at least by implication, much more important than social or moral awareness. It was more important than cross-cultural understanding. It was more important than coming to terms through art with difficult issues in the world such as war, suffering or ecological disaster. This was in marked contrast to views expressed by an earlier generation of art educators, who saw art in schools as a potentially powerful tool for the teaching of concepts such as 'world-mindedness' and international understanding, of use in reducing 'antagonism between racial, religious, social and political groups' (Munro, 1956, p. 153). These views have been echoed more recently in the work arising from the curriculum project, Arts Education in a Multicultural Society.

Eleven years after HMI's contribution to curriculum thinking in art in secondary education, changing social priorities are leading towards a utilitarian view of education. Amid what are often poorly thought-out and hastily implemented plans for vocational education, it is increasingly difficult to resist pressures to train pupils for (that current fiction) the 'real world', a concept previously invoked to support the use of tools and materials! (See Schools Council, 1969.) In this climate, art and design teachers often find it difficult to justify art as an independent subject in the curriculum when school managers are keen to devise curriculum structures which for administrative and resource reasons link art with other subjects.

Art and design teachers have always made creative and often unexpected liaisons with other subjects. Early in my teaching career, a colourful Cambridge-trained biologist coerced me into merging my successful after-school art society with his biology club. The resultant artistic dissections of sheep's eyes and 'scientifically expressionistic' drawings of the same were a testament to a mutually beneficial marriage of subjects – as were a superb set of very large drawings of the world as revealed through the microscope. Later, at another school, art and history were close partners, and whenever we dealt with architectural matters, it was accepted that a mathematics teacher, a former civil engineer, would help with our work, including its assessment. The head of the French department could always be relied upon to do an invaluable stint on Bouchet, Fragonard and Watteau. Whether an open day that saw one John Brindle of the art sixth form dressed as Michelangelo, lying on a scaffolding and transforming the art-room ceiling in one evening into the Sistine Chapel, covered RE as well as art is debatable! Certainly the 'maggots' that dropped from his socks on to unsuspecting parents as part of his thrust for realism had me praying for my job!

Links have always been present between art and other subjects. They have usually been short-lived and based upon personal affinities between teachers, mutual subject benefit and a desire to improve the quality of learning for our pupils. A catalogue of these various relationships would risk becoming mere reportage of the specific, and it is necessary to look beyond transient examples of cross-subject relationships to underlying principles that can guide educational decisions at the levels of both curriculum design and classroom delivery. These principles must have the virtue of being relevant to the subject under consideration (art and design), and be transferable to educational situations that will arise in the future. In other words, the venture must avoid reliance upon the parochial and the fashionable.

In his account of the development of the National Curriculum, Duncan Graham points up a fundamental issue that must be understood if schools are to move forward into a period of even relatively enlightened teaching. He states that 'Art and music are the ultimate expressions of the government's determination to stress knowledge over understanding' (Graham and Tytler, 1993, p. 81). The National Curriculum Council's revisions to the final recommendations of the Art Working Group displayed this 'pure streak' very clearly in the rewriting of the second Attainment Target to include mandatory, named periods and art movements to be addressed in the programmes of study. While most art and design educators realize that over time many modifications will take place in this curriculum, it nevertheless posed the problem of what it is appropriate for young people to know and understand in order for them to be educated in art. Unfortunately, these early revisions lacked clear educational or philosophical underpinning, and displayed an inadequate understanding of both the histories of art and the development of art education in the post-war years. Any attempt to teach that part of the subject that has become known as critical studies through specific, prescribed periods of Western art runs counter to the not unreasonable view about pupils' learning in this sphere propounded as long ago as 1941 by Thomas Munro:

> *What* they like in art is perhaps less important on the whole than *why* they like it and *how* they come to form their judgments of value ... It is absurd to suppose that active boys and girls should prefer Gothic Crucifixions to athletics and dancing, or even to cartoons and motion picture comedies. What they spontaneously like may turn out to have more genuine value for their growth in art in general education than what we mistakenly try to impose upon them. Certain kinds of adult art are too complex and involve types of motivation that are yet foreign to them.
>
> (Munro, 1956, p. 131)

A related point was made earlier by I. A. Richards, who claimed that the first obstacle to understanding poetry was immaturity: 'A lack of experience with poetry must be placed next to general inexperience of life ...' (1929, p. 311).

In other words, art educators need to know much more about 'what kinds of art and what approaches to art' can stir the minds of young people in the various stages of their development and education (see Parsons, 1987). The imposition of highly specified *school knowledge* will do little to encourage genuine understanding – what Gardner (1993, p. 6) calls 'the capacity to apply knowledge, facts, concepts and skills in new situations where they are appropriate'. He comes down heavily on the side of what Barnes (1976) terms 'action knowledge' as a goal of education: that is, that form of understanding that relies upon individuals 'making' their own reality. To do this, as Barnes makes clear, pupils must through talking, writing and (in the case of the art and design lesson) imaging, represent problems or issues for themselves. It is a process through which pupils 'explore the relationship between what they already know and new observations or interpretations which they meet' (Barnes, 1976, p. 81). Art teachers may rightly see part of their job as helping to energize visual perception, but they must remember that this is not simply a matter of training pupils to look, because in Barnes' words, 'we observe not with our eyes alone but with our hypotheses' (p. 58).

A reluctance to accept the fundamental premise that knowledge is not neutral or independent, but that 'subject matter exists in the mind of the perceiver' (Postman and Weingartner, 1971, p. 95), has arguably been at the root of the phenomenon claimed by Gardner, that 'most students in schools all over the world do not understand. In other words, given situations where they must apply their "school knowledge", they do not know what to do' (Gardner, 1993, p. 6).

To recapitulate, in England and Wales, the subject-based National Curriculum has an apparently unstated intention that emphasizes the direct transmission of knowledge over the forming of personal understanding of the kind that is transferable – the making of meaning. Failure to translate the teaching of the National Curriculum into a 'subversive activity' (Postman and Weingartner, 1971) is to deny our children the full possibility of understanding 'the simultaneity of experience' through a *per-*

sonal linking of disciplines. Jerome Bruner's advocacy of learning through discovery supports Postman and Weingartner's conviction that traditional subject boundaries are not helpful to real learning, 'the probing of relationships among subjects, which, in turn, permits the development of a synoptic and frequently original view of knowledge instead of a traditional segmented view' (p. 81).

A truly original view of knowledge is by definition one that is individual and cannot be prescribed in advance. Cross-curriculum links have, in this context, to be characterized by this sense of originality as individuals make meaning for themselves through the questioning process. This in turn bestows on the individual the 'ownership' of what is learned, and fits uneasily into a curriculum framework which lays down the factual content of what must be learned and, through suggested or mandatory cross-curriculum links or themes, the means by which this content should be taught.

A subtle voice in the debate is provided by Mary Warnock. She supports the traditional model of subject specialisms and the concept of depth based upon underlying subject principles – something close to Bruner's 'subject structure'. However, Warnock is no traditionalist and casts serious doubts on the way the curriculum is approached, employing arguments that call into question the educational value of National Curriculum orthodoxy. Her fundamental position is that in every subject there are two possible approaches, the practical and the theoretical (Warnock, 1988). Two of the gains of the last fifteen years in art and design education have been the acceptance that in schools the 'theoretical' is important, and that it is not, or need not be, separated from the practical. As we know, numerous attempts have been made in critical studies to effect a fusion of these two orientations. The same is true of many university art and design courses, where the division between the theoretical and the practical is considered educationally unhelpful, and what used to be called complementary or contextual studies is frequently taught alongside or as a part of 'main' study (itself a changing concept as modularization takes over as the structural principle in many institutions).

Warnock advocates an opening up of the traditional academic curriculum in schools and, in a significant expansion of her definitions, insists that 'The approach I have called theoretical as opposed to practical must have as a major part of its aim not merely the passing on of facts and formulae *but the inculcation of critical and speculative habit*' (Warnock, 1988, p. 52, my italics). This could of course be seen as the major aim of critical studies in art and design. She sketches out a curriculum structure that encourages a genuinely critical approach to study that will 'equip the student with transferable skills and transferable expertise', encouraging pupils to think for themselves and develop habits of 'free, imaginative thought, speculation *and the conceptual connections between one subject and another*' (p. 53, my italics).

To achieve this Warnock maintains, along with Gardner, that priority should be given 'to method rather than content, to a specific manner of acquiring and dealing with information rather than the information itself' (p. 142). An Oxford history graduate may be ignorant of many aspects of history, 'but what he will have is both an awareness of how to find out the nature of historical problems and an ability to distinguish good evidence from bad in seeking solutions ... his skills will be genuinely transferable' (p. 142). According to Warnock, schools, like universities, should teach both the underlying principles of subjects and the ability to express ideas with clarity. This of course is fundamentally at odds with the model of 'Knowledge and Understanding' that initially formed the second Attainment Target for Art in the National Curriculum. This was a linear and highly schematic view of orthodox art history which, with the non-statutory examples of artists to be introduced, implied a heavily didactic approach to critical study.

In the 1970s a number of American art educators, including Efland, articulated positions close to Warnock's. They insisted that

> students should be able to ask some of the same kinds of questions that professionals ask, and the chief task of the curriculum planner is to find ways of representing these questions in a form that students at various levels [could] understand.
> (Efland, 1972, p. 4)

They were looking for a defensible structure in a subject (art) where there are not only many possible structural principles, but many strongly held views as to which principles are important. Herein lies the vitality and risk attached to art in education. Many structures have been proposed and acted out in both the practical and theoretical domains, but like attempts to define the necessary and sufficient characteristics of art itself, none have offered more than a partial approach to the subject. All have been susceptible to change, modification or dismissal.

At present we live in a period when there is an apparent emphasis upon the objective, which usually means figuration. Operational principles for art teaching often coalesce around activities such as observation, recording and analysis. There is an emphasis upon an 'outward-looking search process' (Schools Council, 1978, p. 24) that ignores what many still consider a mainspring of art in education, the inward-looking retrieval of thoughts, feelings and responses externalized in a public medium. The current emphasis upon formalist values (line, tone, texture) or critical frameworks such as Form, Content, Process, Mood (Taylor); or Style, Technique, Context (Dyson), help focus attention but do not constitute an unchanging analytical structure for the subject. That is far more elusive.

The principles of learning discussed so far imply the necessity of allowing, or even expecting, all pupils to make cross-subject links in order to give true and personal meaning to their studies and hence form *real* knowledge and acquire transferable skills. Perhaps at this juncture it should be made clear that the well-rehearsed arguments for and against links across the various arts subjects are to be avoided. Suffice it to say that these are a potentially vital source of enrichment to learning, but they are not the only or necessarily the major avenues of collaboration for the art and design teacher.

In turning from principles of teaching and learning to the subject of art and design itself, a moment's reflection reveals that it is not a unitary discipline. Art, craft and design are not interchangeable, and it would seem foolish to ignore the oft-stated truism that art and design education offers within its own discipline boundaries rich opportunities for 'inter-subject' linking, every bit as important as the more commonly expounded cross-subject links. What art department does not daily, and usually informally, relate art, craft and design activities? The endorsed areas of the GCSE syllabuses formalized the diversity and richness of the subject. Art teachers can employ this particular strength when attempts are made to link art to other subjects in a formal way through faculty or departmental structures or when, to facilitate timetabling, attempts are made to insist that a relatively short and therefore usually superficial introduction to several arts subjects is more beneficial than the range of approaches, practices and outcomes possible from within art as a defined subject.

If making meaning is the assimilation of knowledge for an individual's purposes, then there are two major ways it would seem that art teachers can assist those in their charge. Both imply links beyond the accepted or conventional boundaries of art, but do not dilute the art experience. First, as many before have suggested, every teacher is a teacher of language, both written and oral. 'Speech, while not identical with thought, provides a means of reflecting upon thought processes, and controlling them. Language allows one to consider not only what one knows but how one knows it'; remember, 'we observe not with our eyes alone but with our hypotheses' (Barnes, 1976, p. 58). This means the constant use of language – talking in class. This is where much of the work carried out on the teaching of English can be of inestimable value to the art teacher. In the literature of English teaching we find a wide range of examples of how to employ language related to imagery, including the use of prose, poetry and exploratory speech. Of particular interest is the work of Creber (1990), who draws close parallels between the teaching of English and the teaching of art. He is particularly concerned to generate 'an interest in *the looking act itself*' (p. 81), and offers models of picture interrogation based upon active questioning of the image.

A further rich source of language as an aid to visual understanding is *Voices in the Gallery* (Abse and Abse, 1986). This volume contains the responses of almost eighty poets to works of art (serious, funny, descriptive and moving) that illuminate the work for the onlooker. Ted Hughes', 'To Paint a Water Lily' starts from the familiar *La Bassin aux Nymphéas* by Claude Monet in the National Gallery, a work sadly tamed by exposure from which Hughes evokes a parallel and altogether more sinister world:

A green level of Lily leaves
Roofs the pond's chamber and paves

The flies' furious arena: study
These, the two minds of this lady.

First observe the air's dragonfly
That eats meat, that bullets by

Or stands in space to take aim;
Others as dangerous comb the hum

Under the trees. There are battle-shouts
And death-cries everywhere hereabouts

But inaudible, so the eyes praise
To see the colours of these flies

Rainbow their arcs, spark, or settle,
Cooling like beads of molten metal

Through the spectrum. Think what worse
Is the pond-bed's matter of course;

Prehistoric bedragonned times
Crawl that darkness with Latin names,

Have evolved no improvements there,
Jaws for heads, the set stare,

Ignorant of age as of hour –
Now paint the long-necked lily flower

Which, deep in both worlds, can be still
As a painting, trembling hardly at all

Though the dragonfly alight,
Whatever horror nudge her root.

(Ted Hughes, 1960)

This use of language, which draws upon the fundamental human capacity to form analogies, reflects the ideas of Rawson (1971), whose model of the way in which we form meaning from art implies the widest possible linking with other areas of knowledge and understanding appropriate to the work under consideration. Writing in this instance about ceramics, Rawson says:

> As we live our lives we accumulate a fund of memory traces based on our sensory experience. These remain in our minds charged, it seems, with vestiges of the emotions which accompanied the original experiences ... It is in the realm of these submerged memory traces that creative art moves, bringing them into the orbit of everyday life and making them available to the experience of others by formalising and projecting them on to elements of the familiar world which can receive and transmit them. From the artist's side the projection is done by his activity in shaping and forming. From the spectator's side it must be done by active 'reading' of the artist's forms ... What this art and its reading depend on is the human analogising faculty which lies at the root of all our mental achievements. It is probable that when our memory records an experience it recognises also its analogical resemblance to other experiences of a similar kind and 'accepts' it under the heading of a 'form'. It may also record connections between experiences, many of which may seem to be of different orders or from different sense fields, crossing the boundaries between the accepted categories of the world, as when it recognises that a certain splash resembles a flash, a rose petal resembles a cheek, or a plant stem in spring a burning fuse. The textures, bodies and coloured shapes the potter makes can thus suggest very remote indescribable intuitions. (pp. 15–18)

In other words, we make the reality we perceive rather than passively 'receiving' or 'reflecting' it.

To give one personal illustration of the connecting of experiences referred to by Rawson, I go back a number of years to a particularly memorable production of *The Tempest*. Beforehand I read Wilson Knight's superb essay on the play: 'The Shakespearian Superman'. Here I learned that Caliban was:

> an ugly creature, growing out of our images of brine-pits, ooze, and earthy woodland: he is Shakespeare's imagery of stagnant pools personified. You can't tell whether he is a gorilla or a reptile-dragon. He is a 'puppy-headed monster'. Prospero calls him a

tortoise. He is at least half fish. But he is human too; strong, useful as a labourer, but an unwilling creature, a grumpy yahoo ... But he is a pathetic figure, remembering how he was at first 'stroked' and made much of and taught the names of sun and moon; his eyes opened to the world of thinking beings; and how he, in return, put his half-animal, half-savage, knowledge of 'springs', 'brine pits', barren and fertile spots, at Prospero's service, until his attempted rape of Miranda put an end to friendly intercourse.

(1965, pp. 235–6)

Thoughts immediately turned to Picasso's *Guernica* (I was reading Rudolph Arnheim's fascinating analysis of the painting at the time), and the image conjured was that of the bull. This quickly dissolved into images of other more terrifying Picasso evocations of animality, including frighteningly powerful rapes involving minotaurs and the superb 1935 etching *Minotauromachy* where 'a huge, dark bullman shades his eyes against a light held by a young girl; a dead female torera with bare breasts lies on a disembowelled horse' (Arnheim, 1962, p. 16).

Herbert Read's reflections on Picasso (1974) embrace the realm of Jungian archetypes, and Eric Newton confirmed my own musings from the image of Caliban:

This extraordinary creature [the Minotaur], sometimes a symbol of brute strength, sometimes of Caliban-like bewilderment, sometimes triumphant, sometimes subdued and even slain by beauty, is developed in a series of drawings and etchings that culminated in one of the most pregnant and memorable of all his works, the *Monotauro-machie* of 1935.

(Newton, 1970, p. 263)

Blake's *Nebuchadnezzar, Star Wars'* Chewbacca and Brian Wildsmith's *Wild Things* all flashed into consciousness, along with long-forgotten childhood stereotypes of monsters. At the end of a process that led me on a personal path of imaging and discovery, I may not have grasped the 'correct' reading of *Guernica, The Tempest* or *Minotauromachy*, but I had constructed a powerful personal iconography that mattered to me. This, I believe, is one sense (there are many others explained by Rawson) in which analogizing helped the making of meaning.

This is where concepts of cross-curriculum links become of the utmost importance. No subject or discipline exists in the abstract; it exists in the mind of the perceiver. The responsibility of art educators is to ensure that, by educational procedures deemed to be proper and appropriate, concepts of art are placed in pupils' minds. If teachers fail to do this, as Richards found out in his classic study of criticism (Richards, 1929), responses from pupils will in most cases have little to do with an understanding of art (or the particular art form or work in question). Pupils are unable to construe meaning from art unless they have been taught to construct meaning through debate, hypothesis and the open exploration of meaning in a secure environment. Such an environment, where sharing and not the passive absorption of information is encouraged, time and again appears to be a precondition for the formation of 'real' knowledge. The many protocols recorded by Taylor (1986) bear witness to this, and Patrick Heron gives a beautiful example of an influential teacher who apparently did little more than share his enthusiasms with his pupils. His art teacher was one Ludwig Van der Straeten ('Vandy'). One afternoon, at a time when the young Heron was painting Sickerts and Cézannes ('I wasn't copying Sickert or Cézanne. I was seeing with their eyes'), his teacher took him to London in his Ford V8.

> It so happened that the Courtauld Collection of Post Impressionists was at the National Gallery. He drove straight up to the steps, put the brakes on, got out and we ran up the steps – didn't lock the car or anything! We went directly to the Courtauld pictures, straight up to Cézanne's *Mont Ste-Victoire*, the one he signed in the bottom right hand corner near the trunk of the tree, and just gazed at that, and nothing else, for an hour. Then we got back into the car and the next afternoon I started painting Cézanne watercolours.
>
> (Heron, 1992, p. 3)

This cameo emphasizes the lack of 'teaching' – that is, instructing – that was going on, but emphasizes the personal space allowed by the teacher, who, Heron says, 'could teach anybody anything', and his capacity to make the act of looking a strenuous act of perception.

The potential exists within art and design for the richest, most exciting and most rewarding liaisons, providing defences are dropped and intuitions and feelings are allowed to guide teachers and pupils away from stereotypical modes of response. The principles involved are fundamental to teaching and learning (even if they have been temporarily overlaid with a new 'correctness'). If links are to be made they must assist the process whereby 'pupils think for themselves' (Warnock, 1988, p. 53). Personal links and relationships are best encouraged through the processes of speculation, debate, exploratory speech and free use of the inevitable process of making analogies. None of this is simple or easy, and there are obvious implications in terms of the resources made available to pupils and the way projects are managed. This is where cross-subject and cross-department co-operation is essential. Such co-operation will be school-specific and cannot be legislated for. For art and design teachers, what matters is that whatever temporary or permanent links are put into place, they must not invade the integrity of the subject of study – art, craft and design – but must recognize and celebrate its almost limitless potential for relating to other areas of human experience. An excessive bias in the art curriculum towards the utilitarian should be resisted because in the long run it would deny pupils a full visual education. Instead, efforts must be made to strike a balance between the pressures to offer vocationally linked training and the central task of providing a genuine education into the meanings of art at a personal creative level. If teachers of art and design are driven by a belief in the integrity of their subject and not by short-term expediency, the cross-curriculum dimensions that art will always generate will have coherence and rationality, and will stand every chance of being important to all pupils.

REFERENCES

Abse, D., and Abse, J. (1986) *Voices in the Gallery*. London: Tate Gallery.

Arnheim, R. (1962) *The Genesis of a Painting: Picasso's Guernica*. Berkeley: University of California Press.

Barnes, D. (1976) *From Communication to Curriculum*. Harmondsworth: Penguin.

Creber, P. (1990) *Thinking Through English*. Milton Keynes: Open University Press.

Dearing, R. (1994) *The National Curriculum and its Assessment*. London: School Curriculum and Assessment Authority.

Department of Education and Science (DES) (1980) *A View of the Curriculum*. London: HMSO.

Department of Education and Science (DES) (1983) *Art in Secondary Education 11–16.* London: HMSO.

Department of Education and Science (DES) (1988) *The Curriculum from 5 to 16.* London: HMSO.

Dyson, A. (1987) Style, technique, context: art and design history in the GCSE. *Journal of Art and Design Education* **6**(2), 149–58.

Efland, A. (1972) *Conceptualising the Curriculum Problem in Art Education.* Havant: The National Society for Art Education.

Gardner, H. (1993) Lost youth. *Guardian*, 12 October.

Graham, D., and Tytler, D. (1993) *A Lesson for Us All.* London: Routledge.

Heron, P. (1992) My best teacher. *Times Educational Supplement*, 25 September.

Hughes, T. (1960) *Lupercal.* London: Faber and Faber. Quoted in Abse and Abse (1986).

Knight, G. Wilson (1965) *The Crown of Life.* New York: Methuen.

Munro, T. (1956) *Art Education: Its Philosophy and Psychology.* New York: Bobbs Merrill.

National Society for Education in Art and Design (NSEAD) (1993) *Technology Programmes of Study and Attainment Targets: Recommendations of the National Curriculum Council (Sept. 1993).* Corsham: NSEAD.

Osborne, H. (1970) *The Art of Appreciation.* London: Oxford University Press.

Parsons, M. J. (1987) *How We Understand Art.* Cambridge: Cambridge University Press.

Postman, N., and Weingartner, C. (1971) *Teaching as a Subversive Activity.* Harmondsworth: Penguin.

Rawson, P. (1971) *Ceramics.* London: Oxford University Press.

Read, H. (1974) *A Concise History of Modern Painting.* London: Thames and Hudson.

Richards, I. A. (1929) *Practical Criticism.* London: Routledge and Kegan Paul.

Schools Council (1969) *Education Through the Use of Materials.* London: Evans Methuen.

Schools Council (1978) Art 7–11. *Occasional Bulletin from the Subject Committees.* London: The Schools Council.

Taylor, R. (1986) *Educating for Art.* London: Longman.

Taylor, R. (1988) *Wigan Schools: Critical Studies and GCSE Art and Design.* Wigan: Metropolitan Borough of Wigan Education Department.

Warnock, M. (1988) *A Common Policy for Education.* Oxford: Oxford University Press.

Chapter 12

Approaching Assessment

Martin Kennedy

INTRODUCTION

Assessment of achievement made by pupils following art and design courses has undergone significant development during the last twenty years. An evolution which has been underwritten, and in some cases instigated, by changes in the secondary school curriculum and examination requirements has seen an increase in elaborate schemata designed to facilitate objective appraisal of pupil performance. Since the introduction of assessment systems to meet the demands of the General Certificate of Secondary Education (GCSE), teachers have been more closely involved in both formative and summative evaluation of their pupils' achievement at the end of what is now known as Key Stage 4. They recognize the need to match this achievement to appropriate grades in public examinations. With the introduction of the National Curriculum for Art in 1992, a more rigorous approach to assessment and record-keeping at Key Stage 3 was encouraged, drawing heavily on good practice in GCSE courses.

In this chapter these developments – endorsed by Dearing (1993) – are considered in some detail. The focus is on the opportunities for art and design teachers to formulate assessment systems for their own schemes of work. Just as there is no single way to implement the National Curriculum or teach courses which lead towards the GCSE, there can be no singular didactic assessment format. Nevertheless this chapter will refer to several specific formats derived from schemes that have been 'customized' to suit teachers and pupils working in particular situations. Reference will also be made to the mechanics of assessment, the criteria that inform effective differentiation and the various components of assessment systems: formative assessment, summative assessment, moderated assessment and self-assessment.

The chapter closes with a reference to some of the difficulties experienced when assessing work in art and design, particularly at Key Stage 4, and some comments on ways of integrating assessment into a course conceived as an organic whole. The generic term 'art and design' encompasses a wide range of activities, and schools demonstrate this diversity through specific programmes of study planned, delivered, evaluated and modified by teachers. The development of visual literacy remains central to the symbiotic activities of planning and assessment, which in art and design departments in secondary schools is achieved through 'a continuum of studies ranging from, on the one hand, "expressive" activities such as painting and sculpture, through a range of applied art, to technical and technological studies... on the other' (Binch, 1988, p. 19).

Teachers working with pupils at Key Stage 4 will need to apply assessment criteria (the principle or standard by which achievement is evaluated) that emanate from examination boards in order to judge effectively the extent to which individual pupils have met assessment objectives. Teachers will need to plan programmes of teaching and learning that suit their pupils and at the same time take account of the general aims of the course published by the examination board.

At Key Stage 3 teachers will need to be mindful of the requirements of the National Curriculum when devising the components of their schemes of work inclusive of assessment procedures. Continuity is important as pupils progress through the secondary phase of their art and design education. Within this context the planning of the content and sequence of a programme of work will clearly refer to the ways in which an individual pupil's progress and pace are to be monitored.

The Non-Statutory Guidance (DES, 1992) to support the implementation of the National Curriculum for Art refers to the need for the curriculum to make provision for children with special educational needs, and therefore assessment formats will need to have sufficient flexibility to differentiate across the ability range. This aspect of flexibility is important in art and design assessment, since individual pupils demonstrate their special needs in a subject that places an emphasis on the production of personal responses.

Further guidance from the National Curriculum Council on the issue of assessment can be interpreted to provide the following quality indicators. With reference to Key Stage 3 they should be:

- simple;
- straightforward;
- made by the teacher;
- based on coursework;
- differentiated through outcome;
- flexible;
- not involving national tests or ten-level criteria;
- based upon End of Key Stage Statements;
- utilizing evidence and descriptive judgements;
- taking into account 2–1 weighting between the two Attainment Targets;
- utilizing self-assessment by the pupil; and
- involving minimal record-keeping.

These principal recommendations have since been reinforced and applied in part to the whole curriculum as a result of recommendations made by Dearing (1993). The emphasis is on designing and implementing a high-quality curriculum which allows teachers to fine-tune the management and character of what is taught, while considering a useful spine of reference comprising material that is both statutory and advisory. In this sense assessment is fully integrated within a whole policy for art and design education in a school.

Teachers wish to have easy-to-use, effective *formative* assessment that will ensure that accurate and useful evidence of individual achievement supports any *summative* assessment made. The key word here is *evidence*. At Key Stage 3 teachers will need to be in possession of material that affirms pupil achievement at the end of the Key Stage. This should include realized work along with experimental, diagnostic and research material, probably in the form of a portfolio. However, teachers will need to make provision for the retention of equally valid evidence that exists in less tangible form: for example, a perceptive comment made by a pupil that indicates particular understanding of an element of the second Attainment Target. This will need to be recorded if it is to inform a thorough appraisal of that particular pupil. An example of how this might be done is given later in this chapter.

The Section 4 Order relating to art in the National Curriculum describes assessment as the means by which (my paraphrase):

1. Teachers check that their pupils have made appropriate progress in gaining prescribed knowledge and understanding.
2. Teachers communicate their findings to parents and other teachers.
3. Teachers compile a diagnostic record of attainment to serve as the basis for future (summative) judgements.

The subsequent Non-Statutory Guidance (DES, 1992) provides additional information in section 1.3. It advocates that item 2 should be extended to promote the practice of pupils being informed of their progress as an essential step towards involvement in the monitoring of their own performance. A 'shared vocabulary and criteria' is advocated, thereby letting pupils gain access to the *secret* of evaluation.

Continuity is advocated across Key Stages, and this is where efficient record-keeping by all teachers in an art and design department enables curriculum planning to take into consideration skills, knowledge and understandings previously acquired by pupils.

At Key Stage 4 assessment will, for the immediate future, be made through the GCSE examination system (see SEAC, 1993).

PERIODIC ASSESSMENT

During Key Stages 3 and 4 it is necessary to adopt an appropriate format for monitoring pupils' progress. This can most usefully be seen as forming part of a cycle of development. In other words, assessment should not simply mark the end of a unit or module of work, but should inform and influence the pupil's response to the tasks that follow. This can be useful in underwriting course and Key Stage continuity, and has relevance to the task of integrating the two Attainment Targets at Key Stage 3.

A holistic flavour continues beyond the end of the statutory phase of art and design education, as can be appreciated from the following extract from a GCSE syllabus: 'Genuine continuous assessment is formative in nature. It guides future direction and possible progress at least as much as it documents a series of terminal levels of achievement' (London Examinations, 1994, p. 18).

The models for periodic assessment that spring initially to mind are predictably dominated by the A4 matrix format, offering columns and boxes within which the full diversity of achievement is supposedly to be crammed. The word 'matrix' also means 'womb', and perhaps there is irony here, as many assessment grids convey a sense of rigidity that is anything but fertile. Nevertheless such formats – which can serve to plan as well as to evaluate – doubtless offer, at their best, a direct route to the solution of a complex problem. It is perhaps within the domain of pupil self-assessment that a more imaginative approach will gain greater purchase and consequently provide a fuller picture of progress from the point of view of the pupil.

A teacher working in a south London comprehensive school designed a self-assessment form based on the organic structure of a snail. It supports pupil development and provides an opportunity for self-appraisal (see Figure 12.1). The design of the form seems at first to indicate that art is made in an incremental, sequential way, starting with research and moving through experimentation to realization. It is also apparent that the successful use of the form relies upon the fact that pupils are encouraged by the teacher to select their own paths irrespective of an applied linear progression.

One *spiral* (as the form became known) was issued to each GCSE pupil at the start of successive modules of work. As different activities occurred, appropriate sections of the form were *claimed* by the pupil colouring them in. Four colours were used for the exercise, with pupils deciding whether the specific activity being recorded fell within the domain of Experimentation, Documentation, Experimentation or Realization. Sometimes an activity was most comfortably classified as a combination of these domains (in which case pupils could choose to *weight* their entries using a combination of colours). Pupils were also encouraged to write over the coloured sections to record exactly what they had achieved.

Thus an individual pupil could customize the spiral, and the resulting annotated forms provided further useful evidence when summative assessment was made at the time of the examination. The completed forms were kept in pupils' sketchbooks. Used correctly and with appropriate levels of support, the spiral enabled all pupils to evaluate and criticize their own work and offered sufficient flexibility for the more able pupils to make sophisticated diagnostic records of their progress.

The design of the spiral – which appeared unusual in the context of previously used assessment forms – attracted pupils and encouraged a more thoughtful and conscientious response to the challenge of honest self-appraisal. The document also fitted comfortably with the other types of formative, periodic assessment used, specifically for formal and informal tutorials, teacher-assessment and feed-back from other pupils in the group. This whole package was designed to reflect the methodology of the department in which it operated, and to contribute to the clear communication of that methodology to pupils. In order to integrate planning and assessment, it is essential to consider the question: what is being assessed?

WHAT IS BEING ASSESSED?

The National Curriculum provides clear information concerning the kind of skills and understanding a pupil should be able to demonstrate at the end of Key Stage 3. Statements relating to Attainment Target 1 are concerned with expressive, techni-

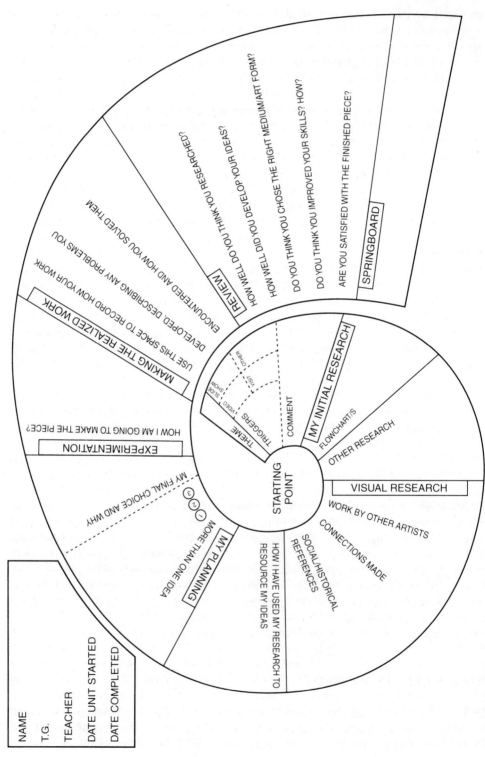

Figure 12.1 *A self-assessment form: the 'snail'*

cal and analytical skills: the ability to develop ideas through investigation and experimentation to resolved form, utilizing a range of materials, tools and techniques. Pupils also need to demonstrate a broad understanding of the basic visual elements, and be able to review and modify work – to know *why* as well as *how*. This aspect is explored further with reference to Key Stage 4 assessment in the last section of this chapter.

The statements relating to Attainment Target 1 cannot be considered meaningful without the accompanying material relating to Attainment Target 2. This is concerned with the identification of artistic conventions from a wide range of periods, traditions and cultures, and the application of methods and approaches found in the work of other artists through the work of pupils.

A viable programme of study at Key Stage 3 might contain a skills *menu* that will describe the 'work made in two and three dimensions and on a variety of scales' (DES, 1992, p. 3). It will also encourage experimentation, rigorous evaluation and modification, and the strand running through issues of ownership and the justification of preference – the 'holy grail' of personal response prioritized for many years in GCSE courses. At Key Stage 3 there is a great deal of information available to support and shape the art and design curriculum. Simple systems for departmental record-keeping can ensure that content is reinforced and extended during the Key Stage rather than needlessly duplicated. Failure to attend to this can result in wasting that most precious resource, time. Once identified, the aims and assessment objectives of a unit of work can determine the content and tasks, which in turn, once applied, can procure the evidence upon which assessment can be based. It should be stressed that the mode of assessment, the way in which evidence is evaluated and recorded, needs to be flexible, user-friendly and fair. Assessment procedures must be capable of accommodating the ways in which the recording of the taught curriculum differs from the planned curriculum – a common occurrence.

One potential difficulty raised earlier in this chapter concerns the viability of recording achievement of a transient quality. An example might be useful here. A group of 13-year-old pupils were investigating ways in which movement can be recorded to represent the passing of time. One week reproductions of Futurist paintings and sculptures were shown alongside images of Duchamp's *Nude Descending a Staircase*. The session closed with some slides of Muybridge's photographic studies of the running figure. At this point a pupil observed that if the photographs were superimposed one on the other, instead of being viewed side by side, the result would be similar in form and energy to the Duchamp image. This astute observation is worth recording. It is directly relevant to the requirements of the second Attainment Target. There is a need to record this achievement during the course of a lesson which perhaps moves into other territory fairly quickly.

How can teachers ensure that such moments are adequately catered for within assessment procedures? This question was considered by a group of heads of departments during an in-service training course on assessment. First, they identified a potential carrier and container for this kind of information. The class register was selected because of its durability as an essential classroom document. Traditionally, teachers have used registers to notate, annotate and record – often in a fairly *ad hoc* fashion – aspects of pupils' performances and progress. The group wondered whether it would be possible to formalize such idiosyncratic but effective practice, and began to design a register that would offer sufficient flexibility to cope with a wide range of assessment and record-keeping tasks.

Although designed for Key Stage 3, it could be utilized at the next Key Stage and used as evidence for GCSE summative assessment. The front view of the folded A3 register-form shows the spaces for class names and provides a broad column to record *non-attendance* of individuals next to three columns for effort, homework and other comments. When unfolded the form shows a directory of codes which can be used to identify pupil progress and achievement within specific contexts. For example, the basic element of Line is represented by the letter **L**. The quality of a piece of line drawing could be indicated by this character followed by a number of arrows. Thus it is possible to indicate that a high standard of work had been achieved, or that the work had been done, but rather poorly. The column headings relate broadly to National Curriculum Attainment Targets.

Like the spiral, the register-form is intended to encourage teachers to identify and respond to the problems of effective assessment from the standpoint of their own experience and departmental methodology. As with all aspects of curriculum implementation, teachers are uniquely placed to create a cohesive mesh that contains the elements of assessment.

SUMMATIVE ASSESSMENT

> summative assessment within a course . . . gives credibility to the internal judgement of the school upon the pupil.
>
> (London Examinations, 1992, p. 18)

Summative assessment occurs at the close of both Key Stages and, in most schools, at strategically placed times during the academic year. The summative assessment that is written for pupils and parents at the end of the first year of secondary education can be seen as having a formative function in relation to the End of Key Stage Statement that will be written at the end of the third year of secondary education. Furthermore, the assessment made at the time of the GCSE examination, both internal and external, is not only summative in nature, but leads directly to the award of a graded certificate (something that the other summative assessment commonly written at the same time, the National Record of Achievement, does not).

At Key Stage 3 statements written about individual pupils will:

- draw upon evidence accumulated through a wide range of formative assessment procedures;
- reflect the progress made by the pupil within the context of the two Attainment Targets;
- utilize self-assessment;
- refer to differentiation through outcome.

It is also known that, whether derived from statement-banks or individually crafted, these summative assessments will need to be accountable and objective, relating to the registered achievement of each pupil against appropriate criteria.

Similarly, at the end of Key Stage 4 teacher assessment will continue to be the most important component in determining the level of pupil performance. This notion of the teacher as central to the process of assessment is found in GCSE moderation procedures as well as being referred to in Dearing's interim and final reports.

In 1993 the Schools Examination and Assessment Council (SEAC) proposed that pupils taking GCSE art and design should be entered within a tiered system that – to an extent – predetermined the final grade. While the principle of tiered entry caused controversy and concern during the subsequent consultation process, the notion of the teacher as the person best placed to make judgements concerning the attainment of pupils was generally accepted.

The assessment of work submitted for the GCSE examination requires teachers to apply grade criteria governed by an appraisal of the degree to which assessment objectives have been negotiated by the pupils. Teachers become the teacher-examiners and, in carrying out the task of assessment, they make an interpretative judgement of the whole presentation of each candidate's work. The separate components of this presentation – which includes a timed test piece, coursework and preparatory work – are examined against the assessment objectives; and the reinforcement that each component may give to another is similarly considered, alongside the balance of strengths and weaknesses displayed in the work overall. This procedure is most comfortably carried out if the work is presented in the form of an exhibition.

The moderation of the mark that is the final outcome of the teacher-examiner's deliberations involves a visiting assessor whose primary function is to secure appropriate evidence to support and endorse the assessment of the candidate made by the teacher-examiner. In other words, the visiting assessor is not re-marking, indeed moderation normally involves little or no alteration to the teacher-examiner assessment, providing that the examination criteria have been properly applied. The London Examinations subject report for the 1992 series of examinations includes the following observations on the matter of assessment:

> The teacher-examiner is the one person who knows exactly what went on in respect of each candidate during the course and in the examination. This privileged knowledge is encompassed in the ... evaluation of each candidate's work ... the teacher-examiners convey all that they know, along with their judgments about the worth of a candidate's work to just one person, the visiting moderator. This is best done where the teacher-examiner documents evidence throughout a course and makes a comprehensive record at the time judgments are made and the reasons for them.
>
> (London Examinations, 1992, p. 7)

In the same document the further point is made that:

> Internal assessment continues to grow in sophistication in most centres. This eases external moderation, allowing the teacher's first hand knowledge of their candidates to be taken fully into account when final grading decisions are made. Such sophistication comes from adopting and applying the official criteria ... (p. 3)

Internal assessment systems, both formative and summative, occupy a vital position as they provide additional pieces of evidence that, alongside the units of work produced by pupils, place the performance of pupils within the boundary of one grade or another. Within the context of assessment at GCSE level, impartial application of the assessment criteria is vital if the moderation procedure is going to take place comfortably and result in fair appraisal for each candidate. Furthermore, it is essential that such criteria be accurately and meticulously applied whatever the grade being awarded. Despite the fact that grading automatically involves hegemony of a sort, it is both educationally and morally correct that the lower-achievement gradings are as carefully considered as the higher ones.

DIFFICULTIES IN MAKING ASSESSMENTS

The collection of essays by Gombrich, Hochberg and Black (1970) was primarily concerned with issues that were very much alive within the arena of assessment of art in schools. Aesthetic and philosophical matters relating to our interpretation of representational painting and sculpture, articulated in particular by Hochberg and Black, could be identified within the approach to assessment prevalent in schools during the 1970s and early 1980s.

This approach could be called 'let's look at the drawing'. To be more specific, the word 'figurative' could be added. During the early years of the GCSE examination, the still-life and life drawing, preferably utilizing a wide range of media, provided a reassuring sanctuary when assessing the work of 16-year-old pupils. The level of pupils' accomplishments could be evaluated – or so it seemed – by comparing their representational efforts against the assessor's benchmark understanding of *reality*. A drawing of a soft-drink can in pristine condition invited direct comparison (through what Hochberg refers to as *active looking*) with the examiner's selective memory of the reality of the form being described. A crushed can, being unique in form, was less easy to criticize in this manner. Perhaps this is why pupils were encouraged to endorse this option so frequently. When looking at such a drawing, assessors might consider the degree of success pupils had achieved in translating reality to a two-dimensional representation and colour information to tone. The depth clues of perspective would also be examined. Indeed, the whole manner in which pupils managed to squeeze the credibility gap between image and reality was analysed, measured and graded.

The broader the base of interpretation, experimentation and applied imagination, the more variety can reasonably be expected in pupils' responses at all Key Stages. However, should this automatically mean that assessment will be significantly more difficult to make? Perhaps at this point it is worth reaffirming that the National Curriculum promotes flexibility in assessment in order to appraise effectively a rich variety of pupil response. Similarly, at Key Stage 4 advisory bodies and examination boards are advocating the broadest possible cultural, historical and artistic base from which to develop work.

In the light of this progress, the agenda for art and design education includes a quite different credibility gap between art made in schools and that made outside, in studios and colleges, and exhibited in galleries. To focus on developments in twentieth-century art is to confront models that are considered to be of important iconoclastic significance within the context of contemporary art. Nevertheless they are frequently considered to be too difficult and inappropriate to be included in contextual and critical studies material presented to pupils.

One reason for this reticence might be that some art forms are feared to be too difficult to assess with confidence and accuracy once transposed from the context of the gallery to that of the school curriculum. Thus, when confronted in a gallery with, for example, a Rothko painting made in 1950, or a Duchamp readymade from 1917, or perhaps a Joseph Beuys of some forty years' vintage, a pupil's response is likely to be dismissive. This is understandable *unless* interpretative criticism has been facilitated through the course of study the pupil is following, and has been further endorsed through the assessment system.

Alas, this problem, while being confronted by some teachers, is being marginalized or even compounded elsewhere. Consider the following extract:

> Those candidates whose work is strongly influenced by chosen 'models' based upon professional art and design practices should make sure that this does not drift wholly towards the pastiche. *Models that are inclined towards minimalistic Art forms may not always be satisfactory in providing a clear declaration of the candidate's ability as is required by the syllabus.*
>
> (London Examinations, 1993, p. 3, italics added)

It is possible that such guidance may result in a dilemma for teachers who, while wishing to provide the broadest possible range of critical and contextual stimuli, would perhaps feel encouraged to advise pupils to avoid particular methods of working. This may be so, even though pupils may have a genuine interest in, and passion for, such an approach and may have seen such work included alongside more *acceptable* work in major collections. The double message seems to be rooted in an apprehension that certain types of work may prove too difficult to evaluate accurately within the context of current assessment criteria.

In order for pupils to recognize, analyse, criticize, internalize and finally utilize knowledge and understanding of art made by others, access to cultural and historic heritage needs to be as far-reaching as possible. The meaning of images and forms relies on contextual, social and historical contexts. In a world where art equals metaphor, pupils, through their art and design studies, can develop cognitive skills and visual literacy. That art and design continues in some schools to be categorized as a practical subject, with a tradition as a *doing* rather than a *thinking* discipline, poses a particular threat to the further development of assessing the work of pupils accurately.

Assessment frameworks in secondary schools need to adequately identify and reward achievement generated through any cultural, aesthetic and intellectual route, rather than operate within a predetermined and prescriptive cul-de-sac. They also need to serve as accurate and flexible diagnostic tools that, with the partner frameworks concerned with planning, facilitate effective teaching and learning programmes.

REFERENCES

Binch, N. (1988) *Towards an ILEA Policy on the Arts.* London: ILEA.

Dearing, R. (1993) *The National Curriculum and its Assessment* London: SCAA.

Department of Education and Science (DES) (1992) *The National Curriculum: Art for Ages 5–14.* London: HMSO.

Gombrich, E.H., Hochberg, J., and Black, M. (1970) *Art, Perception and Reality*. Baltimore and London: Johns Hopkins University Press.

London Examinations (1992) *Subject Report GCSE 1000–1020, 5000, 5015*. London: University of London Examinations and Assessment Council.

London Examinations (1993) *Advanced Level and Advanced Level Supplementary Art and Design: Notes for Guidance*. London: University of London Examinations and Assessment Council.

London Examinations (1994) *Syllabus for Art and Design 1000: May–June 1994*. London: University of London Examinations and Assessment Council.

National Curriculum Council (1992) *Art Non-Statutory Guidance*. York: National Curriculum Council.

Schools Examinations and Assessment Council (SEAC) (1993) *Draft GCSE Criteria for Art*. London: Schools Examinations and Assessment Council.

Index